The Transformative Potential
of LGBTQ+ Children's Picture Books

Children's
Literature
Association

Children's Literature Association Series

The
Transformative
Potential
of
LGBTQ+
Children's
Picture
Books

Jennifer Miller

University Press of Mississippi | Jackson

The University Press of Mississippi is the scholarly publishing agency of
the Mississippi Institutions of Higher Learning: Alcorn State University,
Delta State University, Jackson State University, Mississippi State University,
Mississippi University for Women, Mississippi Valley State University,
University of Mississippi, and University of Southern Mississippi.

www.upress.state.ms.us

The University Press of Mississippi is a member of
the Association of University Presses.

First printing 2022
∞

Library of Congress Cataloging-in-Publication Data

Names: Miller, Jennifer, Ph. D., author.
Title: The transformative potential of LGBTQ+ children's picture books / Jennifer Miller.
Other titles: Children's Literature Association series.
Description: Jackson : University Press of Mississippi, 2022. | Series: Children's literature associa-
tion series | Includes bibliographical references and index.
Identifiers: LCCN 2022000617 (print) | LCCN 2022000618 (ebook) | ISBN 9781496839992
(hardback) | ISBN 9781496840004 (trade paperback) | ISBN 9781496840028 (epub) | ISBN
9781496840011 (epub) | ISBN 9781496840042 (pdf) | ISBN 9781496840035 (pdf)
Subjects: LCSH: Picture books for children—Bibliography. | Picture books for children—Educa-
tional aspects. | Sexual minorities—Juvenile literature—Bibliography. | Queer theory—Juvenile
literature—Bibliography. | Homosexuality—Juvenile literature—Bibliography. | Transformative
learning.
Classification: LCC LB1044.9.P49 M55 2022 (print) | LCC LB1044.9.P49 (ebook) | DDC 011.62—
dc23/eng/20220124
LC record available at https://lccn.loc.gov/2022000617
LC ebook record available at https://lccn.loc.gov/2022000618

British Library Cataloging-in-Publication Data available

To Owen Robert Arditi

(my heart in the world)

Contents

(Anti-)Acknowledgments

I wrote *The Transformative Potential of LGBTQ+ Children's Picture Books* while working as an adjunct assistant professor at the University of Texas at Arlington, often cobbling together a full-time schedule by teaching one or two classes from several departments and programs, including sociology, English, interdisciplinary studies, and women's and gender studies. Whereas tenure-track faculty have a reduced course load and institutional support that may include research and writing sabbaticals, I wrote this book while teaching over six classes a semester. For instance, during the Spring 2020 semester I taught two online sections of Introduction to Popular Culture for UTA's Sociology Department, one face-to-face section of Introduction to LGBTQ+ Studies for the Women's and Gender Studies Program, and one face-to-face section of Representations of Children and Childhood, as well as two face-to-face sections of Developmental English for the English Department. I share this for political reasons, for the opportunity to reflect on what work is and isn't supported, what scholars are and are not supported, and what knowledge we are losing due to lack of institutional support for LGBTQ+ studies and children's literature, two subjects that it is too often assumed anyone can teach and no one needs to research.

A traditional acknowledgments narrative would list all the wonderful support the author has received. Mine reads as the sad and sometimes catty confession of an unfunded, poorly compensated, and overworked adjunct. In retrospect, the creation of this book shares significant similarities with the creation of the LGBTQ+ children's literature it analyzes. Both LGBTQ+ children's picture books and this book were created in contexts of scarcity, with deficient material resources and insufficient intellectual and creative support. Also, like LGBTQ+ children's picture books, this book about them is a product of love inspired by absence. Many of the picture books I discuss are by amateurs, outsiders to the field of children's literature who were either LGBTQ+ or loved someone who was. Noticing a lack of children's books about LGBTQ+ experiences and identities, they responded by producing their own texts. My path is similar; as a cisgender bisexual white woman married to a man, I was very invested in incorporating queer stories into my child's life. Luckily, I found dozens, then hundreds of picture books to share with my child. If I hadn't, instead of this book, I may have tried my hand, disastrously I'm sure, at writing children's literature. Although I found loads of LGBTQ+ children's picture books, I didn't find much scholarship. And so, like LGBTQ+ children's picture books, this book is a response to an absence I identified and sought to remedy.

Although my position within the university is precarious, I experience very real privilege as a university faculty member. I have access to a university library and a community of scholars willing to read my work. If I were not working at a university, I couldn't have accessed the many primary sources needed to compile a rich and representative archive. I was able to use my library's interlibrary loan service to track down even the most obscure titles, with few exceptions. Additionally, Diane Shepelwich, a librarian at UTA, provided invaluable support. Diane located Merrikay Everett Brown, whose MA thesis about Lollipop Power Inc. was essential to my understanding of 1970s feminist publishing. The dissertation was not digitized, so I also need to thank Merrikay for digging it out of her attic, scanning it, and sending me a copy.

This book also benefited greatly from the generous feedback of friends and colleagues. Tim Morris read the complete manuscript and provided feedback that helped me clarify my arguments in meaningful ways. David Arditi also read the book, commenting helpfully. Additionally, he identified high-resolution images and saved them as JPEGs. All the images in this book are a result of his diligence. Sara Austin commented on several chapters and has always generously provided information about the field of children's literature, which I clumsily entered after graduate school. Additionally, Amy Hodges provided technical expertise to make indexing a bit less tedious. Access to a university library as well as access to academics played a significant role in the development of this book.

I am also indebted to authors and publishers who have shared their motivations and experiences writing and publishing LGBTQ+ children's picture books as well as their work itself. Jane Severance, author of the first LGBTQ+ children's picture book to be published in the US, has been a wonderful source of information. The prolific Lesléa Newman has shared her experiences and even some of her books. Flamingo Rampant Press provided me access to its entire collection. Several other authors, including Cheril Clarke with My Family!/Dodi Press; Daniel Haack, author of *Prince and Knight*; and Suzanne DeWitt Hall, creator of the Rumplepimple series, offered fascinating insights into the field.

Finally, I want to thank UPM senior acquisitions editor Katie Keene and my copy editor, Elizabeth Farry. Katie contacted me to discuss my research while I was attending the Children's Literature Association's annual conference way back in 2018. At our meeting she expressed interest in seeing me develop my work into a manuscript, which I did over the next three years. Research and writing moved slower than I liked due to my teaching commitments, which were exasperated by a global pandemic, but I was able to submit my final manuscript in May 2021. UPM provides generous support to authors including professional copyediting services, and I'm grateful for Elizabeth's attention to detail and astute suggestions. It has been a pleasure to work with UPM to bring this text to life.

The Transformative Potential
of LGBTQ+ Children's Picture Books

Chapter One

What Can Picture Books Do?

The Politics of LGBTQ+ Children's Literature

In November 2019, I attended the National Women's Studies Association (NWSA) annual conference in San Francisco. Coincidentally, while waiting for a panel about children's picture books to begin, I opened Makeda Zook and Sadie Epstein-Fine's *Spawning Generations: Rants and Reflections on Growing Up with LGBTQ+ Parents* (2018), a book I had picked up earlier that day in the conference exhibit hall. I wasn't expecting the collection of essays by children of LGBTQ+[1] parents to begin with a reflection on cultural representations, particularly children's books, but to my surprise it did. In the book's introduction, the editors lament the absence of families like theirs in children's picture books while they were growing up in the 1980s and 1990s. They propose that the recent expansion of LGBTQ+ children's picture books makes the "queerspawn" of LGBTQ+ parents feel "incrementally less scattered" (1). This indicates that children's picture books can foster a sense of collective identity and help develop an imagined community by encouraging readers to understand their experiences as part of a larger story. Readers of LGBTQ+ children's picture books, whether they are queer identifying themselves or are the cisgender, heterosexual children of queer parents, find their experiences affirmed in children's culture that accounts for queer identities and experiences.

Having one's queer experiences acknowledged and affirmed in the relentlessly and deliberately cisgender, straight world of children's culture is politically significant, and it is an example of the transformative potential of LGBTQ+ literature. In other words, stories, like those found in LGBTQ+ children's books, undertake essential sociocultural work. They make legible, and by extension knowable, what would otherwise hover below the surface of our collective consciousness. For instance, Stefan Lynch, the first director of Children of Lesbians and Gays Everywhere (COLAGE), a networking and support organization for children with LGBTQ+ parents that was founded in 1990, coined the term *queerspawn* (Epstein-Fine and Zook 5–6). For Epstein-Fine and Zook, the word serves as an anchor. They write that it "situates [queerspawn] within a political and personal landscape of community belonging" that can be important because of similar experiences of homophobia and transphobia as a result of the proximity to queerness the children of LGBTQ+ parents experience (5–6). In other words, although queerspawn may identify as cisgender and heterosexual, they are "queered" because of their love for gay, lesbian, bisexual, or transgender parents. Additionally, queerspawn may share affinity with queer cultures and communities because of growing up queerly. The importance of collective queer language and culture in encouraging modes of queer relationality and modeling queer possibilities is discussed throughout this book, which explores representations of living, learning, and loving queerly in LGBTQ+ children's picture books.

This study introduces and builds the argument that LGBTQ+ children's picture books have the potential to create imagined queer collectives that can have real consequences on experiences of community belonging and building as well as social and psychic transformation. Benedict Anderson introduced the term *imagined community* in his 1983 study of European nation-states and nation building, in which he conceives of the nation as an imagined community. According to Anderson, individuals identify with images depicted in cultural texts and imagine themselves as similar to others as a result of the shared culture and experience. This encourages identification and fellowship with a network of strangers (Anderson 6). I find this description of the imaginative work required to make and sustain a nation and identification with a nation quite compelling and think LGBTQ+ cultural texts can accomplish similar identification with an imagined collective. Even more, this initial imaginative work can have real effects on material worldmaking and community building. LGBTQ+ children's picture books write the lives of LGBTQ+ persons so often omitted from cultural representation into the field of social and cultural visibility, enabling both collective identification and identity affirmation among those who may be quite isolated from others with similar experiences of gender and sexual identity. As a result, studying the types of representations written into intelligibility and types of collectives imagined is essential to understanding the transformative potential of LGBTQ+ children's literature. What is imagined affects what is possible.

In addition to a worldmaking project, LGBTQ+ children's picture books are a historical archive that elucidates what was thinkable and possible at different historical junctures. Writing in the late 1990s, Kenneth Kidd persuasively argued that lesbian and gay young adult novels are a useful "index to changing attitudes toward homosexuality" (114). He noted that in studying young adult fiction, one could trace a shift away from representing homosexuality as a social problem and toward representing homophobia as a social problem (114). Creating an archive large enough to map content shifts in LGBTQ+ picture books similar to those described by Kidd within young adult literature was one of my central investments in researching and writing this book.

The politics of inclusive children's picture books and the political work these texts can do have long been explored by scholars of multicultural children's literature. For instance, Rudine Sims Bishop's impactful 1990 essay "Windows, Mirrors, and Sliding Glass Doors" has served as a rallying cry for the multicultural literacy movement (Bishop). Bishop's poetic opening asserts:

> Books are sometimes windows, offering views of worlds that may be real or imagined, familiar or strange. These windows are also sliding glass doors, and readers have only to walk through in imagination to become part of whatever world has been created or recreated by the author. When lighting conditions are just right, however, a window can also be a mirror. Literature transforms human experience and reflects it back to us, and in that reflection we can see our own lives and experiences as part of a larger human experience.

For too long it has been difficult for queerspawn and queer children to see their "own lives and experiences as part of a larger human experience" (Bishop). Instead, as Zook and Epstein-Fine assert, queerspawn and queer children have felt isolated in their experiences, unable to make connections and imagine community.

In addition to helping children see themselves as part of the human network who share experiences with other people, Bishop indicates that children's literature can help us imagine ourselves and one another differently, because children's books can both affirm the self and introduce us to others. This textual and aesthetic introduction to others is an essential component of LGBTQ+ children's picture books' transformative potential. These texts don't only normalize lesbian, gay, bisexual, and trans experiences. They also decenter the normalcy of cisgender heterosexuality. This decentering can help all readers see the straight world, often hidden by its own ubiquity, and critique its inadequacies. For instance, in many of the children's picture books discussed here, the heterosexual family is revealed as insufficient, unable to meet the needs of the queer child. In other instances, cisgender heterosexuality is represented as drab. In these instances, queerness is envied even as its vilified, needed even as it is rejected.

Very recent LGBTQ+ children's picture books are radically inclusive, boldly celebratory, and have no time for stigma or shame. These books show queerness taking up space in public spaces. This is particularly apparent in recently released children's books that celebrate drag culture. For example, 2020 releases like Little Miss Hot Mess's *The Hips on the Drag Queen Go Swish, Swish, Swish*, Ellie Royce's *Auntie-Uncle: Drag Queen Hero*, Desmond Napoles's *Be Amazing: A History of Pride*, Michelle Tea's *Tabitha and Magoo Dress Up Too*, and *RuPaul Charles*, a board book biography from Little Bee Books' People of Pride series, all introduce young readers to queer culture and gender play joyfully and unapologetically (Little Miss Hot Mess; Royce; Napoles; Tea; Little Bee Books). The partial, precarious, and still incomplete normalization of drag marks a shift in queer culture's position in dominant culture; drag is moving toward the center of our cultural imaginary as family fun entertainment, and, I would suggest, shifts like this are transformative. It is essential to think like historians of the present in order to identify cracks in oppressive gender and sexual ideologies and make change as well as acknowledge when change is being made.

Although experts in literary studies, sociology, education, and library studies have created convincing, evidence-based scholarship about the importance of making LGBTQ+ children's picture books accessible to young readers, recent studies demonstrate that teachers are not prepared, administrators are not willing, and community members frequently rally against attempts to include LGBTQ+ children's literature in public school curriculums and on library bookshelves (Sears; Letts and Sears; Janmohamed; Hermann-Wilmarth and Ryan; Ryan and Hermann-Wilmarth, *Reading the Rainbow*; DePalma;

Goodrich and Luke; Curwood et al.; Garry; Sanders and Mathis; Brand and Maasch; Dodge and Crutcher; Hyland; Swartz; K. Jiménez; Burke and Greenfield; K. Robinson). In fact, Laura B. Smolkin and Craig A. Young's 2011 essay "Missing Mirrors, Missing Windows: Children's Literature Textbooks and LGBT Topics," which references Sims Bishop's important work in its title, suggests that young readers are being "denied their rights" to LGBTQ+ children's books by adults who see LGBTQ+ people and culture as "morally wrong and wish to obliterate high-quality books that portray the families and, therefore, the children of same-sex relationships" (217). Smolkin and Young's study of children's literature textbooks proves that few future teachers are introduced to LGBTQ+ content, which they attribute to "commonly held misconceptions about LGBT families and children," including the idea that LGBTQ+ identities and experiences are not relevant, relatable, or appropriate for consumption by children (217). These "commonly held misconceptions" also include belief in the inferiority, indecency, and deviancy of homosexuality as well as the belief that children lack an understanding of gender and sexuality. The tension between the ever-growing field of LGBTQ+ children's picture books available and the censorship controversies that often keep these texts out of the hands of children is explored throughout this book.

In 2015, Christian conservative "Jacqueline" wrote a popular tirade against LGBTQ+ children's picture books on her blog *Deep Roots at Home*. Like many Christian conservatives, she is invested in reproducing hierarchal adult-child dynamics that position adults, especially parents, as protectors of children. This claim is used to make impassioned censorship arguments. Jacqueline writes: "Yep, I'm pretty sure you've heard about library books that promote the homosexual lifestyle for kids as young as kindergarten—but are you aware of the agenda to force in-depth sexuality and perverse lifestyles on your kids in public schools—and likely yours?" (Jacqueline). In the post, she references Lesléa Newman's frequently contested *Heather Has Two Mommies* (1989) as a case in point and argues that books like this can "unlock" the minds of children. Jacqueline's concern that children's minds might be unlocked (a.k.a. opened) is quite revealing. She appears to recognize the pleasures of queerness and the likelihood that children will find queer content compelling. It's not so much individual children she is concerned with, but instead children's role in reproducing society, which she believes should replicate a narrow set of Christian ideals. In fact, she goes on to write: "A nation can be lost in one generation, and we are losing America now. The future depends upon what your kids are being taught now" (Jacqueline). Whereas Smolkin and Young suggest children's rights are violated by excluding queer content from public school curriculum, Jacqueline's claim hinges on parental rights, which she claims are violated if queer content is included in public school curriculum. Parents' rights claims reify normative understandings of the adult-child relationship that demands adults protect vulnerable, malleable children. Importantly, LGBTQ+ children's books often become legible to cisgender heterosexuals through panic narratives such as that performed by Jacqueline. This moralizing framework introduces LGBTQ+ children's picture books as a problem to be solved through censorship, not as a possible solution to the problems of homophobia and transphobia.

In addition to rhetoric, policies, and practices driven by overt homophobia and transphobia, several scholars convincingly argue that dominant concepts of children and childhood make it difficult to build a compelling case for LGBTQ+-inclusive curriculum even when explicit homophobia isn't present. As a case in point, in "Doing Anti-Homophobia and Anti-Heterosexism in Early Childhood Education," education scholar Kerry Robinson argues that "hegemonic discourses of childhood and sexuality . . . operate to render sexuality (especially non-heterosexuality) issues as 'taboo' and irrelevant to the lives of children." In other words, ideologies of children and childhood warrant the cloak of silence that wraps around all things queer. Robinson explains that it is impossible to include LGBTQ+ content in curriculum without challenging these entrenched sociocultural norms about gender, sexuality, and adult-child relationships. Even more, she argues that LGBTQ+ representations "disrupt the inequitable discourses that operate to constitute sexuality as fixed within a naturalized hierarchical heterosexual/homosexual binarism, which normalizes heterosexuality and renders non-heterosexual relationships as deviant and abnormal" (K. Robinson 178). It is the disruptive potential of LGBTQ+ children's picture books that I return to throughout this book, even when I recognize and lament attachments to white, middle-class ideals, even when I identify and critique hetero- and homonormativity. To paint a full picture of the cultural work LGBTQ+ children's picture books do, it is essential to articulate the disruptive work their very existence accomplishes. Because of the stigmatization of queer gender and sexuality in children's culture, a stigma currently being contested, I suggest that whatever else LGBTQ+ children's books do, they *also* denaturalize the still present dominant notion that nonheterosexual relationships are deviant, abnormal, and unfit for children.

This is a significant point because LGBTQ+ children's picture books have often been dismissed as homonormative, didactic, and antiqueer (Huskey; Lester; Taylor). In fact, the accusation of homonormativity has been central to scholarship production about LGBTQ+ children's picture books, and, I suggest, it limits more productive and nuanced readings of these texts (Huskey; Taylor; Lester). *Homonormativity* is a term queer activists and scholars use to critique mainstream civil rights organizations' assimilation tactics. Queer theorists who are skeptical of inclusion suggest that as privileged gays and lesbians gain increased acceptance into mainstream institutions, it is becoming possible to "forget" personal and collective histories based on shame, which hinders community building and justice-oriented activism. Privileged gays and lesbians are usually understood as white, middle class, and cisgender. Inclusion refers to access to social institutions, like marriage and the military, that have excluded LGBTQ+ individuals. Those who are skeptical of inclusion argue that the contingent acceptance and inclusion of some LGBTQ+ persons further stigmatizes others—for instance, BIPOC[2] and transgender individuals—who may not be able to, or may not want to, be included in social institutions that reproduce social hierarchies (Duggan, *Twilight of Equality?*; Duggan, "New Homonormativity"; Puar; Warner).

I agree that homonormativity stands in the way of transformative action. I also agree that most LGBTQ+ children's picture books are homonormative. For instance, in a study of lesbian and gay children's picture books, April M. Sanders and Janelle B. Mathis found that most of the texts analyzed construct lesbian- and gay-parented families as similar to heterosexual-parented families in all significant ways. They write: "The child in each of the books only demonstrates a happy and content disposition from having LGBT parents; the situation is presented as normal instead of an anomaly from heterosexual parenting" (Sanders and Mathis). My findings mirror those of Sanders and Mathis. I actually go further, suggesting that representations of gay and lesbian parenting in LGBTQ+ picture books often reify white, middle-class experiences and values, particularly by placing families in white suburbs and identifying gay and lesbian parents with middle-class occupations and consumption patterns. These markers are often visual—for instance represented by large homes, material possessions, and even mobility, such as the ability to go on vacations or participate in transnational adoptions. My readings of these texts link homonormativity to racialized class privilege. Additionally, my findings show that books with racially and ethnically diverse characters often take place in urban settings like apartment buildings and highlight public spaces in addition to the private space of the home. Far fewer in number, these books are also likely to thematize the normalcy of different family units, but they frequently represent difference more expansively to include single parents and extended family. At no point do I shy away from a critique of clearly present homonormativity; I just refuse to see it as the whole story, suggesting instead that even at their most homonormative, LGBTQ+ children's picture books transform the field of cultural visibility simply by existing. Although representation is not enough, it is significant. I am equally committed to identifying and interpreting the transformative potential of LGBTQ+ children's picture books and their collusion with hegemonic social ideologies.

It is true that *almost* all pre-2000 LGBTQ+ children's picture books are about lesbian and gay adults parenting presumably cisgender, heterosexual children. It's also true that in LGBTQ+ children's picture books, gay- and lesbian-parented households have often been presented as a "problem" to be solved by normalizing the queer family unit, which is usually accomplished by downplaying queer difference and focusing on love as a common feature of all families. As a result, there is little internal complexity to these texts. But this is not the whole story. First, most early LGBTQ+ children's literature was written for a small audience of LGB adults—most often parents—and their children. Additionally, most LGBTQ+ children's picture books focused on gay and lesbian parents were written with the express purpose of providing children in lesbian- and gay-parented families representations of lives that looked, at least a little bit, like their own, in order to counter dominant cultural erasure or misrepresentation. Second, there are books that stray from the formula. Third, looking at the discourses surrounding these texts as well as the contexts that both enable and constrain them provides critical insights into the cultural work the field accomplishes as well as its transformative potential.

LGBTQ+ Children's Picture Books vs. Queer Children's Picture Books

The American Library Association (ALA) defines picture books as a "visual experience" with "a collective unity of story-line, theme, or concept, developed through the series of pictures of which the book is comprised" ("Caldecott Medal"). Working with the ALA definition of picture books, I identify LGBTQ+ children's picture books as texts that meet the formal specifications outlined above while also depicting adult, child, or nonhuman characters who identify or can reasonably be identified as homosexual, bisexual, gender-creative, transgender, or queer. I have intentionally identified the object of my study as LGBTQ+ children's picture books as opposed to queer children's picture books. I struggled with this choice. I remain concerned that the term LGBTQ+ implies inclusion that is absent in children's picture books. For instance, I have yet to identify a single bisexual character, and I'm not alone in this observation (Coletta; Epstein). Still, I decided to identify the literature discussed in this book as LGBTQ+ to make it clear to readers that my project engages explicit LGBTQ+ representations, even if all the identities are not equally represented in the existing field of children's picture books. I also wanted to differentiate my project from more common scholarly endeavors that do not engage explicit LGBTQ+ representations. As noted above, most scholars who consider LGBTQ+ children's picture books at all have written them off as didactic and homonormative. Additionally, a fair amount of scholarship reads popular children's picture books through a queer theoretical framework, finding queerness where it is not explicitly present but instead coded or perhaps present peripherally in the author's identity. Although I recognize the significance of engagement with latent queerness, my project does very different work than most of the previous scholarship.

Popular children's literature scholar Kenneth Kidd warns that working within binaries like implicit/explicit or hetero/homo is too "limiting" a framework for understanding children's picture books (115). His own work in the field often collapses the distinction between implicit and explicit representations. Although I concede that binaries are far too crude to account for complex social phenomena, I do not by extension feel that distinctions are unhelpful or inherently problematic. Instead, I produce a nonce taxonomy à la the brilliant Eve Sedgwick. A nonce taxonomy encourages the naming of peripheral and often ephemeral expressions and identification (Sedgwick, *Epistemology of the Closet*). By generating a nonce taxonomy, this project produces a temporal map that identifies and articulates shifts in dominant and emerging understandings of gender and sexuality as presented in the pages of picture books. Far from limiting what we see, the kind of nonce taxonomy of queer gender and sexual expressions that follows in this book hopes to reveal the queer intricacies and shifting normativities that both constrain and generate our social world.

As mentioned, those who have analyzed explicit representations of LGBTQ+ expressions and identities in children's picture books tend to dismiss them as didactic and homonormative. For instance, Melynda Huskey critiques LGBTQ+ children's books as tethered to a wish for acceptance through normalization, which renders them politically ineffective. Her reading of explicit representations warrants her claim that queerness is most present in books where explicit homosexuality is absent. This leads Huskey to argue that popular children's books are more likely to represent queer challenges to regimes of normativity than explicitly LGBTQ+ children's books. She writes: "There's no shortage of queer picture books if you're looking in the right places, or with the right eye. For, while foregrounding homosexuality, whether deliberately or in flight, robs the picture book of its queerness, seeking it where it 'isn't' establishes it more fully" (Huskey 68). As mentioned, this move away from LGBTQ+ children's literature to find queer potential in children's literature is typical of much scholarship in the field. *Over the Rainbow: Queer Children's and Young Adult Literature* (2011), an edited collection by Kenneth Kidd and Michelle Ann Abate, is another example. The editors bring together previously published scholarship, most of which "queers" popular children's literature or analyzes lesbian and gay young adult fiction. A couple of notable exceptions identify and explore explicit representations, including Robert McRuer's "Reading and Writing 'Immunity': Children and the Anti-Body" and Elizabeth A. Ford's "H/Z: Why Lesléa Newman Makes Heather into Zoey," both of which I discuss at length in the next chapter. Additionally, Jody Norton's fascinating article "Transchildren [*sic*] and the Discipline of Children's Literature" (which I will return to shortly) is reprinted in the collection. However, children's books that explicitly engage LGBTQ+ identities and experiences are not the focus of the collection. In fact, the queerness Huskey and several authors in Abate and Kidd's collection reference is void of LGBTQ+ embodied experience, cultural specificity, and queer community.

To take a case in point, Huskey develops a queer reading of Margaret Wise Brown's *Goodnight Moon* to theorize the possibility of a "counter-discourse" in popular literature that emerges from "an awareness to lesbian and gay issues" as well as the author's sexuality and motivation for writing (Huskey 69). Specifically, Huskey contends that knowledge of Margaret Wise Brown's intimate relationships with women might influence our relationship to her books (69). However, I wonder who exactly "our" refers to in Huskey's essay. All readers? Young readers? Queer readers? I don't think queer readings that rely on knowledge of an author's romantic life are available to most children, or adults for that matter. Instead, the "our" Huskey references is most likely a small group of queer literary scholars, which both limits the potential of these books to be read queerly and the transformative potential of queer reading.

Eschewing the idea that queer coding and subtext is more transformative than explicit representation, Jennifer Coletta's work about bisexual representation in children's picture books argues that "effective representation of bisexual characters first includes a clear naming of bisexuality within the text; in addition, it challenges normative binaries and stereotypes in an attempt to make these characters—and subsequently the young readers they represent—fully visible" (86). Coletta notes the risk of explicit labeling. She writes: "On the one hand, employing labels can advance hegemonic discourse; on the other, it can be seen as enabling the recognition of marginalized voices and simultaneously repudiating heteronormative default assumptions, particularly for bisexual people" (Coletta 86). She uses Allison Weir's theory of transformative identification as a model for thinking about solidarity without sameness as well as for developing the idea that identity can be mobilized for change (91–92).

There can be very practical reasons to develop queer reading strategies in order to take advantage of queer subtexts in popular literature. In fact, educators, librarians, and other gatekeepers who must negotiate transphobic and homophobic institutions don't always have the freedom to introduce children to explicit LGBTQ+ children's books because of the controversy surrounding them. In these instances, helping young readers develop a queer lens that challenges nonnormative intimate and social relations as well as gender and sexual desires, expressions, and identities may be necessary. In Caitlyn Ryan and Jill M. Hermann-Wilmarth's 2013 essay, "Already on the Shelf: Queer Readings of Award-Winning Children's Literature," the authors explain that in several states, policies prohibit discussing LGBTQ+ content in the classroom. For instance, in 2011 the state senate of Tennessee passed a "Don't Say Gay" bill that prohibited openly discussing LGBTQ+ identities (143). The authors note that the bill simply codified an unspoken rule: "Schools in general and elementary schools in particular are spaces where only heterosexuality—and its accompanying categories of feminine girls and masculine boys—is assumed, approved, and allowed" (143). In this case, generating reading strategies that encourage students to identify and critique taken-for-granted assumptions about gender and sexuality is a necessary alternative to silence and erasure, since legal constraints can put teachers' careers at risk. Ryan and Hermann-Wilmarth argue that a queer lens can encourage readers to "tease out and discuss experiences and subjectivities that have been too frequently considered inappropriate for school, including issues of sexuality and gender identity" (143). It is because of this still enforced construction of LGBTQ+ identities and experiences as unfit for youth consumption that I suggest even the most homonormative LGBTQ+ children's books do the important work of disrupting a cisgender heterosexual field of cultural visibility that either erases or demonizes, with little room for humanizing, LGBTQ+ persons.

In her popular 1999 publication "Transchildren [*sic*] and the Discipline of Children's Literature," Jody Norton identifies another constraint to engaging LGBTQ+ children's literature, particularly representations of transgender characters, by noting that few exist.[3] Norton writes: "If, in the interests of an ethical as well as an aesthetic realism, we seek explicit representations of transchildren [*sic*] in children's literature itself, we will, as we might expect, seek largely in vain—for the taboos of the adult operate, as a crucial political determinant of the adult-child distinction, to define and circumscribe the culture of the child" (298). Norton's assessment of the dismal state of transgender representations in children's picture books was correct when her article was first published in 1999 and still held true when it was updated and republished in 2011. However, transgender representations are slowly making an appearance in children's picture books, most notably with Marcus Ewert's 2008 publication *10,000 Dresses*, as well as more recent publications like *Sam!* (2019) and *Jack, Not Jackie* (2018). Although the field of transgender picture books has hardly reached a point of "ethical and aesthetic realism," it appears to be moving in that direction.

Like Ryan and Hermann-Wilmarth, Norton develops an interpretive strategy in response to material constraints that prohibit critical engagement with explicit LGBTQ+ content in children's picture books. Norton refers to the strategy she develops as transreading and suggests that using it to interpret texts can prompt transgender-affirming interpretations of popular children's picture books and, in doing so, trouble unchallenged conflations of sex and gender as well as gender as a binary construct. According to Norton: "Pending the creation of a substantial body of specifically transchildren's [*sic*] literature, we can intervene in the reproductive cycle of transphobia through strategies of transreading: intuiting/interpreting the gender of child characters as not necessarily perfectly aligned with their anatomies" (299). To accomplish this, Norton draws on Jessica Benjamin's work and suggests that we consider gender not as an identity but instead as a series of shifting identifications (301). According to Norton: "Implicit in Benjamin's conception of gender as identificatory rather than identical is the potential for variable (trans) gender subjectivities, and even coincident multiple gender identifications" (303). Identification assumes flexibility and changeability as opposed to the fixity identity connotes. Like Norton, I think children's books can position readers to experience difference, not as otherness, but as a potential point of identification that enables radical empathy across difference, much like queerspawn identify with queer culture and identity because they have affectively experienced queer shame, queer pride, and queer love as their own. It is this identification *with* queerness, even if readers don't quite identify *as* queer, that I suggest has transformative potential.

Although Norton, Ryan, and Hermann-Wilmarth identify a clear need to construct queer reading strategies, they are all passionate about the importance of explicit LGBTQ+ representations. In fact, this is the subject of Ryan and Hermann-Wilmarth's 2018 book *Reading the Rainbow: LGBTQ-Inclusive Literacy Instruction in the Elementary Classroom*, in which the authors suggest that reading LGBTQ+ literature will help students gain a more complex and critical understanding of society. Additionally, in her essay, Norton expressed hope for an archive of children's literature that will "include a range of child subjectivities so broad, and at the same time so individually distinct, as to constitute what I have called a sublime realism" (309). Norton's desire for a realism so inclusive and nuanced that it is sublime echoes Sammy Sass's assertion that for queerspawn "speaking with nuance when you are expected to maintain the standard story" is radical (33). Like Norton, I wish to see the archive of LGBTQ+ children's picture books expand, grow more nuanced, and account for racial, ethnic, religious, and regional differences as well as difference in age and ability. An expanded archive could encourage identification based on affinity, experience, and pleasure while simultaneously recognizing the importance of embodied differences in a social matrix that doesn't enable shared access to power. However, researching the field of LGBTQ+ children's picture books published through 2018, I am grateful for the growing archive of LGBTQ+ children's picture books that does exist, and accounting for this archive with the care it deserves was my motivation for developing a book-length project. Although we haven't reached the point of "sublime realism," I truly see us moving in that direction.

My Archive

For this project, I've identified approximately two hundred LGBTQ+ children's picture books published between 1972 and 2018. As noted, the scope of this project is deliberately limited to explicit representations of lesbian, gay, bisexual, transgender, nonbinary, and queer identities, expressions, and cultures, although I occasionally discuss proto-LGBTQ+ children's books, most often those that demonstrate a commitment to critiquing binary gender norms. Additionally, this text is limited to English-language LGBTQ+ children's picture books available in the United States between 1972 and 2018. This doesn't mean that all books discussed were originally published in the US. Although most were, others were published in Europe or Canada. The books I include were, however, distributed in the US.

My main challenges were identifying and accessing LGBTQ+ children's picture books. I used existing bibliographic and scholarly work to identify relevant books, including Jaime Campbell Naidoo's *Rainbow Family Collections: Selecting and Using Children's Books with Lesbian, Gay, Bisexual, Transgender, and Queer Content* (2012) and B. J. Epstein's *Are the Kids All Right? Representations of LGBTQ Characters in Children's and Young Adult Literature* (2013). In 2008, the ALA started a "Rainbow Book List," which was quite useful (American Library Association, "Rainbow Book Lists"). Digital networks of cultural circulation such as blogs and social media platforms including Twitter and LinkedIn were essential to the project. One blog, Dana Rudolph's *Mombian: Sustenance for Lesbian Moms*, has been a particularly valuable resource. Rudolph founded *Mombian* in 2005 after noticing that few sites focused on culture and politics from the perspective of LGBTQ+ parents. Her blog includes reviews of LGBTQ+ children's picture books, and in January 2021, Rudolph began publishing a database that includes over six hundred searchable LGBTQ+ cultural texts ("Mombian Database").

Although I accessed many books through the University of Texas at Arlington's interlibrary loan system, out-of-print, independently published, self-published, or very new books couldn't be accessed through the library. As a result, I contacted many authors and publishers directly to request copies of their work as well as material about their publishing experiences. Many authors, including Jane Severance, Lesléa Newman, Suzanne DeWitt Hall, Daniel Haack, Deborah Underwood, Jordan Scavone, and Rob Sanders responded, generously answering my questions and sharing their work.

Additionally, some publishers shared review copies of publications, particularly Penny Candy Press and My Family!/Dodi Press. Even more, Flamingo Rampant, a micro press based in Canada, gave me access to several years of their publications as well as promotional materials.

Although I do not claim my archive is exhaustive, it is by far the most extensive collection of books to be identified and analyzed in a scholarly manuscript to date. When I began this project, I knew it was essential to create a large archive from which evidence-based claims could be made. I collected my preliminary research into a prose table in Microsoft Word. The table includes author's name, illustrator's name, publication year, publisher, themes/tropes, and racial/ethnic representation. The tables (available in the appendix) helped me identify a variety of historical shifts and trends in the field of publishing as well as in the content of LGBTQ+ children's picture books.

After preliminary research was complete, I identified dominant tropes. I use the term *trope* to discuss recurring themes, modes of representation, and even available identities and identifications. I suggest that the appearance of specific tropes as well as their disappearance or persistence across time reveals how gender and sexuality are understood at specific historical junctures. For instance, queer youth being bullied as well as queer exceptionalism are persistent and reoccurring themes found in even the earliest LGBTQ+ children's picture books. In early texts, children don't identify queerly even though they are often depicted as desiring queerly, by which I mean wanting things deemed inappropriate within a normative sex-gender-sexuality system.[4] This is important, because lacking articulatable identifications with queerness meant there could be no coming out moment. As a result, it stands to reason that youth coming out, by which I mean articulating a queer identification, is a relatively recent trope that reflects a growing self-awareness among younger children as well as the availability of language to describe one's queer desires. Even more, my research demonstrates that the identifications and identities present in children's picture books change. For instance, in the 2000s, the "sissy boy" of early LGBTQ+ children's picture books morphs into the far more celebratory "pink boy." By creating, analyzing, and historicizing a nuanced taxonomy of tropes found in LGBTQ+ children's picture books, I am able to support the argument that LGBTQ+ children's picture books reflect and prompt changing understandings of gender and sexuality, adult and child relationships, and the function of family.

The Importance of a Comprehensive Archive

In literary and cultural studies, the archive we engage is the data set we theorize from. Most existing literary scholarship makes generalizations about LGBTQ+ children's picture books from too small a data set, which leads scholars to draw conclusions that misrepresent the field. I myself am guilty of this. In one of my previous publications, I referred to post-2000 LGBTQ+ children's picture books as "new queer children's literature" to distinguish them from what I referred to as "old" queer children's literature.[5] I wrote:

> I suggest that in contradistinction to the "old" queer children's literature, which is committed to a narrow vision of normalcy, the new queer children's literature introduces the possibility of queering the straight world. New queer children's literature represents the coexistence of straights and queers in the most intimate of domestic spaces: kitchens, living rooms, playgrounds, and bookshelves. As a result, new queer children's literature takes the most normative of institutions—the family—as an object of critical queering. ("For the Little Queers" 1646)

Although I still think the mingling of straight and queer characters in familial spaces contains transformative potential à la the kind of affective and experiential queering of straights discussed vis-à-vis queerspawn, I no longer stand behind my periodization or my binary construction of "old" and "new" LGBTQ+ children's picture books. At the time, I was working from an archive of about two dozen books. Ironically, in the article I am quite proud of myself for engaging what I considered, at the time, to be a robust data set. Additionally, in the article I'm quite critical of other scholars for generalizing about LGBTQ+ children's picture books based on archives I considered too small. In hindsight, after completing my current research and identifying about two hundred LGBTQ+ children's picture books, I recognize that my earlier distinction between "old" and "new" was not nuanced enough to account for the queerness of many early texts or to acknowledge how disruptive to social norms many LGBTQ+ books published prior to 2000 actually were considering the sociocultural norms prevalent at their publication. Additionally, it doesn't account for the affective investments in normalcy that so often appear in post-2000 texts. The field is far more complex than I accounted for in my early work.

Like my early work, the few articles that engage LGBTQ+ children's picture books are constrained by a limited archive that leads authors to inaccurately describe and assess the field. This is the case with Nathan Taylor's 2012 exploration of LGBTQ+-themed children's books titled "U.S. Children's Picture Books and the Homonormative Subject." Taylor draws his conclusions from a four-book archive of texts available through the Columbus, Ohio library system: *Uncle Bobby's Wedding* by Sarah Brannen (2008), *Molly's Family* by Nancy Garden (2004), and two board books by Lesléa Newman, *Daddy, Papa, and Me* (2009) and *Mommy, Mama, and Me* (2009) (Taylor 141). After studying these books, he argues: "There are no drag queens, no signs of affection between same-gendered adults, no flower boy instead of a flower girl, and no different forms of kinship (e.g., a single, African American, gay male with children)" (141). It is true that the books he identifies have limited representations of LGBTQ+ experiences and embodiments, but the archive itself is limited to four books. Even more, he doesn't seem to consider that the library's purchasing policy likely emphasizes the homonormative. I suggest the archive says more about the Columbus, Ohio library system than it does LGBTQ+ children's picture books, but this doesn't stop Taylor from identifying LGBTQ+ children's picture books as "potentially politically paralyzing and nontransformative" (Taylor 137). Taylor misses books like Laurel Dykstra's *Uncle Aiden* (2005), which hints at polyamory; Rigoberto González's *Antonio's Card* (2005), about a boy embarrassed by his mom's girlfriend who his peers think "looks like a guy"; and Marcus Ewert's *10,000 Dresses* (2008), which is an important early depiction of a transgender girl. If his archive had included these texts, he would likely have drawn very different conclusions.

A critique of LGBTQ+ children's picture books, similar to Taylor's, appears in a 2002 *The Lion and the Unicorn* article by Melynda Huskey. Huskey's article was published at the start of the surge in LGBTQ+ children's picture books that occurred at the turn of the millennium. As a result, her analysis focuses on Alyson Wonderland Books publications from the 1990s, including the second edition of Lesléa Newman's 1989 picture book *Heather Has Two Mommies* (1990), Michael Willhoite's *Daddy's Roommate* (1990), and Johnny Valentine's *The Duke Who Outlawed Jelly Beans* (1991). Alyson Wonderland Books was the children's imprint of Alyson Books, a press specializing in gay and lesbian fiction. Huskey writes:

Picture books compulsively exhibit gay or lesbian adults connected by family ties to nonsexual, presumptively latently heterosexual child/children. There are no gay or protogay children in these texts—that would open too clear a route to the forbidden realm of desire. What these books must avoid at all costs is any affect that might activate the pernicious myth of recruitment." (68)

Huskey seems to suggest that LGBTQ+ children's picture books of the early-1990s were neither disruptive not transformative. I suggest, more generously, that representations of gays and lesbians in children's picture books do indeed disrupt a visual economy that depicts LGBTQ+ persons as deviant when visible at all. Even more, Huskey's assessment that authors self-censor to avoid controversy doesn't hold up, as the books she discusses were met with repeated challenges. In other words, there is no winning path that will allow creators to avoid "activat[ing] the pernicious myth of recruitment." One example of the controversy caused by both Willhoite's and Newman's work took place in the 1990s when Oregon Citizens Alliance, a conservative Christian political activist organization founded by Lon Mabon, used their picture books to fuel arguments that would amend Oregon's state constitution to legalize anti-LGB discrimination (Egan). LGBTQ+ children's picture books continue to be censored, their authors frequently have events canceled, and many states have policies in place to keep LGBTQ+ children's picture books out of classrooms and libraries (Pitman; Curwood et al.; Garry). Regardless of how seemingly assimilatory and nontransformative some queer scholars find LGBTQ+ children's picture books, many conservatives perceive them as a threat. I suggest that, like Taylor's, Huskey's claims about LGBTQ+ children's picture books misrepresent the field in part because she works from a limited archive.

To be clear, I am not rejecting Taylor's and Huskey's critiques of homo-normativity entirely. Instead, I'm suggesting that interpreting LGBTQ+ children's books as homonormative is a hasty move, and I am arguing that a more nuanced reading of LGBTQ+ children's picture books is enabled if we broaden the archive and study it more optimistically. Additionally, I argue that new historicist and cultural studies strategies can help us understand the cultural work that LGBTQ+ children's picture books do. To date, no project has mapped the field of LGBTQ+ children's picture books, making them knowable to a wide audience while also identifying characteristics of the field at its early stages and mapping shifts in content, production, and distribution through its development. This book moves from decade to decade, identifying dominant tropes, discussing the production and distribution of LGBTQ+ children's picture books, and interpreting these books to identify their constraints and transformative potential.

Throughout this book, I make several interrelated claims about LGBTQ+ children's picture books. First, I argue that LGBTQ+ children's picture books can illuminate dominant social realities and should be read as a historical archive that reveals changing sociocultural norms related to gender, sexuality, family, and even adult-child relationships generally. Second, I suggest that LGBTQ+ children's picture books have the power to challenge dominant social realities by revealing the ways social identities, ideas, and institutions create a world that fails to do justice to queer children and adults. Third, I suggest LGBTQ+ children's picture books are worldmaking projects that can usher in new ways of perceiving and acting in the world. Relatedly, I suggest that LGBTQ+ children's picture books can prompt affective identifications with queerness, similar to that experienced by "queerspawn." In other words: LGBTQ+ children's picture books: 1) show us the world as it is, 2) show us what isn't working, and 3) prompt us to imagine and enact change.

Methodology

My book project explores the politics and possibilities of LGBTQ+ children's picture books by identifying and interpreting a rich archive of texts distributed in the US from the 1970s to 2018. As suggested previously, in literary and cultural studies, the archive we create and theorize from is essential to understanding sociocultural phenomena and the worldmaking work they do. Just as important are the critical lenses we use to apprehend the object of our analysis as it manifests at various points on the Circuit of Culture, a term coined by Birmingham School of Cultural Studies scholars to explore the relationship between various aspects of culture, including production, consumption, and regulation. In this section, I describe the theoretical frameworks I use to: 1) analyze the archive and produce a foundational understanding of LGBTQ+ children's picture books as a field, 2) analyze subfields of LGBTQ+ children's picture books (e.g. pink boy texts), 3) analyze individual texts within the field, and 4) theorize the transformative potential of the field.

Cultural Studies

My genealogical approach emerges out of my commitment to cultural studies, particularly the work of Birmingham scholars like Raymond Williams, Paul du Gay, and Stuart Hall. Raymond Williams's understanding of society as dynamic, power as decentralized, and culture as in flux is essential to how I interpret the field of LGBTQ+ children's picture books as a historical archive that reveals shifts in the meaning and materiality of gender, sexuality, family, and adult-child relationships. It also influences my understanding of LGBTQ+ children's picture books as worldmaking projects that reflect, revise, and reinvent the social world, often intervening in dominant sociocultural meanings by modeling new ways of thinking and acting in the world.

Williams's discussion of dominant, emergent, and residual cultural forms in *Marxism and Literature* (1997) inspired my genealogical approach as well as my interest in identifying tropes and analyzing historical shifts in representations of queerness. Williams writes:

> In authentic historical analysis it is necessary at every point to recognize the complex interrelation between movements and tendencies both within and beyond a specific and effective dominance. It is necessary to examine how these relate to the whole cultural process rather than only to the selected and abstracted dominant system. (121)

By this he means that it is important to identify and describe dominant culture and how it operates in a given social world and historical epoch, but it is also important to understand the dominant as one site of meaning making within a larger sociocultural field that reverberates with a multiplicity of meanings and materialities with dynamic relations, not just to the dominant, but to one another. Even more, Williams suggests we look at culture not just as moving through linear stages of transformation but as being essentially nonidentical to itself at any particular historical moment. In other words, residual, dominant, and emerging coexist.

Williams introduces the terms *residual* and *emergent* to discuss the dynamism and distinguishable forces influencing meaning and materiality at any given time. By *residual* he means that "which has been effectively formed in the past" but "is still active in the cultural process, not only and often not at all as an element of the past, but as an effective element of the present" (122).

Williams further explains that dominant culture will try to incorporate and control the oppositional potential of residual culture by means of "reinter-pretation, dilution, projection, discriminating inclusion and exclusion" (123). Williams uses the term *emergent* to suggest that "new meanings and values, new practices, new relationships and kinds of relationships are continually being created" (123). For him, the trick is to understand and differentiate new iterations of the dominant and instances of emergent culture that oppose it. Williams theorizes that truly oppositional emergent culture will be identified and incorporated by dominant culture much as dominant culture incorpo-rates the residual in order to control it. He suggests that incorporation can look like acknowledgment and acceptance but is motivated by the need to neutralize opposition. Williams is a Marxist focused on socioeconomic class, and he is invested in understanding the reproduction of capitalism and its buttressing logics. My project is clearly quite different. However, like capital-ism, the sex-gender system must be constantly reproduced and maintained. Also, like capitalism, the sex-gender system is a construct whose material effects are made to seem natural and inevitable, but one that is, nonetheless, vulnerable to oppositional forces.

In addition to Williams's theory of dominant, residual, and emergent culture, I found the Circuit of Culture model popularized by Birmingham School cultural studies scholars in the 1990s useful. The Circuit of Culture model illustrates the complexity of making meaning in society and theorizes the sociocultural work that cultural texts partake in. According to Paul du Gay, "Rather than be seen as merely reflective of other processes—economic or political—culture is now regarded as being as constitutive of the social world as economic or political processes" (xxix). This theory of culture sees it as playing a significant role in the creation of social realities. When I refer to LGBTQ+ children's picture books as worldmaking projects, it is with an understanding of the meaning making that cultural texts partake in and the influence these meanings have on social practices, institutions, and identities. To put it plainly, texts have material effects.

The Circuit of Culture model encourages cultural studies scholars to ana-lyze "the biography of a cultural artefact" (du Gay xxx). In other words, to understand the meaning, not just of individual LGBTQ+ children's picture books, but of the field itself, it is necessary to understand the articulation of several processes. In this context, articulation refers to "the form of the connection that can make a unity of two or more different elements, under certain conditions"(du Gay xxx). To look at it another way, several interrelated elements weave together to enable and constrain the way cultural texts emerge in the world as well as the meaning the texts make and the meaning that is made of them.

The Circuit of Culture model helps identify the elements that, taken together, reveal the shifting, situated, and contingent meaning of cultural objects. As noted, these elements include: 1) representation, 2) identity, 3) production, 4) consumption, and 5) regulation. Analyzing the representation of a cultural object requires one to identify discourses about the object in which meaning is made of the object. Earlier, I suggested that moralistic panic narratives about the influence LGBTQ+ children's books may have on children frame how individual texts are received, since many cisgender heterosexuals are introduced to them as a problem to be solved through censorship as opposed to a solution to the problem of homophobia. By identifying the ways LGBTQ+ children's picture books emerge as an identifiable cultural object, one can begin to understand the meaning made of these books as a whole and, by extension, their position in a larger matrix of sociocultural meaning and materiality.

Identity refers to "various groups and types of people" associated with the cultural object (du Gay xxi). Here, we can develop a more robust understanding of a cultural object by naming its target audience as well as various stakeholders. In the case of LGBTQ+ children's picture books, I consider who authored, illustrated, published, distributed, read, wrote about, and censored specific texts. Of course, there is an inevitable incompleteness to this project. My hope is that the work begun here will generate future scholarship.

Production encompasses how meaning is encoded, or embedded, in a cultural text via genre, focalization, tone, and other storytelling techniques. The formal elements of a text or series of texts are a significant part of the work they may accomplish, which is why I discuss focalization throughout my interpretations of texts. There is, of course, much more work to be done in this area than I was able to accomplish in this book.

Consumption refers to the process by which audiences decode a text, and this process will be affected by various factors. Du Gay writes: "In other words, meanings are not just 'sent' by producers and 'received' passively by consumers; rather meanings are actively made in consumption, through the use to which people put those products in their everyday lives" (xxxii). This understanding of cultural consumption suggests that readers play an active role in interpreting cultural texts rather than simply receiving messages. For example, young children with an LGBTQ+ parent or parents may bring a different understanding of family formation to texts than children with cisgender, heterosexual parents. The meaning made of texts isn't static but is as dynamic as the field of cultural production itself. Stuart Hall has elaborated on the relationship between production and consumption extensively (Hall, "Encoding/Decoding"; Hall, "Introduction to Media Studies at the Center"; Hall, *Representation*).

Finally, regulation refers to conditions that influence the production, distribution, and consumption of texts. Throughout this project, I consider technological shifts that both enable and constrain the creation of LGBTQ+ children's picture books. For instance, the availability of platforms like GoFundMe permits creators to connect with potential audiences and raise money to create products with minimal personal financial risk, encouraging the creation of self-published texts (GoFundMe). Additionally, censorship initiatives to keep LGBTQ+ children's picture books out of schools and libraries as well as assumptions about their limited market appeal regulate the archive. A full picture of the sociocultural work that LGBTQ+ children's picture books do and the social forces both enabling and constraining them can only be drawn by studying the Circuit of Culture. Even more, it is essential to note that this must be an ongoing project. In other words, because culture is fluid and changing, no aspect of it can be known fully or once and for all.

Theoretical Influences

My interpretive readings of both individual LGBTQ+ children's picture books and the field as a whole are indebted to queer theories of affect and social transformation as well as queer critiques of homonormativity and social hierarchy. Several texts were particularly significant as I developed two concepts that inform my interpretations of LGBTQ+ children's picture books: critical optimism and queer love. Although very much influenced by queer theory, throughout the book I do not engage specific theorists at length for many reasons, primarily to optimize the text's accessibility to a wide audience. That being said, I do want to briefly acknowledge the scholars and scholarship that have shaped my thinking about the significant influence culture has on our understanding of self, other, and world. First, Eve Sedgwick's "Paranoid Reading and Reparative Reading, or, You're So Paranoid,

You Probably Think This Essay Is About You" encouraged me to consider the politics and privilege of skepticism as well as the queer potential of optimism. Sedgwick's investment in hope is also present in work by queer scholars of color, including Jose Estaban Muñoz's *Cruising Utopia: The Then and There of Queer Futurity* and Joshua Chambers-Letson's *After the Party: A Manifesto for Queer of Color Life*. Muñoz theorizes the political potential of art and culture to encourage the development of a radical imagination capable of thinking and enacting a just future. Joshua Chambers-Letson engages Muñoz's work to consider how specific cultural texts and performances by minoritarian creators are rehearsals for future forms of sociality as well as practices of freedom in the present. In addition to this highly theoretical work, Charlene Carruthers's *Unapologetic: A Black, Queer, and Feminist Mandate for Radical Movements* draws on the author's experience organizing Black youth in Chicago as well as the Black radical tradition to strategize justice-oriented community building and self-care initiatives.

Along with scholarship that considers the relationship between culture and social transformation, Mari Ruti's work on affect in *The Ethics of Opting Out: Queer Theory's Defiant Subjects* has informed my understanding of identifications with queerness as well as radical empathy. Ruti considers the potential collapse of distinctions between self and other, which I suggest describes the affective identification with queerness experienced by queer-spawn as well as the parent-advocates of queer kids that I refer to as queer love and discuss in later chapters. Teasing out the transformative potential of LGBTQ+ children's picture books is, in part, about strategizing ways to change and transform the subject of hetero- and homonormativity. Although I identify attachments to oppressive regimes of gender and sexual, as well as race and class, hierarchy in LGBTQ+ children's literature, I also acknowledge the desire for change, the hope for a better world, that permeates the field. I refer to this reading strategy as critical optimism, as opposed to naïve or even cruel optimism (Berlant).

Critical Optimism

I read LGBTQ+ children's picture books through an interpretive lens characterized by critical optimism to highlight the field's transformative potential as a queer worldmaking project while accounting for, perhaps inevitable, attachments to regimes of normativity and social hierarchy so frequently present. As an interpretive lens, critical optimism assumes LGBTQ+ children's picture books can be productively read multiple ways and that the reading strategies one employs are political. I find critical optimism to be a far more productive interpretive framework than the homonormative panic narrative performed by scholars like Huskey and Taylor, which I argue obscures more about the queer potential of LGBTQ+ children's picture books than it reveals. My own approach to LGBTQ+ children's picture books remains committed to identifying and critiquing attachments to identities, ideas, and institutions that reproduce power inequities, while graciously and gratefully reading the archive for the worldmaking potential that emerges within it—in other words, for its transformative potential. I acknowledge that the creators of these texts were and are putting representations of LGBTQ+ identities and experiences into a world that often receives them with hostility. As previously suggested, LGBTQ+ children's picture books disrupt a field of sociocultural possibility that privileges heterosexuality by rendering queer genders and sexualities invisible or undesirable when represented. In 1980, Adrienne Rich introduced the term *compulsory heterosexuality* to describe the ubiquity of heterosexuality in dominant cultural and concomitant representations of lesbians as deviant. She convincingly claimed that culture overdetermines heterosexual identification and reifies heteronormativity (636). LGBTQ+ children's picture books refuse the mandate of erasure, particularly the imperative to erase LGBTQ+ people and culture from children's view. Instead, LGBTQ+ children's picture books demonstrate that LGBTQ+ persons are already part of children's worlds. Even at their most homonormative, and this is frankly most of the time, LGBTQ+ children's picture books demand LGBTQ+ visibility and challenge stigma associated with LGBTQ+ identities and experiences. This certainly influences dominant culture. If it didn't, the radical Right wouldn't work so hard to censor these materials.

Queer Love

To again conjure Rudine Sims Bishop's metaphor, LGBTQ+ children's books do the important work of providing windows and mirrors of queer lives. These books offer affirming reflections of queer lives that LGBTQ+ children as well as cisgender heterosexual children raised in proximity to queerness can see themselves and their experiences in. These images are essential windows that humanize LGBTQ+ identities, expressions, and communities for children who may have no access to queer worlds outside of picture books. However, it is the potential of LGBTQ+ children's books to be "sliding glass doors" that emboldens my understanding of queer love, which is where I find the most transformative potential in LGBTQ+ children's picture books. Bishop claims books can be sliding glass doors, inviting readers into the world created in the texts. When it is a queer-affirming world that children step into, young readers can be provoked by the pleasures of queerness, they can think and act queerly—purposefully, playfully, and strategically troubling regimes of gender and, to a lesser extent, sexual normativity. As a result, I suggest that in addition to changing "attitudes towards difference," which is certainly a significant project, we need to theorize children's picture books' potential to help us identify and release attachments to privilege as well as to desires that require us to support oppressive institutions that reproduce the world as it is—racist, patriarchal, heteronormative (trans- and homophobic), ableist, and so on. Inspired by Rudine Sims Bishop's metaphor of sliding glass doors as well as Ruti's understanding of self and other, I suggest the transformative potential of LGBTQ+ children's picture books is located in the momentary shattering of the distinction between self and other, a moment that can prompt affectively oriented identifications across difference. In other words, can we all be queered by children's picture books, and what potential does that queering hold? To consider the queer possibilities of LGBTQ+ children's picture books, I introduce the term *queer love* and identify some of its manifestations within and outside of LGBTQ+ children's picture books.

Many contributors to Zook and Epstein-Fine's project note that they experienced queerness as children and that queerness remains a feature of their adult lives. This proximate experience of queerness is one place where I find the potential for radical empathy across difference. Another example of identification with queerness from a position outside of queer identity can be found in the work of cisgender heterosexual parent-advocates who work to make the world a queerer world for the love of their LGBTQ+ children. In fact, my theory of queer love first emerged while I worked on a research project about Lori Duron's mommy blog, *Raising My Rainbow*, where she posts about raising a gender-creative child (Miller, "Queering the Straight World?"). My close readings of her posts prompted me to think about the intellectual and affective labor that mothering a child whose oppression is tethered to your privilege must entail. It is here that I began theorizing queer love as a mode of radical empathy. I work with this concept throughout the book, but especially in chapter four, which considers parent-advocates' attempt to create a pink boy category to garner acceptance for their gender-creative sons.

To be queered by proximity and affinity, like queerspawn or the cisgender, heterosexual parents of queer children, is to experience queer love. Amplifying queer love is the hope that haunts this book like a ghost from a not-quite-imaginable queer future. My theory is that queer love can disrupt clear distinctions between self and other, queer and straight, even in children's books that are reasonably described as normalizing and assimilationist. In other words, the proximity of queerness and straightness represented in most LGBTQ+ children's picture books contains the possibility of a new type of queer subjectivity to emerge, a new kind of queer world to be imagined and created.

Imaginative Labor, Transformative Possibilities

Writing more generally about the transformative potential of children's literature, in "A Plea for Radical Children's Literature," author and educator Herbert Kohl makes several observations about the imaginative work children's literature can encourage or constrain. Kohl argues that few children's picture books challenge "the economic and social structure of our society and the values of capitalism" (59). As a result, children aren't encouraged to question inherited social realities; instead, as Kohl convincingly contends, they are indoctrinated with ideas and ideals that naturalize and reproduce privilege and oppression. This, he reasons, is due to the focus in children's literature on individualism (60). He explains: "The stories we provide to youngsters have to do with personal challenge and individual success. They have to do with independence, personal responsibility, and autonomy. The social imagination that encourages thinking about solidarity, cooperation, group struggle, and belonging to a caring group is relegated to minority status" (63). I find Kohl's critique cogent and applicable to LGBTQ+ children's picture books.

Dismally few LGBTQ+ children's picture books consider queer community and activism. Of course, there are notable exceptions, but these exceptions are few and far between. *A House for Everyone* (2018), written by Jo Hirst and illustrated by Naomi Bardoff, is one example of a text that focuses on community cooperation and queer worldmaking. Gender is troubled throughout the text as a group of children, sans adults, work together to build a house they can all enjoy. The children decide what to do and accomplish the task cooperatively. Bardoff's thoughtful images depict a variety of races and queer gender expressions. For instance, Ivy, a young girl with tan skin and short, dark hair, is the fastest runner in the group, so she runs all around the playground collecting sticks for the house. Ivy's hair and boyish clothes could mark her as a boy, but she is cisgender even though she does not conform to gender expectations. Another child, the pale-skinned Alex, uses the pronoun *they* and does not identify as a girl or boy. Sam, a long-haired boy whose black hair contrasts with his light, pink-toned skin, collects plants and flowers. He decorates the house, so it will look beautiful. A brown-skinned, curly-haired boy named Jackson likes to wear dresses. He is very strong and carries heavy rocks to put inside the house to "make comfortable seats for everyone." Tom, a boy with tan skin, likes to spell and arranges rocks to create a "welcome" sign in front of the home. When he was born, everyone thought he was a girl, but now they understand he is a boy. Gender possibilities are part of the text's reality, but they are not presented as a problem to be solved. The characters challenge the dominant sex-gender system as well as the conflation of gender identity and gender expression. Even more, it shows children working together, cooperating to create something for all of them.

Another example is a Flamingo Rampant Press publication, *The Zero Dads Club* (2015), which is written by Angel Adeyoha and illustrated by Aubrey Williams. The story unfolds around Father's Day. Two children with dark brown skin, Akilah and Kai, sit next to each other at a desk. Akilah complains to Kai about painting an image of a tie. She is upset because neither of their families includes a father. The activist-minded Akilah suggests they protest Father's Day, but after some discussion, they decide to instead start a club, which they name the Moms Only Club. As the club's membership grows, the young activists change the name to the Zero Dads Club to account for members who have neither moms nor dads. Their flexibility and accountability to one another serves as an inclusive activist model, demonstrating that aspects of an organization can change without compromising its integrity.

The group of first graders in the Zero Dads Club meets to support one another and make cards for the grown-ups they love. A celebration of multiple family forms ensues. Cards are created for a transgender mom, lesbian moms, a single mom, an abuela, and a tía. This picture book is noteworthy since children work collectively to solve an institutional problem made by adults. Their family forms are rendered invisible, and by extension unworthy, by the school, which assumes the presence of a father in all families. Even more, this picture book provides young readers with an inspirational vision of solidarity, cooperation, and belonging they can imitate.

Although *A House for Everyone* and *The Zero Dads Club* are rare examples of LGBTQ+ children's picture books centered on community solidarity, the field of LGBTQ+ children's picture books does contain many books that "fundamentally question the world" and that offer "new possibilities for living and acting" in the world (Kohl 63). Herbert Kohl is convinced of the transformative potential of children's literature. He suggests that "what is read in childhood not only leaves an impression behind but also influences the values, and shapes the dreams, of children" (61). By thinking broadly about what transformative or, to use Kohl's language, radical children's literature might look like, I find more reason for critical optimism. This is because even the most homonormative LGBTQ+ children's literature makes LGBTQ+ identities, expressions, and communities thinkable. LGBTQ+ children's literature makes queerness possible, even desirable. And, yes, it too often does that by representing lesbian and gay adults as like heterosexuals, but it posits a forceful challenge to dominant culture and dominant cultural values. Kohl writes:

> The imagination gives rise to the idea of possibility, and to the contrast between what is and what might be. The power of the imagination comes from our ability to entertain alternatives to what we have experienced or have been told. The existence of imagination is perhaps the originating force of the ideas of freedom, choice, and the possibility of personal, social, and political change. If we were not able to imagine the world as other than it is, then taking an active role in change would be unthinkable. (62)

The overwhelming cisgender heterosexuality of children's literature is troubled by the existence of LGBTQ+ children's picture books that encourage students to consider alternatives to oppressive gender roles and naturalized heterosexuality.

Toward Historical and Sociopolitical Understanding

In addition to envisioning a transformed world, as implied by Kohl, picture books can help readers confront the world as it is, which reveals the gap between the justice we desire and the reality we too often settle for. In *Critical Multicultural Analysis of Children's Literature: Windows, Mirrors, and Doors*, Maria Jose Botelho and Masha Kabakow Rudman "advocate for reading that goes beyond stretching children's cultural imagination, to reading that fosters historical and sociopolitical imagination" (xiv). They assert: "Children's books offer windows into society, they are sites for struggle among shifting, changing, overlapping, and historically diverse social identities" (2). According to Botelho and Rudman, children's books are sites of cultural struggle and transformation in which warring ideologies, values, and perspectives collide to encourage readers to develop critical consciousness of privilege, power, and oppression.

Writers like Rudine Sims Bishop, Herbert Kohl, and Maria Jose Botelho and Masha Kabakow Rudman influence my understanding of LGBTQ+ children's picture books as historical archives and worldmaking projects as well as my understanding of the exchange between these elements. This book maps the field of LGBTQ+ children's picture books to foster an understanding of the field's internal characteristics and complexities as well as the outside forces that influence everything from content to consumption.

Chapter Summaries

I begin my genealogy of LGBTQ+ children's picture books in chapter two, "A Genealogy of LGBTQ+ Children's Picture Books: The Early Years." This chapter covers the 1970s, 1980s, and 1990s. Although I am surely missing some texts, I sought to be thorough in my research so all my claims about LGBTQ+ children's picture books would be derived from an archive that truly represents the field. In this chapter, I identify popular tropes that emerged in the "early years" of LGBTQ+ children's picture books and begin to trace their development. Additionally, I discuss shifts in publishing and distribution practices that have shaped the field of LGBTQ+ children's picture books. Although there are very few literary analyses of explicitly LGBTQ+ children's books available, I identify and engage relevant scholarship throughout the book. The taxonomy of tropes introduced in this chapter becomes the organizational framework of subsequent chapters, which focus on specific tropes introduced in the early years of LGBTQ+ children's picture books while introducing new ones that emerge after 2000.

In chapter three, "Virtually Normal: Lesbian and Gay Grown-Ups in Children's Picture Books," I identify and analyze representations of lesbian and gay marriage and family life post-2000. Using new historicist methods, I contextualize representations of same-sex marriage within a larger socio-political framework by considering public sphere debates about marriage equality throughout the 2000s and 2010s. Representations of lesbian and gay family life found in this chapter are further taxonomized to identify nuanced trends. I read representative texts through a framework of critical optimism to suggest that although many LGBTQ+ children's books do represent lesbian and gay adults within homonormative frames, a critique found in most of the scholarship, they also challenge parenting as the property of heterosexuals and suggest that the world can be made better by queerness.

In chapter four, "Beyond the Sissy Boy: Pink Boys and Tomboys," I explore the short-lived phenomenon of the pink boy, a category parents of effeminate boys tried to normalize from around 2005 to 2010. I analyze published inter-views with the authors of what I refer to as pink boy books to demonstrate that they were motivated by activism and advocacy to secure representational and physical space for pink boys. I suggest that the parents of pink boys experience "queer love" because of their affinity with their queer children, which has the potential to queer them. I am also critical of several aspects of these books, including the association of effeminate boyhoods with play, which I suggest inadvertently diminishes the transformative potential of gender disruption. I also critique the taken-for-granted assumption that masculine girls have easier childhoods than feminine boys, which is implied in attempts to create the pink boy category as an identification possibility similar to that of the tomboy.

In chapter five, "Queer Youth and Gender: Representing Transgender, Nonbinary, Gender-Creative, and Gender-Free Youth," I consider LGBTQ+ children's picture books that challenge the naturalness and inevitability of the sex-gender system. Although books featuring transgender and nonbinary children were infrequent prior to 2010, they now compose a sizeable subfield within LGBTQ+ children's picture books. I introduce recent sociological studies about transgender children to historicize and contextualize the emer-gence of LGBTQ+ children's picture books about transgender and nonbinary children within a large-scale shift in the meaning of gender.

In chapter six, "Queer Youth and Sexuality: Camp Flamboyance, Queer Fabulousness, and Even a Little Same-Gender Desire," I explore texts that gesture toward children's potential homosexuality, often coded through flam-boyance or fabulousness. I introduce Susan Sontag's idea of camp as well as Madison Moore's recent theorizations of fabulousness (Moore; Sontag). In this chapter, I also consider representations of adult homosexuality that children can identify *with* as a result of the character's representation as someone's child and, at times, as childlike (Bansch; Haan and Nijland). I read key texts through the framework of critical optimism to demonstrate the transformative potential of representations of queer desire.

In chapter seven, "Queer Histories: The Politics of Representing the Past," I discuss nonfiction LGBTQ+ children's picture books. As of 2018, there were only half a dozen LGBTQ+ children's picture books exploring activist biographies and histories, and this chapter considers what history is imagined as inheritable by creators of LGBTQ+ children's picture books. After identifying what queer histories are currently available, I consider the attachments to neoliberal cultural, political, and economic ideals embedded in the texts.

Chapter Two

A Genealogy of LGBTQ+ Children's Picture Books

The Early Years

This chapter focuses on English-language LGBTQ+ children's picture books that were published or readily available in the US prior to 2000. It maps the emergence and development of dominant themes and tropes in these books. Sections are divided by decade into the 1970s, 1980s, and 1990s. I've identified fewer than fifty LGBTQ+ children's picture books published in this thirty-year period, but those that were form a significant historical archive that reveals shifts in dominant understandings of gender and sexuality as well as adult-child relationships. Several representative books from each period are analyzed through the framework of critical optimism to make sense of literature within the historical context of its creation as well as to explore children's picture books as creative worldmaking projects that disrupt heteronormative children's culture. Subsequent chapters explore postmillennial LGBTQ+ children's picture books and are thematically clustered around the tropes introduced in this chapter as well as new ones that emerge after 2000.

Teresa de Lauretis introduced the term *queer theory* at a University of California, Santa Cruz conference about lesbian and gay sexualities in February 1990 (Miller, "Thirty Years of Queer Theory"). At the conference, which was later collected in a 1991 special issue of *Differences: A Feminist Cultural Studies Journal*, de Lauretis argued that, by resisting the imperative of heterosexuality, lesbian and gay sexualities introduce nonnormative and potentially transformative intimate and social relations into the world. Although much queer theory pivots around explorations of sexuality, in the original conference proceedings, de Lauretis noted that queer theory had the potential to reveal and respond to "constructed silences" around race, ethnicity, class, and gender ("Queer Theory" vi). Throughout this book, I use the term *queer* to describe that which resists discursive and institutional regimes of normativity. I identify as queer both gender and sexual identities and expressions that challenge the dominant sex-gender-sexuality system. Importantly, which representations I identify as expressing queer genders or sexualities at a particular historical juncture change over time because regimes of normativity are themselves changeable. For instance, a girl committed to wearing jeans and being a doctor when she grows up is a queer representation in the 1970s, but in the 2010s, jeans-wearing girls who want to be surgeons are no longer challenging dominant gender expectations. As a result, in this chapter, I discuss early representations of tomboys in picture books, not as precursors to later representations of nonbinary and transgender children, but as themselves queer. Additionally, I trace representations of sissy boys and, later, pink boys to consider shifts in the meaning of gender as well as changing parental attachments to and investments in gender normativity represented in picture books. As I hope to demonstrate, queer genders, like queer sexualities, introduce new, possibly transformative ways of relating to self, other, and society. Even more, throughout my analysis of genders and sexualities, it will be clear that although gender and sexuality should not be collapsed, they have a complicated relationship to each other.

An understanding of capitulations and refusals of dominant social norms is essential to my theorization of LGBTQ+ children's picture books as a field and the cultural work the field accomplishes, which is why I've introduced critical optimism as an interpretive framework. It allows me to identify homonormativity, while suggesting that homonormativity should never exhaust our analysis of LGBTQ+ children's picture books. To that end, I'm interested in interpreting the forms that inclusion takes as well as what happens to the dominant (straight) social world when queerness is interjected into "straight" spaces like home and school. Additionally, I describe and analyze multiple instances in which representations in LGBTQ+ children's picture books "queer" dominant understandings of gender, sexuality, children/childhood, and adult-child relationships.

In the 1970s, 1980s, and 1990s, LGBTQ+ children's picture books were most often published by small, mission-oriented, nonprofit presses, which allowed creators to produce content without the pressures of appealing to a large audience or bringing in a large profit. The few presses that produced LGBTQ+ children's picture books were often committed to publishing anti-sexist and antiracist books, even if the lack of diverse editorial and creative staff often led to poor implementation of espoused goals (Everett). Authors and illustrators were usually paid a modest one-time fee for their work, and profits made by presses were put into producing more books (Everett). In her history of feminist children's picture book press Lollipop Power Inc., Merrikay Everett Brown notes that the nonprofit

> felt that children needed to see different ways of living and acting between the sexes and in families. Along with the non-sexist theme, they also wanted to portray members of minority and low-income groups more realistically, and they hoped, by producing books with the non-sexist, non-racist themes, that they could help free the minds of children, and eventually, adults. (7–8)

Independent presses like this were central to the early development of LGBTQ+ children's picture books before 2000, which is when more established presses as well as the ease of self-publishing began to open new paths to publication. Without the pressure to turn a profit and guided by a mission to challenge unjust social relations by critiquing racism, sexism, and homophobia, LGBTQ+ children's picture books of the 1970s, 1980s, and 1990s often offered visions of a transformed world. However, books were just as likely to, perhaps inadvertently, reproduce stereotypes or represent a narrow vision of the good life anchored to white, middle-class values and ideals. Caught between attachments to an imperfect world and desire to envision a transformed social reality, LGBTQ+ children's picture books are best read using critical optimism as an interpretive strategy to acknowledge when books are caught by a reality that constrains imagination and an imagination that desires radical change.

Persistent Tropes in Early LGBTQ+ Children's Picture Books

As noted, fewer than fifty LGBTQ+ children's picture books were published prior to 2000. Some of the books I discuss in this chapter, particularly those representing tomboys and "sissy boys," might not even be identified as queer by many scholars. However, I suggest that they are important parts of queer literary history that influence more recent and more decidedly queer representations. The first cluster of three tropes I identify is primarily associated with child characters and includes 1) the "sissy boy," 2) queer exceptionalism, and 3) "boy-meets-skirt." The second cluster of tropes that emerges includes 1) "virtually normal" lesbian- and gay-parented families, 2) family diversity, and 3) the gay uncle.

The "sissy boy" trope is introduced in the 1970s and is reintroduced and transformed in subsequent decades. The sissy boy is a young effeminate boy with a proclivity for objects and activities associated with women and girls. The sissy boy is not necessarily coded as gay. This distinction is important, because after 2000, child characters are more explicitly coded gay through association with "camp," a point discussed at length in chapter six. In the 2000s, the "sissy boy" trope is slowly replaced by a new trope, that of the "pink boy." This representational shift, and the cultural transformations it reflects, is discussed in chapter four. In early LGBTQ+ children's picture books, the "sissy boy" trope often appears alongside the trope of "queer exceptionalism."

Children's books that include the trope of queer exceptionalism may at first appear to celebrate queer difference, but actually render it banal by putting queerness at the service of dominant cisgender, heterosexual society. Queer exceptionalism requires queer adversity, which is often linked to the policing of gender and sexual norms or "difference" more broadly construed. In other words, queerness, most often boyhood effeminacy, is represented as a problem to be solved in sissy boy books. The solution isn't performing masculinity, but instead demonstrating that boys can have feminine qualities and be useful to the cisgender, heterosexual world. Queer difference is celebrated, or at least tolerated, once the queer character proves themself worthy. When this trope appears alongside the "sissy boy" trope, it shows how the sissy boy can move from a position of social ostracization to one of social purposefulness.

The last trope in this cluster is the "boy-meets-skirt" trope. Like queer exceptionalism, the "boy-meets-skirt" trope often appears to celebrate difference while most often neutralizing its transformative potential. The theme first appears in Bruce Mack's 1979 picture book, *Jesse's Dream Skirt*, but it is not until the 2000s that, through repetition, it emerges as a trope. Recent books that use this trope represent skirts (or similar objects associated with femininity) as queer objects of desire. Although the grown-up world of drag may haunt these texts, it is never explicitly engaged in them. Possession of the skirt is often presented as an end in itself. In other words, although the skirt certainly queers the child, it does not imply homosexuality, transgender identification, or even gender transgression, since one of the primary tasks of the representation is normalization, at least in its post-2000 iteration, when it is most frequently paired with the "pink boy" trope.

Importantly, in 2020, several children's picture books that explicitly engage drag were published, including Little Miss Hot Mess's *The Hips on the Drag Queen Go Swish, Swish, Swish*, Ellie Royce's *Auntie-Uncle: Drag Queen Hero*, Desmond Napoles's *Be Amazing: A History of Pride*, Michelle Tea's *Tabitha and Magoo Dress Up Too*, and *RuPaul Charles*, a board book bio from Little Bee Books' People of Pride series. These all introduce young readers to queer culture and gender play joyfully and unapologetically. Whereas boy-meets-skirt tales focus on children who enjoy wearing skirts and dresses, representations of drag focus on adult characters. Additionally, the emphasis is on queer culture in the latter texts, not negotiating straight society. I do not see recent representations of drag as similar to boy-meets-skirt narratives. If anything, they more closely resemble the very few representations of queer culture available, most notably those focused on Pride parades.

The second cluster of tropes emerges in LGBTQ+ children's picture books about adult LGBTQ+ characters. The "virtually normal" trope constructs gays and lesbians, most often gay and lesbian parents, as indistinguishable from their straight counterparts. Gay conservative Andrew Sullivan popularized this claim in his 1995 publication *Virtually Normal: An Argument about Homosexuality*. Sullivan argues that because gays and lesbians are just like heterosexuals, the state should treat them the same as heterosexuals. This logic leads him to argue in support of same-sex marriage and against antidiscrimination laws (Sullivan). Sullivan-style gay and lesbian politics has been labeled homonormative by many queer theorists, as discussed in my introduction (Duggan, *Twilight of Equality?*; Duggan, "New Homonormativity"; Warner). Others have labeled it gay pragmatism to suggest that the liberal logics informing the position—logics that foreground the individual and equality before the law—obstruct the transformative potential of queer politics by only serving the interests of elite, white, upper-middle-class, gay men (Muñoz). For instance, queer theorist José Esteban Muñoz claimed transformative queer thought and action were under siege by the "pragmatic gay agenda," which is crystallized by activists and commentators like Andrew Sullivan (7–10). For Muñoz, gay pragmatism limits the potential of queerness to transform society and do justice to the most marginalized LGBTQ+ individuals. Sullivan-style assimilation politics assumes everyone desires the same things: a home, a monogamous partner, children, and money.

LGBTQ+ children's picture books that engage this trope tend to foreground queer families' similarities to straight families, ignoring the specificity of queer experience. This similarity is usually expressed through acquiescence to white, middle-class family ideals and values, such as two married adults living in a single-family home with a variety of material comforts. Extended family is rarely present, urban settings are scarce, signs of financial stress are ignored, and queer community is absent as the focus is specifically on the family unit.

Whereas the "virtually normal" trope represents a narrow view of family life that remains attached to markers of race and class privilege, the "family diversity" trope does the opposite. The "family diversity" trope depicts families that look quite different: single parents, grandparents, foster parents, gay and lesbian parents, blended families, and so forth. However, within these texts, diversity is visual and located on the surface of the text. The deeper message is that all families are essentially the same, are essentially united by love.

Finally, the "gay uncle" trope depicts gay men as a nonthreatening accessory to the heterosexual family unit. Importantly, in this period, the gay uncle maintains a position both within and outside the family—a visitor. This trope, like several others, changes post-2000 as uncles are invited into the family through the creation of their own marriages. Earlier representations often cloak the gay uncle's queerness in secrecy and quasi shame. In fact, several explore the sickness and death of uncles as a result of HIV/AIDS.

The persistence of common tropes across decades of LGBTQ+ children's picture books reveals that similar concerns have dominated the hearts and minds of creators working to write queer existence into children's culture. I argue that shifts in representations and representational practices, by which I mean what is represented and how it is represented, both reflect and inform shifts in dominant sociocultural understandings of gender, sexuality, parenting, and family. Even more, when reading literary texts as historical texts, I can support claims about the role of children's picture books in transforming attitudes, perceptions, and actions. This is why I refer to LGBTQ+ children's picture books as both a historical archive and worldmaking project.

Although identifying, mapping, and interpreting tropes in LGBTQ+ children's picture books is a significant part of this study, I am critical of the ubiquity of certain tropes. Tropes become constraints that run the risk of limiting our ability to imagine alternative worlds and ways of being in the world. By this I mean that when certain images, ideas, and identities, as well as modes of representing those identities, begin to dominate the field, this truncates the transformative potential of LGBTQ+ children's picture books. Like Norton suggests in her article about transreading, transgender representations, and children's literature, I think children's literature has unrealized transformative potential. Norton calls for a "sublime realism" that represents queerness in all its nuances so that queer representations themselves do not become prescriptions for gender expression, sexual desire, family formation, community building, and queer worldmaking. The majority of LGBTQ+ children's picture books normalize accommodationist modes of relating to straight society. These texts most often position queers as similar to cisgender heterosexuals instead of constructing queerness as aspirational and transformative.

The 1970s

When Megan Went Away (1979), written by Jane Severance and illustrated by Tea Schook, is about the breakup of a lesbian couple raising a child together in the late-1970s. It was published by Lollipop Power Inc., a small cooperative feminist press that evolved out of a women's consciousness-raising group and was responsible for much of the LGBTQ+ children's literature of the 1970s and early 1980s (Everett). Lollipop Power Inc. plays a vital role in very early LGBTQ+ children's picture books. The press was responsible for publishing the first two overt representations of lesbian family life along with picture books that challenged gender norms. The other press that shaped the field's early development, Alyson Wonderland, didn't begin publishing children's books until 1990. Since there were so few LGBTQ+ children's picture books published prior to 2000, these presses play an important role in shaping the field.

When Megan Went Away is the first children's picture book to represent lesbian family dynamics, and it is fascinating that the lesbian relationship represented is one that has already dissolved. Severance's book explores the immediate aftermath of a lesbian couple's breakup from the point of view

Figure 1 *When Megan Went Away* (1979), written by Jane Severance, illustrated by Tea Schook, published by Lollipop Power Inc.

of the child, Shannon, the couple had raised together. Shannon experiences a sense of loss when Megan leaves. She is depicted walking through her home taking note of all the things that went away when Megan left: a loom, a rocking chair, a plaid jacket, a little box of tools. Throughout the text, Megan exists like a phantom, only present in Shannon's memories, and the weight of Megan's absence is measured by conjuring the lost objects that she took with her when she left.

When Megan Went Away centers Shannon's relationship to her mother, not her mother's relationship to Megan. This mother-daughter relationship troubles normative parent-child dynamics in which the parent is protector and nurturer. Here, neither Shannon nor her mother can be protected from pain and loss. Even more, care and nurturance are depicted as reciprocal. Shannon wants to talk about her feelings to her mother, but her mother is emotionally unavailable while processing her own pain. Roles are temporarily reversed as Shannon attempts to take on caregiver responsibilities by making tuna fish sandwiches for dinner. When her mother refuses to eat, Shannon's feelings of guilt and sadness transform into anger. She screams and knocks over her milk, finally getting her mother's attention. The two curl up together, comforting each other (figure 1). Although the amateurish cover image of Severance's picture book may immediately suggest normative adult-child relations are being reproduced, since Shannon is depicted wrapped in a blanket on her mother's lap, the text itself challenges any normative readings by showing an emotionally complex mother-child relationship that includes various instances in which the child attempts to nurture the mother.

In Sadie Epstein-Fine and Makeda Zook's *Spawning Generations: Rants and Reflections on Growing Up with LGBTQ+ Parents*, they claim queerspawn "have been taught that airbrushing our lives is the best form of survival" (3). Severance's account of lesbian family takes the opposite approach, tenderly painting a picture of a flawed lesbian mom, her flawed relationship, and the kid who is okay regardless. Severance's *When Megan Went Away* acknowledges lesbian specificity, and consequently, provides an important historical record of lesbian family life in the 1970s and 1980s. As Thomas Crisp notes: "Severance's career and books provide an alternative look at queer life and themes in children's literature, a vision that may be more emotionally honest."

The emotional honesty Severance represented in *When Megan Went Away* came at a cost. In a personal correspondence, Severance described receiving a lot of "flack" for not airbrushing lesbian family life. She defends the book, noting that she wrote what she saw in the lesbian community she participated in throughout the 1970s and 1980s. She speculated that having little institutional and familial support caused lesbian parents to struggle on their own with mental illness and addiction, which, in conjunction with poverty, left many ill-prepared to parent. On the other hand, Severance notes that she observed instances of lesbian parents creating innovative alternatives to two-parented households, such as the communal living situation explored in her second children's picture book about lesbian family life, *Lots of Mommies* (1983), also published by Lollipop Power Inc. (see appendix for full correspondence).

The rest of the LGBTQ+ children's picture books published in the 1970s explore children whose gender expressions trouble rigid binaries. I include these books even though they are not overtly LGBTQ+ for several reasons. First, they show child characters negotiating gender using the ideas and language available to them at a time when a complex vocabulary to explore and express gender didn't exist. Second, they trouble taken-for-granted gender norms, particularly gender roles, and model resistance. Third, in many instances they gesture toward then inarticulable queer desires that, in subsequent decades, became increasingly speakable and livable.

An early iteration of the sissy boy trope appears in *William's Doll* (1972), written by Charlotte Zolotow and illustrated by William Pène du Bois. The text opens with the simple declaration: "William wanted a doll." Desiring a doll is presented as a problem from the start. Unable to convince an adult gatekeeper to give him a real doll, William is depicted playing with a make-believe one. When his brother and a boy neighbor witness William nurturing his pretend doll, they call him a sissy, performing their disapproval while policing his gender. Although William's father does not resort to name-calling, his refusal to buy William a doll and overt attempts to redirect William's attention to more boyish toys makes his position clear. No mother is depicted in the story, which is significant as mothers are often represented as more accepting of gender nonconformity in children. This is of further interest since the father is positioned as the two boys' primary caregiver. William does have a grandmother who serves as a mother proxy and eventually buys him a doll. When his father gets upset about the purchase, she explains that having a doll will help William be a good father.

Read through the lens of critical optimism, we can see the story's full complexity. For instance, Zolotow reproduces gender norms even as she critiques them. She characterizes the only woman in William's life, who is also the only woman in the story, as both understanding and nurturing, while depicting William's brother and father as committed to masculinity through both their performance and policing of it. This produces normative gender roles as the framework through which William's gender expressions and desires are read. Then, William's grandmother calms down his angry father by redeeming William's "sissy boy" behaviors for heterosexual reproduction. The doll is practice for when William will become a father like his father; the promise of his future heterosexuality appeases the straight father. For the "sissy" to be accepted, fear of the effeminate boy becoming a gay man must be addressed and neutralized (Sedgwick, "How to Bring Your Kids Up Gay"). Of course, this is just one interpretive reading; it could be suggested that William may grow up to be a gay father, but the appeal to fatherhood is a neutralizing one, made to make William's desire for a doll appear less transgressive, which also means straighter.

Critique and optimism are both needed to understand the queer hopes and normative attachments embedded in LGBTQ+ children's picture books. I am drawn to *William's Doll* because of the persistence of William's desire for a doll as well as his queer resilience when confronted with gender policing. William wants a doll more than he wants familial acceptance. He doesn't modify his behaviors or desires to nullify those around him. He doubles down and repeats his demand for a doll. Queer persistence and resilience are significant features of LGBTQ+ children's picture books that feature queer youth. These texts do not suggest that "it gets better"; instead, they acknowledge the oppressive presence of the straight world while demonstrating that queer desires will prevail and are worth the risk of familial and social rejection. In other words, these texts offer models of queer resistance, resilience, and reward.

Renowned gay author and illustrator Tomie dePaola's *Oliver Button Is a Sissy* (1979) is another early example of the sissy boy trope. Oliver would rather pick flowers and dance than play ball. Effeminate Oliver is bullied at school and discouraged at home because he doesn't enjoy stereotypically boy activities. Recognizing that they cannot change their child, Oliver's parents enroll him in dance classes. He is such a good dancer that his teacher recommends he enter a local talent show. Although he doesn't win, Oliver gains confidence and his parents are proud of his performance. The kids at school also recognize Oliver's talent and stop mocking him. The shift in the behavior of those who initially police Oliver's gender, his family and peers, gestures toward queer exceptionalism, another trope that develops early in LGBTQ+ children's picture books. Oliver's acceptance appears contingent on his ability to impress everyone with his talent. The rejection of masculine stereotypes found in both *William's Doll* and *Oliver Button Is a Sissy* as well as the theme of acceptance through exceptionalism found in the latter text have influenced the subsequent development of more explicitly queer representations.

Lollipop Power Inc.'s *Jesse's Dream Skirt* (1979), written by Bruce Mack and illustrated by Marian Buchanan, introduces what I fondly refer to as the boy-meets-skirt trope.[1] The opening image of *Jesse's Dream Skirt* shows a semicircle of ethnically diverse men wearing traditional cultural attire, from kilts to togas, that is coded as masculine. The men frame the title character, Jesse, a young boy wrapped in a sheet. The image creates a visual genealogy that is reinforced in the book's opening: "There are and were and always will be boys who wear dresses and skirts and things that whirl, twirl, flow and glow." Image and text position the title character within this imagined community of men with a queer desire for "dresses and skirts." Importantly, neither the men nor Jesse are feminized vis-à-vis their interest in skirts and dresses.

Jesse shares his dreams of skirts with his mother and asks her to help him make one. She willingly agrees, while acknowledging that some people might make fun of him. She doesn't attempt to protect him from his queer desire, instead empowering him with knowledge about possible consequences. Although children are often depicted as agents in picture books—that is, after all, part of their appeal to children—they are less often depicted as agents within the family unit, which is where adult gatekeepers tend to act on them. This difference is an important one that can be found in many

LGBTQ+ children's picture books, which depict the familial home as an essential site of identity construction and child-agency.

Jesse understands that he may be mocked, but he wants a dress more than the acceptance of his peers. Like William's desire for a doll, Jesse's desire for a dress persists even after he understands the consequences of failing to meet gender expectations. When Jesse enters his preschool classroom wearing the skirt that he made in collaboration with his mother, readers are introduced to his teacher, a Black man named Bruce. Representing a preschool teacher as a Black man deliberately disrupts cultural expectations that women are consummate nurturers. Even more, when Bruce sees Jesse, he acknowledges the significance of wearing a skirt to school and tells the boy that he looks like "a butterfly that has just come out of its cocoon" (Mack and Buchanan). This suggests that Jesse has undergone a transformation and that the transformation is natural. It also positions an important man in the text as accepting of diverse gender expressions, which is quite rare in LGBTQ+ children's picture books. As discussed, men tend to be positioned as gender police. By the end of the book, instead of begrudgingly offering acceptance contingent on exceptionalism, as seen in *Oliver Button Is a Sissy*, Bruce and several of Jesse's peers don dress-like clothing in an act of queer identification and camaraderie. Stories that represent the queering of the straight world, by which I mean the rejection of dominant gender and/or sexual norms, hold the most transformative potential. These stories model radical acceptance and community building for young readers while creating the possibility for identifications with queerness. Although books like this are few and far between, they do the work that so many Christian conservatives are afraid they will do: they open minds to the pleasure of queerness and embolden young people to reject gender policing.

Like many LGBTQ+ children's picture books, *Jesse's Dream Skirt* sparked concerns from adults invested in maintaining a cisgender, heterosexual status quo. Merrikay Everett Brown notes that even during production *Jesse's Dream Skirt* met with negative reactions. For example, *Jesse's Dream Skirt* was explicitly linked to homosexuality. One illustrator "flatly refused to have any part of such a 'silly' story and in the creation of more homosexuals" (Everett 58–59). Although gender and sexuality shouldn't be collapsed, there is frequently slippage between the two in the dominant cultural imaginary with feminine boys and masculine girls being read as proto-homosexuals. For instance, a 1986 *New York Times* article reported:

MOST young boys who persistently act like girls grow up to be homosexuals or bisexuals, a 15-year study of "sissy boys" has shown. According to the findings, neither therapy designed to discourage the extremely feminine behavior nor ideal child rearing could guarantee that the boys would develop as heterosexuals, although parental discouragement of the boys' girlish behavior tended to result in a more heterosexual orientation. (Brody)

The popular press article summarizes a study by Dr. Richard Green, who published a full-length manuscript a year later called *The "Sissy Boy Syndrome" and the Development of Homosexuality*. Throughout the 1970s and 1980s, studies linking feminine behaviors in boyhood to adult homosexuality were frequently published in scientific journals, and these ideas found their way into the dominant imaginary (Green, "One-Hundred Ten Feminine and Masculine Boys"; Green "Significance of Feminine Behavior"; Green, "Sissy Boy Syndrome"; Green et al., "Playroom Toy Preferences"; Green et al., "Masculine or Feminine Gender Identity"; Lebovitz; L. E. Newman; Stoller; Tuber and Coates). Another such example, an article titled "Playroom Toy Preferences of Fifteen Masculine and Fifteen Feminine Boys," linked toy preferences to other expressions of femininity noting, "if given a choice of masculine and feminine items, boys designated feminine on the basis of cross-dressing, female playmate preference and female role-taking in fantasy games will select toys culturally typical of girlhood play" (Green et al., "Playroom Toy Preferences" 487). Discourses about "sissy boys" surely informed the creation and reception of books like *William's Doll*, *Oliver Button Is a Sissy*, and *Jesse's Dream Skirt*, which challenged the idea that boys playing with dolls, collecting flowers, and wearing skirts need to be corrected. These books model acceptance as well as queer resistance, persistence, and reward.

Some readers may disagree with my identification of *William's Doll* or *Jesse's Dream Skirt* as queer. For instance, in his recent article "What Having Two Mommies Looks Like Now: Queer Picture Books in the Twenty-First Century," Derritt Mason suggests that the content of LGBTQ+ children's picture books has developed alongside, and responded to the same changes as, LGBTQ+ studies. According to Mason, the content of LGBTQ+ children's picture books has shifted from lesbian and gay adults with the aim of trying to "explain gay adults to readers" to books that "make space for the queerness of children" (111). He reads this as a linear progression, much like LGBTQ+ studies shifted away from identity-oriented scholarship to a more critical approach to gender and sexuality in the 1990s that foregrounded the idea of fluid identifications (Miller, "Thirty Years of Queer Theory"). In fact, Mason argues: "In the context of picture book history, the queer child seems to be a contemporary phenomenon" (111). Although Mason discusses *William's Doll* and *Oliver Button Is a Sissy*, he doesn't identify these texts as queer, even as he notes their queer potential, writing, "queerness appears only as a veiled signifier: primarily through attachments to 'non-masculine' objects, relations, and activities" (113). He goes on to argue that the protagonists, William and Oliver, do not "engage in activities that allow us, as readers, to concretely identify them as such. Instead, their latent queerness haunts the texts" (113). My own reading of these texts moves beyond the picture books to the discourses surrounding them, from scientific journals to popular newspapers, to support my reasoning for reading the protagonists as queer. In the 1970s, desiring dolls or being identified as a sissy signified homosexuality. The signifiers "doll" and "dress" are not "veiled" as suggested by Mason but, at least in the 1970s and into the 1980s, signified homosexuality. That doesn't mean that these representations are unambiguously queer. Instead, I suggest that in the 1970s, and even in the 1980s, ambiguously is the only way for queer children to appear in any cultural text because of the limited vocabulary available to name and, in naming, render visible. Even more, there is a necessary lack of stability at the center of queerness. It is okay for the signs that signify queerness to shimmy and shift; in fact, it is inevitable. So, the 1970s bring us dress-wearing and doll-loving queer boys, to express and explore two desires that may indeed become less queer the less ardently normative gender expectations and roles are adhered to in dominant culture.

One of the benefits of generating and studying a large archive of LGBTQ+ children's picture books is the ability to identify historical shifts in desires and expressions that signify queerness As chapter four demonstrates, the skirt itself is often degendered in post-2000 LGBTQ+ children's picture books, a project introduced in *Jesse's Dream Skirt*. Skirts and dresses are increasingly presented as gender-neutral clothing items by authors and illustrators who connect them to power and play. This work is being undertaken by activist-authors working to create a pink boy category that parallels the tomboy category, which is often read, and I would argue misread, as socially accepted. Even more, attempts to degender skirts and dresses, so they are seen as neutral, like a pair of jeans, can be read as attempting to render skirt-wearing boys banal, innocent, and disconnected from the effeminacy often linked to homosexuality. In other words, whereas boys desiring dolls and dresses signified homosexuality through gender effeminacy in pre-2000 children's picture books, in post-2000 children's picture books there is an attempt to construct these items as gender neutral and unrelated to sexuality.

Lois Gould's short story *X: A Fabulous Child's Story*, published by *Ms.* magazine in 1972, was revisited six years later. In 1978, illustrator Jacqueline Chwast complemented the text with evocative images, and the story was published as a picture book by Daughters Publishing. The feminist tale tells the story of X, who is part of an experiment. X's parents do not share the child's sex assignment, much to the chagrin of family and friends who are uncomfortable relating to a child without a sex-gender identity. The clever story holds up a mirror to the world, showing readers the degree to which gender permeates social expectations, interactions, and institutions. The degree to which we identify and sort people by gender is so naturalized as to be taken for granted, but this text provides readers with some distance to critique the ubiquity of these practices.

School is particularly daunting for X because everything, including lining up, playing, using the bathroom, and friendship, is gendered. Although X is initially bullied at school, their peers soon realize that "X is having twice as much fun" as them. In fact, many of the children are "queered" by X, once they realize they can challenge gender stereotypes as well. In one instance, a boy football player, understanding that he doesn't need to choose between "girl" and "boy" things, starts bringing his sister's doll to school.

The children's parents are not happy. One by one, they refuse to let their children play with X, and they eventually claim collective authority as parents to demand X be examined. The goal of the examination is to identify X as a girl or boy, and presumably to try to make them conform to gender role expectations. X is subjected to an examination by experts who decide that X is not mixed up about their identity. Although the criteria used to identify X's "true" sex-gender identity are not revealed, most readers are likely to assume the experts are subjecting X to a genital exam. Gould's representation of adults attempting to deny children agency, in order to reproduce social norms, highlights both the social nature of gender and the policing power of adults, particularly parents.

Although there is much to appreciate about *X: A Fabulous Child's Story*, it dates itself by capitulating to the idea that the truth of sex is located on the body as represented by experts' examination of X. This is typical of feminist understandings of the period. For instance, Gayle Rubin's canonical 1975 publication "The Traffic in Women: Notes on the 'Political Economy' of Sex" describes sex as biological and suggests that culture turns the "raw material" of sex into gender through acculturation into binary gender identities. In the 1990s, largely as a result of feminist theorist Judith Butler's early work on gender, scholars began to see the sexed body as culturally constructed—not the actual materiality of the body, but the meaning we make of it in a society that demands gender be read within a binary opposition (*Gender Trouble*; *Bodies That Matter*). Additionally, X is problematically referred to as "it," whereas in the 2020s we would more likely use the term *they*, as I have in my description. In fact, *they* is Merriam-Webster's 2019 word of the year (Merriam-Webster). Neither critique changes the fact that the story remains an insightful account of gender segregation and the enforcement of strict gender roles. A more problematic element of the text is the objectification of X for the purposes of an experiment. Although X is free of gender, they are not free of adult intervention into the assignment of gender, or lack thereof. The child's agency and ability to self-define remain circumscribed as adults, at every turn, remain in a position of authority over the child. This is, perhaps, inevitable but does gesture toward a limitation of the imagination to conjure a truly radical adult-child relationship and envision a child agent.

The 1980s

Very few LGBTQ+ children's picture books were published in the 1980s, although Lollipop Power Inc. did put out a couple additional LGBTQ+ titles before closing in 1986. One of these titles, *The Boy Toy* (1988) written by Phyllis Hacken Johnson and illustrated by Lena Shiffman, subtly challenges gender stereotypes on multiple fronts. The protagonist is a boy named Chad whose grandmother made him a doll named Dan. Readers are immediately introduced to an adult-child dynamic that differs greatly from that foregrounded in *William's Doll*, which set this publication apart from its predecessor. Chad's grandmother appears to have made the doll without being solicited, and no one in the family has an issue with it.

When Chad starts school, he meets a boy named Sam who polices gender norms—for instance, suggesting that girls can't be doctors. Chad wants to impress Sam and is afraid Sam will find out he has a doll and make fun of him, so he gives his doll to his sister. A sudden illness brings Chad to the hospital, where he must stay for several days. Chad brings his doll, Dan, to keep him company, although he is apprehensive about being mocked while at the hospital. Chad's doctor is a woman, which subtly challenges Sam's earlier claim that women can't be doctors. In addition to depicting Chad's surgeon as a woman, Hacken Johnson represents his father in a nurturing role throughout. This is also significant since many LGBTQ+ children's picture books represent fathers as emotionally distant or, even worse, as gender bullies. The book certainly supported the press's mission to publish antisexist children's picture books.

When Chad is released from the hospital, Sam visits him at home and brings him a teddy bear, which prompts Chad to tell Sam about his doll. Although Sam notes that he's never met a boy with a doll, he admits he thinks it is kind of cool. *The Boy Toy*, like *Jesse's Dream Skirt*, represents desire for "feminine" objects as benign. One could argue that, because of this, these texts are not queer. I suggest instead that they represent a queer possibility for a world beyond gender or, at least, beyond the oppressive enforcement of oppositional gender roles. In this way, they can be said to offer more realistic visions of a transformed world than Lois Gould's more speculative *X: A Fabulous Child's Story*. Additionally, I include them in a book about LGBTQ+ children's picture books because they are critical to understanding the social significance of more recent representations as well as mapping larger shifts in representational practices over time.

In addition to *The Boy Toy*, Lollipop Power Inc. published Jane Severance's second book about lesbian family life, *Lots of Mommies* (1983), which was illustrated by Jan Jones. *Lots of Mommies* tells the story of a little girl raised by several women in the late 1970s or early 1980s. Severance creates a robust cast of diverse lesbian characters; Annie Jo, Shadowoman, Vikki, and Jill all live together and appear to co-parent a child named Emily who has Asian facial features and long dark hair. The short picture book provides readers with a snapshot of Emily's first day of school, where she is confronted with the uniqueness of her family.

Annie Jo and Shadowoman walk Emily to school. Like many children, Emily is nervous when her parents leave her alone for the first time. However, Emily quickly finds her teacher standing among a group of children. The children are talking about their families and Emily joins in the conversation, telling students she has "lots of mommies." Her incredulous peers call her a liar, and Emily dejectedly leaves the group to play alone. Lesbian- and gay-parented families are frequently represented as a "problem" in LGBTQ+ children's picture books, as something children (and adults) have trouble understanding or even believing. This is another reason I suggest that LGBTQ+ children's picture books, no matter how much they may demonstrate attachments to troubling social norms, also do the important and disruptive work of rendering gay and lesbian families visible. Severance's book goes even further and shows a queer communal model of family.

While playing by herself on a jungle gym, Emily slips. Everyone on the playground runs to her aid. Several adults who witnessed the event try to track down Emily's mother, but everyone identifies a different woman. Miraculously, *all* of Emily's mothers are found and they rush to her side. When the children realize Emily was telling the truth about having lots of mommies, the "problem" is solved. After all, seeing is believing, and illustrator Jan Jones provides visual proof of Emily's queer family life. No one appears to be bothered by the situation; in fact, upon seeing Annie Jo's toolbelt, one little girl wistfully exclaims that she wishes she could build things. The women soon go to work, leaving a confident Emily behind to start her first day of school.

Like Severance's early children's picture book *When Megan Went Away*, *Lots of Mommies* provides a rare snapshot into lesbian living and loving in the 1970s and 1980s. Both picture books also offer an affirming alternative to the nuclear family. However, although there are benefits to publishing with small presses, such as control of content, there are also drawbacks. Children's literature scholar Thomas Crisp suggests that Severance's publications with feminist press Lollipop Power Inc. likely remain peripheral to the LGBTQ+ children's picture book archive because of their poor physical quality, which was typical of independent presses of the time. I am thrilled to include them in this archive, since both of Severance's books, and other independently published picture books, make significant contributions to the field.

It was not until five years later that another children's picture book about lesbian mothers became available. Lesléa Newman, a central figure in LGBTQ+ children's literature, published *Heather Has Two Mommies* in 1989. As in Severance's *Lots of Mommies*, the "problem" of lesbian parenting is introduced when a young child is confronted with heterosexual norms upon starting school. However, whereas Severance's book features racially diverse characters with working-class jobs—for instance, one of Emily's parents is a school bus driver—the lesbian couple represented in Newman's book is white and clearly middle-class; one is a doctor. Both books expand images of family life. However, it is Newman's that has become a classic, and despite the far more normative familial situation of the lesbian-parented family the story is about, it has also proven far more controversial than the less popular, albeit more subversive, *Lots of Mommies*.

As mentioned, in the 1970s and 1980s few presses published explicitly lesbian and gay children's picture books, and Lollipop Power Inc. dissolved in the mid-1980s. Lesléa Newman came up with an inventive strategy for getting her story into the world. She describes publishing *Heather Has Two Mommies*:

> Though *Heather Has Two Mommies* isn't self-published, I did actively participate in its publication. My business partner at the time, Tzivia Gover, and I came up with the term co-publishing. She had a desktop publishing business and when no traditional publisher was willing to publish *Heather*, we decided to do it ourselves. We raised $4,000 via a letter writing campaign, found an illustrator and a printer, and brought the book out in December of 1989.

Newman's innovative strategy resembles crowdsourcing, ironically, a popular way many more recent LGBTQ+ children's books have been funded. Crowdsourcing allows creators or publishers to find financial backers for creative projects, and these backers help pay for production costs. Then, contributors receive the products they "sponsored." This is a practical strategy for putting content into the world when it is deemed too risky by major publishers.

Over thirty years after its original publication, the recently updated picture book remains in print, which certainly proves wrong the traditional presses that shunned it in the late 1980s. In the original book, readers are introduced to a round-faced, curly-haired Heather as she plays outside with her pets. Readers soon meet her two moms: Mama Jane (a carpenter) and Mama Kate (a doctor). Both women are white with similar haircuts, although one has dark hair and wears glasses and the other's hair is much lighter. Subtle symbols of lesbian culture make their way into the text's illustrations. For instance, in one image, Kate wears a labrys necklace, a double-headed ax often used as a feminist and lesbian symbol. In early versions of the picture book, the specificity of lesbian family formation is also detailed. Jane and Kate make the decision that Jane will carry the baby, and Jane's insemination by "a special doctor" is described in age-appropriate detail. Newman writes,

"After the doctor examined Jane to make sure that she was healthy, she put some sperm into Jane's vagina. The sperm swam up into Jane's womb. If there was an egg waiting there, the sperm and the egg would meet, and the baby would start to grow." Above the text, Jane sits in front of a woman doctor with a cloth modestly draped over her body. When Jane and Kate realize Jane is pregnant, they "hugged each other and kissed each other." Newman captures the couple's intimacy and joy at beginning a family. The couple even opt for a home birth attended by a midwife. These details are omitted in later versions of the text, a point I return to shortly.

When Heather is three years old, her moms put her in a playgroup. This is the first time her lesbian-parented family becomes an issue. Heather enjoys part of the day playing with new friends. However, when a student asks her about her father's occupation, she becomes confused and wonders if she is the only child without a father. Her teacher, Molly, intervenes, asking all the children to draw pictures of their family, at which point they realize all families are different. The message present in many books that focus on lesbian- and gay-parented families is that all families are the same because, in essence, family is love. By including images of multiple families, this book gestures toward the family diversity trope that has become quite popular in the past decade. Books that use this trope represent family forms as taking many shapes, but the focus is on love as a common feature of all families.

Heather Has Two Mommies was acquired by newly founded Alyson Wonderland Books soon after its original publication. Alyson Wonderland Books, an imprint of Alyson Books, was responsible for many lesbian and gay children's picture books published throughout the 1990s. In 2000, the press reissued the picture book. At this time, details that gave the text its lesbian specificity, including Kate's labrys necklace and Mama Jane's insemination, were removed. In a personal correspondence, I asked Newman to explain what promoted the change. She responded:

> When I originally wrote the book and sent it out to editors, one New York editor was interested in the book. He said that kids know two moms can't make a baby, and I needed to address this. So, I inserted the alternative insemination scene. The editor ultimately did not take the book. I left the scene in there, as I thought that an editor at a big New York house knew more about children's books then I did. In the ten years that followed, I heard from many parents who said that they were hesitant to bring the book into their

children's classrooms, not because Heather had two moms, but because of
the alternative insemination pages. So, when I had the opportunity to revisit
the book, I decided to remove those pages, making the book more "reader-
friendly." I had other reasons as well. In hindsight, I realized that a flashback
to before Heather was born could confuse young readers, interrupted the
flow of the narrative, and made the book too long. So, I was happy I had the
opportunity to remove the scene. It lifted out so easily and made the book
read in a much smoother way.

This change does make the book less didactic and more "reader-friendly."
Of course, most bedtimes stories do not contain detailed explanations of
conception. But, as mentioned, the lesbian specificity present in the 1989 and
1990 versions is lost as a result of making the book more accessible. Instead,
the diverse family trope that appears in many LGBTQ+ children's books
after 2000 dominates the text, rendering the story less "sublimely realist," to
refer to Jody Norton.

In his analysis of the tenth anniversary edition, Derritt Mason maintains
that the changes "vanish the lesbian backstory and position Heather's conception and birth as sites of the text's danger" (120). He continues: "Certainly, the
characters of Jane and Kate are not without their homonormative elements,
but I wonder: is there not something subversively queer about the act of
detailing lesbian reproduction in the context of a children's picture book—
something that disrupts heteronormativity by making explicit a method
of conception that does not require a daddy?" (120). I agree that the first
version of the text is more radical in its specificity than the later version. To
me, this is because of its realist representation of reproduction as well as the
closed sphere of women, including the doctor and midwife, who are integral
figures in Heather's conception and birth. I tie this to a shift in intended and
actual audience. LGBTQ+ children's picture books published in the 1980s
and 1990s were written for a queer audience. However, post-2000, when the
ten-year anniversary edition of a revised *Heather Has Two Mommies* was
published, the intended and actual audience of LGBTQ+ children's picture
books was expanding. Instead of demonstrating to children in lesbian- and
gay-parented families that their family was "normal," as well as providing a
model for negotiating stigma, by the late 1990s, LGBTQ+ picture books had
begun to infiltrate the straight world, including schools, which created new
pressures and new possibilities.

Newman's *Heather Has Two Mommies* has prompted a fair amount of scholarly criticism, which the field of LGBTQ+ children's picture books tends to lack more generally. In his 1998 article, "Innocence, Perversion, and Heather's Two Mommies," Eric Rofes analyzes one dozen LGBTQ+ children's picture books to understand "conceptions of childhood currently valorized by lesbian and gay men" (5). Rofes's archive highlighted Alyson Wonderland publications, although the only book discussed in detail is *Heather Has Two Mommies*. Rofes argues that in LGBTQ+ children's picture books "the world of the child is centered around the family unit" (18). He also contends that "the gay and lesbian authors of these children's books continue to paint a traditional, untroubled picture of family life and produce a body of work filled with oppressive images of children" (19). According to Rofes, images are oppressive if they depict children as reliant on adults with no agency or ability to act on the world. Additionally, he is concerned with images that depict children as "simple people, free of complex and conflicting emotions" (19). I agree with Rofes's assessment of *Heather Has Two Mommies* as a celebration of lesbian family life, since the book clearly seeks to normalize lesbian-parented families. However, I find his reading of both individual titles and the archive of LGBTQ+ children's picture books simplistic and, at times, sloppy. For instance, to demonstrate that Heather is depicted as "innocent," he quotes a description of her as an infant. In the quote, infant Heather is described as "very little," and it is noted that "she smiled and sometimes cried." Rofes complains that "this is how many Americans see young children and how children's books traditionally have represented young children" (19). Rofes sloppily conflates infants and small children to illustrate his point. The problem is, his entire argument hinges on this and a couple of other decontextualized quotes. His claim that modern constructs of homosexuality and childhood emerge and develop together is far more convincing. Rofes states that children have been constructed as innocent, and that protecting their innocence has been a significant warrant for denying adult homosexuals access to full citizenship rights and cultural visibility.

As mentioned in my introduction, archive is *almost* everything; close readings matter too. If, for example, Rofes's archive included books published by Lollipop Power Inc., like *When Megan Went Away* and *Jesse's Dream Skirt*, his description of the field would be quite different. As I discussed in my analysis, *When Megan Went Away* depicts an emotionally complex child character and illustrates reciprocal care between child and adult, which disrupts dominant representations of adult-child relationships within the family. Additionally, *Jesse's Dream Skirt* focuses on Jesse as an agent of desire who is capable, with some help from his mother, of materializing his desires. Even more, he introduces queer desire to his teacher and classmates, effectively queering the classroom.

Beginning in 1989, a handful of texts about HIV/AIDS and gay men were published, evincing a slight cultural lag with the emergence of the AIDS crisis in the early 1980s. *Losing Uncle Tim* (1989), an Albert Whitman publication written by MaryKate Jordan and illustrated by Judith Friedman, was the first children's picture book to acknowledge the HIV/AIDS-related loss of a loved one from the point of view of a child. Books about HIV/AIDS tend to partially embrace an investment in childhood innocence, but they also depict emotionally complex child characters. Like several later children's picture books that depict uncles with HIV/AIDS, the sexual identity of the uncle is unclear in *Losing Uncle Tim*. I incorporate these texts, much like I incorporate picture books depicting "sissy boys," because they were released into a world that read sissy boys and HIV-positive men as gay. Additionally, the uncles in these books, like overtly gay uncles represented in other picture books, are depicted as both inside and outside of the heteronuclear family. Also, like books featuring gay uncles more generally, these texts tend to depict the uncle and child as sharing a very close, joyful relationship. Often, the child character identifies the uncle as their favorite relative.

I am not interested in arguing that Uncle Tim is gay, although I think he is. Instead, I claim that this representation has enough in common with more overt ones to be included. It helps us understand the field of LGBTQ+ children's picture books by demonstrating shifts in representational strategies.

Losing Uncle Tim explores the relationship between a boy named Daniel and his uncle, Tim, who is depicted both prior to his AIDS diagnosis and during it. Throughout the text, soft illustrations in earthy blues, oranges, and browns create a meditative state, making this a good book for discussing love and loss with children. The story unfolds through the point of view of Daniel. It begins with image and text harmoniously showing readers how close the two characters were. They're often found outside, making forts with old blankets and sledding in the snow. Daniel describes Uncle Tim as "more fun than any other grownup," and theirs is the primary relationship represented in the text.

Daniel notices his beloved uncle's health deteriorating and asks his mother what is happening. She doesn't try to protect him from the truth but instead explains that Uncle Tim has AIDS. Furthermore, she tells him that most people with AIDS die. Uncle Tim's health gets worse with every turn of the page. Now, instead of playing outside in the snow, uncle and nephew play checkers inside. At one point, a frightened Daniel asks his father if he can get sick by spending time with his uncle, but his father reassures him he cannot. At the end of the book, Uncle Tim dies. In the last image, Daniel sits at his desk, facing a window. He sees his uncle's face in the window and has one hand on a wooden duck they used to play with and the other hand on the checkers set. Uncle Tim has clearly made a lasting impression on his nephew.

Although AIDS is named in the text, it is not represented with much specificity. The only exception is when Daniel asks his father if he can get sick by spending time with Uncle Tim, which hints at panicked fears about HIV/AIDS that were rampant in the 1980s. The abstraction of both sexuality and HIV/AIDS is explored in Robert McRuer's 1998 publication "Reading and Writing 'Immunity': Children and the Anti-Body." McRuer suggests that "the story of AIDS may demand the text of the gay male body, but the body is an 'anti-body' as far as children's literature is concerned" (134). By this he means that gay men as gay men are largely absent from children's literature about AIDS. I concur with McRuer. Gay men as gay men both are and are not there. According to McRuer, "The liberal reinscription of AIDS, from the late 1980s on, as 'everyone's disease' ironically functions within the text of children's literature—as it has elsewhere—to make gay men living with AIDS invisible" (134). McRuer understands the absence of gay specificity in most children's picture books about HIV/AIDS as an extension of liberal discourse that seeks to decouple HIV/AIDS and gay men. In doing so, liberal discourse makes HIV/AIDS an individual, rather than a community-specific, health crisis.

McRuer is critical of *Losing Uncle Tim* because it never mentions Tim's sexuality or attempts to provide any practical knowledge or advice about HIV/AIDS. In fact, he ends the essay powerfully arguing, "Gay and proto-gay (and heterosexual and proto-heterosexual) children do exist, and these children need to learn not only that they should be compassionate toward those people already living with AIDS, but rather that AIDS may affect them directly if they share needles or engage in unprotected sex. Without such interventions, educators can expect that a sequel—'Losing Uncle Daniel,' perhaps—will eventually need to be written" (141). Although he doesn't bla-tantly state it, McRuer's critique suggests that picture books about HIV/AIDS seek to preserve children's sexual innocence by representing HIV/AIDS as someone else's problem even as it is brought into proximity with the child.

I agree with McRuer's assessment of this text, and his critiques hold for the handful of books about gay uncles and HIV/AIDS that I discuss in the next section. However, as mentioned before, the insider/outsider position of gay men, which is essential to the gay uncle trope, likely reflects how most children experienced these scenarios; queerness and HIV/AIDS were both open secrets they witnessed without quite understanding (Sedgwick, *Epistemology of the Closet*). The "open secret" of queerness and HIV/AIDS receded in LGBTQ+ children's picture books of the 1990s with titles like *Whisper Whisper Jesse, Whisper Whisper Josh* and *My Two Uncles* explicitly naming homosexuality.

1990s

I've mentioned Alyson Wonderland Books before. In 1980, Sasha Alyson founded Alyson Publications, a press focused on lesbian and gay fiction and nonfiction for adult audiences. Ten years later, Alyson Wonderland Books, a subsidiary of Alyson Publications, was created with the express purpose of publishing lesbian and gay children's picture books. This press was responsible for the majority of LGBTQ+ children's picture books published in the 1990s.[2] In a 1998 *Bookbird* interview, independent bookstore owner River Artz explained that the timing was perfect because of the early 1990s "gay baby boom" (Yampell 31). Although there was growing demand for LGBTQ+ children's picture books, other issues made it difficult to succeed financially in LGBTQ+ children's picture book publishing. For instance, the 1990s saw a rise in chain bookstores, so independent publishers could no longer rely on their natural alliance with independent bookstores to guarantee retail shelf space (Yampell 32). This was particularly challenging for publishers focused on LGBTQ+ content, since large chain stores sought to appeal to the masses instead of niche markets (Yampell 32). Still, more LGBTQ+ children's picture books were published in the 1990s than in the 1970s and 1980s combined. As a result, I am able to identify clusters of texts that explore similar themes, including lesbian and gay parenting, uncles with HIV/AIDS, LGBTQ+ culture, and even the emergence of texts that address queer youth desire.

Lesbian and Gay Parents

One of Alyson Wonderland's first publications was the previously discussed *Heather Has Two Mommies*, which it reissued with no changes in 1990. In 1990, Alyson Wonderland also published *Daddy's Roommate*, which was written and illustrated by Michael Willhoite. The story is narrated by a young boy a year after his parents' divorce. At this point, his father has moved in with a man named Frank. Colorful illustrations depict Frank, the boy's father, and the boy in typical family scenes. For instance, the cover image depicts them in a rowboat on a serene lake. Ducks flock the boat, and the boy feeds them as the men look on. Additionally, several images paired with brief descriptive text show the child and his father engaged in everyday household activities, including cleaning and eating. Taken as a whole, the picture book depicts a harmonious father-son relationship. The boy's relationship with Frank mirrors the father-son relationship shown. Frank and the boy are depicted playing catch, reading books, and catching bugs. The boy's mom explains to him, and by extension to the reader, that Frank and his dad are gay, which the boy accepts as just another way to love someone. This early depiction of gay parenting represents two men sharing a home and parenting a child as normal. It is important to note that no intimacy between the two men is depicted.

Although both *Daddy's Roommate* and *Heather Has Two Mommies* have been convincingly interpreted as homonormative, as I've suggested, that is not all they are. Both books challenge the naturalized social construction of homosexuality as a threat to children. As previously noted, in his critique of Newman's *Heather Has Two Mommies*, Eric Rofes argued that homosexuality and childhood have developed as constitutive oppositions. He argues that "the social, economic, and culture forces that have created 'the innocent' in the body of the child, have created 'the pervert' in the body of the homosexual, and that the two are historically and conceptually linked" (5). If Rofes is right, and I think he is, representing homosexual adults and presumably heterosexual children in familial spaces challenges that dominant construction of homosexuality as dangerous to children.

Asha's Mums, written by Rosamund Elwin and Michele Paulse and illustrated by Dawn Lee, is similar in theme to Severance's *Lots of Mommies* and Newman's *Heather Has Two Mommies* but focuses on a Black Canadian family. All three texts share a central problem: the children of lesbian parents go to school, where they are met with disbelief when they share that they have two (or more) mothers. Whereas it is children who do not believe in the possibility of lesbian-parented families in Severance and Newman's texts, it is a teacher who challenges Asha's familial reality. These books counter the impossibility of lesbian parents and demonstrate that visibility itself is interventionist. They all proclaim that queer families can and do exist.

Asha's Mums opens in a classroom. The students are racially diverse, and the teacher is a plump woman with Asian features. Asha has light brown skin and short loose curls. Students are excited about an upcoming field trip that they can't attend without a signed permission slip from a parent or guardian. Both of Asha's mothers sign the permission slip. When Asha turns it in, her teacher insists she can't have two moms and demands the permission slip be signed by her real parents. Although Asha tries to stand up for herself, her teacher seems unable to imagine the possibility that a student in her class might have two moms. Asha tells one of her moms what happened and is assured that her parents will speak with the teacher.

The next day in class, students are drawing pictures of their family. Asha draws a picture of her family and shows the class. One student asks why she has two mommies. Another, echoing her teacher's response to the signed permission slip, assures Asha that she cannot have two moms. Asha's friends stand up for her, more discussion ensues, and one student shares that her father said having two moms is bad. Asha explains that her family loves each other and isn't bad. Another student asks the teacher for her expert opinion on the acceptability of two moms raising children, but the bell rings before she can answer. Both of Asha's moms come to pick her up from school. She is excited when they tell her they spoke with her teacher and that she will be able to go on the field trip. After the lively discussion about her family in class, everyone now believes she has two mothers. As mentioned, like Severance's and Newman's similarly themed picture books, *Asha's Mums* represents lesbian-parented families as a problem because both children and adults cannot imagine them as possibilities. However, *Asha's Mums* is the only one to deal directly, albeit subtly, with overt homophobia.

Interestingly, in Newman's and Severance's picture books, readers are invited into the homes of children who are parented by two, or even three, moms. These texts normalize the queer family by depicting it as similar to heterosexual families. The creators of *Asha's Mums* are less invested in portraying the normalcy of lesbian-parented families. In fact, within the text there are only two images of Asha at home. One shows her being comforted by one of her parents as she explains that her teacher doesn't believe she has two moms. The other depicts her alone in bed with a stuffed toy. Although Asha mentions a brother, he is never visually represented in the text, other than in the family picture she draws and presents at school. In addition to two images of family life depicted within the text, the book cover offers an awkward image of the family. In it, Asha is depicted with her mothers in their living room, but the image lacks a strong sense of family intimacy. Asha's upper torso is shown in a close-up, her expression neutral, as her upper body tilts unnaturally to the side. Her mothers are shown in the background, sitting next to each other on a couch. Their faces are out of the frame, and their bodies form an awkward V on the couch, legs leaning toward one another even as their upper bodies seem to pull in opposite directions. I draw attention to these images of Asha in her home to suggest that *Asha's Mums* attempts different cultural work than other picture books about lesbian- and gay-parented families. In this book, the focus is on the homophobia entrenched in straight society, which is demonstrated by the unthinkability of lesbian families even when clearly confronted with the reality.

Many firsts in LGBTQ+ children's picture books can be attributed to Lesléa Newman. *Belinda's Bouquet* (1991), an Alyson Wonderland publication written by Newman and illustrated by Michael Willhoite, is no exception. It's one of the first picture books to represent incidental queerness, by which I mean representations that are explicitly of LGBTQ+ characters and cultures but do not make either the main theme of a text. The story is narrated by a young boy named Daniel, although it focuses on his best friend Belinda's challenges with positive body image following a disturbing bullying experience at summer camp. Belinda is a chubby, red-haired girl full of confidence until the camp bus driver rudely refers to her as fat. Daniel tells one of his moms what happened. She gives Belinda a compelling lesson in body autonomy and the difference between being skinny and being healthy. The lesson is brought home by Daniel's other mom, who tells her that children need to be big and strong to help in the garden. The cheerful girl heads home with a plump bouquet of healthy, well-nourished flowers.

Daniel is clearly being raised in a lesbian-parented home, but queer families are not the "problem" in the text. The problems include fatphobic adults and body image. Newman's portrayal of the adult bus driver as a bully interjects a nonnormative representation of adult-child relations into the text by demonstrating that adults do not always have the best interests of children in mind. Even more, whereas gays and lesbians are usually positioned as a threat to children in dominant social discourses, it is Daniel's mothers who nurture Belinda. Importantly, they do not try to protect her from the bully. Instead, they empower her to see her body and her relationship to her body in a positive way by replacing the ideal of being skinny with the importance of being healthy.

Several other books about gay and lesbian parenting were published in the 1990s, many by Alyson Wonderland, including *The Generous Jefferson Bartleby Jones* (1991), written by Forman Brown and illustrated by Leslie Trawin. This delightfully quirky children's picture book is about Jefferson Bartleby Jones's unconventional but enviable family life. Jefferson spends three days of the week living with his dad and his dad's "friend" Joe, and the remaining four days with his mom. As in *Daddy's Roommate*, queerness is coded, but not very subtly. Also, like *Daddy's Roommate*, the child of divorce and queer parenting is perfectly content with his life. This is not the case for Jefferson's friends. His friends' dads are often too busy to play with them, and the children are emotionally hurt by the absence of attention from their fathers.

Jefferson decides to share his fathers with his friends, so they can share in his happiness. He generously lends his friend Kim one dad and his friend Chad the other. Of course, this means he has no dads, which leaves him feeling abandoned until both fathers and both friends show up to take him for ice cream. *The Generous Jefferson Bartleby Jones* doesn't just represent queer families as acceptable; it represents them as enviable, specifically as models of emotionally caring, joyful family units. The book challenges the idea that nuclear heterosexual families can meet the emotional needs of children. Jefferson's dads are represented as "better" than his friends' fathers because of their playfulness and availability. Kim's and Chad's fathers are busy with responsibilities. They are constantly working to make money. The text subtly critiques capitalism for reinforcing values that fail to serve families. This book, unlike most others that focus on gay- and lesbian-parented families, compares straight and gay families and thematizes the gay difference as anchored in emotional connection and pleasure.

Although not as prolific as Alyson Wonderland, throughout the 1990s other independent presses helped develop the field of LGBTQ+ children's picture books. Written by Lesléa Newman and illustrated by Annette Hegel, *Saturday Is Patty Day* (1993) was published by lesbian-feminist press New Victoria Publishers a decade after Jane Severance's *When Megan Went Away*

(1979). Newman's picture book puts a far more positive spin on lesbian parenting and separation than Severance's earlier book. The story unfolds from the point of view of Frankie, a young child whose parents are separating. Before his moms, Allie and Patty, separate, Frankie can hear them fighting at night as he cuddles his stuffed dinosaur, Doris Delores Brontosaurus. After the separation, he deals with sadness and anger, but both moms support him and demonstrate a continued commitment to co-parenting. Frankie will live with Allie most of the time, but Saturday will be "Patty Day." Patty's new apartment has a shelf Frankie can keep his things on and a pullout sofa he can sleep on when he is there. Frankie's emotional state and experience of his family life prior to and during the separation aren't romanticized. He hears his parents fighting prior to their breakup and has an emotionally complex reaction to their separation, similarly to Shannon in *When Megan Went Away*. However, whereas *When Megan Went Away* illustrates both the adult's and child's reaction to family dissolution, in this book, neither Allie's nor Patty's emotional reaction is depicted. We see their anger prior to their separation focalized through Frankie, but adults are not represented with much emotional complexity, which is quite different from Severance's earlier text. I highlight these two early texts about lesbian-parented families that focus on separation to better illustrate a shift in representations of gay and lesbian families post-2000.

LGBTQ+ Culture

Amy Asks a Question . . . Grandma—What's a Lesbian? (1996), written by Jeanne Arnold and illustrated by Barbara Lindquist, romantic partners and cofounders of the Mother Courage Press, is one example of a picture book that made queer culture accessible to young audiences. The book focalizes Amy, a young girl with lesbian grandmothers. Although the text doesn't problematize their relationship, it does explore Amy's ignorance about the meaning of *lesbian*. After winning a soccer game, Amy and several of her teammates hug one another. Seeing the girls' typical response to victory, some bullies call Amy lesbian. Amy is confused and later asks her mother what "lesbian" means. Amy's mother brings her to Grandma Bonnie, who provides a detailed and celebratory description of what being lesbian means to her. Several aspects of lesbian culture, including Pride parades, rainbow flags, pink triangle pins, and commitment ceremonies/handfasting are shared with

Amy and, through Amy, with young readers who are positioned to identify with her as she acquires queer knowledge. I appreciate the project, but the idea that an eleven-year-old with lesbian grandmothers wouldn't know what the term *lesbian* means is quite implausible. Importantly, this is one of few books published in the 1990s that sought to introduce readers to LGBTQ+ culture, which it does very well.

Gloria Goes to Pride (1991), an Alyson Wonderland publication, written by the prolific Lesléa Newman and illustrated by Russell Crocker, also introduces young readers to LGBTQ+ culture. Crocker's drafty but realistic pencil drawings focalize Gloria while enveloping her within queer family and community. The first image frames Gloria and her two mothers in a large heart. Gloria is in the middle, a mother on each side. All three characters hold a Valentine's Day gift in their hands. The text is narrated in the first person and describes how Gloria and her mothers celebrate Valentine's Day. The family's Halloween and Chanukah traditions are depicted in subsequent images and text. Descriptions of family celebrations set up the introduction of Pride, another "special holiday" the family celebrates.

The family begins their Pride festivities early in the morning by making signs. One of Gloria's mother's signs reads, "Gay Nurse Healing the Earth." Her other mother's sign reads, "Gay Mechanic Healing the Planet." Gloria's sign reads, "I Love My Mommies." After completing their signs, the family heads to the Pride parade. At the Pride parade, Gloria sees lots of people she knows, including her mail carrier and music teacher. Along the parade route, community members line up to watch and cheer. Newman writes, "When we get near the park, everyone starts clapping and singing: 'Two-four-six-eight, being gay is *really* great!' The people standing on the sidewalk clap and sing with us. They smile when we pass" (*Gloria Goes to Gay Pride* 23). The positive reception of Pride seems almost utopian as the line between queers and straights collapses into a harmonious chant. However, the next page offers a different reception, one that illustrates the partiality and precarity of LGBTQ+ acceptance. Three angry people are depicted, one with a sign that reads, "Gays Go Away." Newman shows readers a glimpse of pure acceptance only to quickly direct readers to its opposite. Crocker's image candidly expresses the lingering commitment to homophobia that haunts the text. Gloria is not shamed by the homophobic taunts; instead she is confused. She simply cannot understand why anyone would protest her family. Although Gloria cannot understand shame, and the book rejoices in visibility, Pride is represented as a special day in which lesbian parents can hold hands freely. At one point, when joining the parade, Gloria even notes, "Usually my mommies don't hold hands when we go out, but today they do because today is Gay Pride Day, and that makes them smile" (20). The special occasion sanctions the publicness of queerness, a publicness that partially relies on the invisibility demanded of queerness the rest of the year. This play between queer presence and absence manifests in a variety of ways in the field of LGBTQ+ children's picture books.

HIV/AIDS, Homophobia, and the Gay Uncle

As mentioned in my discussion of the 1980s, beginning in 1989, a handful of texts about HIV/AIDS that incorporate and help develop the gay uncle trope were published. These include Eileen Pollack and Bruce Gilfoy's *Whisper Whisper Jesse, Whisper Whisper Josh: A Story About AIDS* (1992), Patricia Quinlan's *Tiger Flowers* (1994), and Lesléa Newman's *Too Far Away to Touch* (1995). All three books are told from the point of view of children processing the illness and subsequent death of beloved uncles. Also, similarly to Jordan's text, and as passionately critiqued by Robert McRuer, they detach AIDS from the gay community. Additionally, they depoliticize AIDS by focusing on grief and loss while providing little sociohistorical context. In other words, the beloved uncles are present as beloved uncles only; this may be necessarily so, since they appear through the eyes of their young nieces or nephews. However, because they are represented almost exclusively in their role as uncles, everything else they also are is rendered absent, or at least auxiliary, to this primary relationship, which perhaps sanitizes queerness for an audience struggling with homophobia.

Whisper Whisper Jesse, Whisper Whisper Josh: A Story About AIDS (1992), written by Eileen Pollack and Bruce Gilfoy, explores losing an uncle to AIDS. The text-heavy story pairs prose with detailed sketches of Jesse processing the loss of his uncle, Josh. Unlike most stories that explore similar themes and foreground the close relationship between uncle and nephew or niece, Jesse is estranged from Josh. The story is told from Jesse's point of view as he recalls the secrets and whispers that envelop his uncle. Jesse's mother tells him that his father and uncle had a fight, which is why he doesn't have a relationship with Josh and why his father doesn't like to talk about him. The reader, like the child, does not learn the cause of the adults' fight.

Josh abruptly moves in with the family, which makes Jesse's mother happy, because she missed her brother. The young boy helps bridge the relationship between his uncle and father. However, as the family bonds, Uncle Josh grows sicker. He eventually ends up in a hospital, more news Jesse's parents are not forthcoming about. It is Jesse's cousin who tells him Uncle Josh has AIDS. This knowledge is enveloped in bigotry and moralization as Jesse's cousin tells him that Uncle Josh contracted AIDS because "he was a bad man." Silence reproduces a sense of shame and stigma around AIDS, which is reinforced by the unchallenged "bad man" characterization. Uncle Josh's death is as abrupt as his arrival, and as veiled by secrecy. He is rushed off in the middle of the night as Jesse sleeps. The text, like others that explore AIDS through possibly gay uncles, isolates the uncle from any semblance of a queer community, and in this instance extended family members are also absent.

Like most of these picture books, *Tiger Flowers* (1994), written by Patricia Quinlan and illustrated by Janet Wilson, is told from the point of view of a boy who loses his uncle to HIV/AIDS. The warm and accessible picture book directly engages HIV/AIDS but has a subtler approach to addressing homosexuality. The book's cover depicts a pensive young boy with white skin and rosy cheeks, framed by tiger lilies, a vivid flower referenced throughout the text. Readers are introduced to the young boy, Joel, as his sister wakes him up to ask about their uncle, Michael. Joel reminds her that Uncle Michael has died. After this scene, the reader gets snippets of memories, familial experiences shared by Joel, Michael, and sometimes Michael's "friend" Peter. *Tiger Flowers* makes the uncle's partner present in the text, while never directly addressing homosexuality. In fact, Joel is sandwiched between Michael and Peter in many memories that serve to illustrate the intimacy of the boy's relationship with his uncle. In one two-page spread, text faces an image of Peter, Michael, and Joel standing in front of a model train. All three are smiling. The text reads: "A few years ago Peter got sick. He had a disease called AIDS. Michael told me that when someone has AIDS, it's easy for them to get lots of other illnesses. Peter was sick for a long time and then he died." Although this book, like others that thematize uncles with HIV/AIDS, only gestures toward a description of AIDS, it is notable for recognizing the uncle's loss. Following his partner's death, Michael is described as "sad," and his nephew acknowledges this sadness.

Michael moves in with his family after Peter's death, and readers learn that he is ill as well. In a two-page spread, Uncle Michael is illustrated on a couch with his niece and nephew. Tara, Joel's sister, wraps her arms around their uncle's neck as the family makes paper airplanes. The children's mother is shown behind them, smiling at the scene. The accompanying text explains that some of Michael's friends "didn't want to be with him anymore because he had AIDS." Gay love and community are relegated to the past once Michael moves in with the heterosexual family. I don't say this to suggest that Quinlan intentionally moves Michael away from markers of queerness when he moves into his sister's home, but that is, in effect, what happens.

Too Far Away to Touch (1995), thoughtfully written by Lesléa Newman and movingly illustrated by Catherine Stock, follows a young girl as she processes her beloved uncle's AIDS-related illness. The story opens with Zoe sitting alone on an overstuffed brown couch as she waits for her uncle and his friend Nathan to pick her up for a trip to the planetarium. While she waits, Zoe envisions an elaborate plan to play a joke on her uncle. She has two marbles she is going to hide in his hair, so she can joke that he's losing his marbles.

The next image is of Zoe hugging her uncle at the door. When she asks about Nathan, Leonard tells her Nathan had to work and won't be joining them. Zoe decides to save her marble trick for later, because her uncle is wearing a beret. She is unperturbed on both accounts, and the two go to the planetarium, where they enjoy sitting together while looking up at the stars. When Zoe asks Leonard how far away the stars are, he wisely answers: "Too far away to touch, but close enough to see." This phrase reoccurs through the text, a melancholy mantra that foreshadows loss to come. After the show at the planetarium, Leonard purchases a surprise for his niece at the gift shop and they go to a café.

While at the café, Zoe remembers the trick she wants to play on her uncle and asks him to remove his beret. When he does, she is surprised that his thick hair has transformed into thin spotty wisps. Leonard explains that the hair loss is part of his illness. Zoe asks if he will get better soon, but he doesn't placate her with false optimism. He tells her that he doesn't know. Back at Zoe's home, Leonard banishes her from her bedroom and sets up the surprise he purchased for her in the gift shop. When she reenters her bedroom, it is to a ceiling full of stars reminiscent of the planetarium. In its brilliance and depth, the night sky plays a significant role in the short picture book, which neither imagines children as innocent nor protects them from pain. The night sky is unknowable, like the illness making Leonard sick, like what will happen to him when he dies.

These questions are in fact articulated by Zoe several weeks later when Nathan and Leonard take her to a beach, where she can see stars in the night sky. The sky makes Zoe feel "very small and a little lonely" (28). Looking up at the sky, Zoe asks her uncle if it's where people go when they die. He tells her he doesn't know, allowing himself to be vulnerable, uncertain, and sad. To comfort her he says, "Too far away to touch, but close enough to see." The primary relationship represented in the book is Zoe and Leonard's, and the honesty they reciprocate with each other subtly troubles normative adult-child relationships. Zoe asks questions, and instead of trying to protect her from the complexity and ambivalence of his illness and of death, he answers honestly. Zoe is also allowed emotional complexity and depth. Even more, throughout the story she offers her uncle comfort by holding his hand when he is sad. Young readers are permitted, even encouraged, to feel sad while reading this book, which is dominated by moody indigos and blues, complex emotions, and ambiguity. Many critiques of LGBTQ+ children's picture books suggest that they reify adult-child relationships, simplify children's emotional state, and seek to sanitize queer identities and cultures for general consumption. I think it's essential to identify and critique problematic content, but the frenzy of critique can inhibit more nuanced analysis of texts that undertake complex, often contradictory cultural work. *Too Far Away to Touch* revels in uncertainty about sickness, death, and an afterlife. If read as a bedtime story, it doesn't promise sweet dreams.

Many cultural theorists critical of capitalism's constraining influence on cultural texts suggest that "to produce an economically successful product, cultural meanings, norms and values are crucial," and they are absolutely correct (Leve 7). However, most early LGBTQ+ children's picture books did not aspire to be "economically successful." Of course, regardless of motive, all cultural texts are produced, distributed, and consumed within a capitalist system. My issue is not with critiques of capitalism, which I share, but rather the negating essence of critique as an end in itself, which can obscure the transformative potential of texts. Scholars who make assumptions about the production of LGBTQ+ children's picture books simplify the motivations of queer content creators and often fail to pay considerable attention to content of texts. My research involves identifying historical changes that affect the Circuit of Culture through which LGBTQ+ children's literature is put into the world and made to have meaning in the world. This approach counters problematic readings of LGBTQ+ children's picture books that assume a profit motivation, which I suggest isn't always, or even usually, the primary motive of LGBTQ+ children's picture book creators. For instance, prior to 2000, most presses that published LGBTQ+ children's picture books were nonprofit, mission-oriented institutions. They often paid authors and illustrators under one hundred dollars for their work, and any profit made went back into developing new products.

I interject these points here because one such critique has been leveled against Newman's early work. Elizabeth A. Ford's "H/Z: Why Lesléa Newman Makes Heather into Zoe," originally published in 1998, performs the kind of critical analysis I suggest conceals more than it reveals. Focusing on illustrations, Ford analyzes the gender expression of Zoe in *Too Far Away to Touch* and Heather in *Heather Has Two Mommies*. Ford rightly claims that Zoe is represented as more feminine than Heather. Her claim that this is motivated by a desire to make *Too Far Away to Touch* more commercially viable is less convincing. Ford suggests, "Authors who choose gay themes and who write for children must also choose whether or not to be commercially viable. Those who want to sell books must learn, as Lesléa Newman seems to have learned, to maintain a 'safe' distance between child and gay adult characters" (2003). This "distance" she notes is presumably not familial, not spatial, as Zoe is depicted hugging her uncle, holding his hand, and lying next to him. Although it is true that the queer adult character(s)'s relationship to the child protagonist and focalizer changes from lesbian parents in *Heather Has Two Mommies* to a gay uncle in *Too Far Away to Touch*, the adult-child relationship is far more intimately portrayed in the latter text. Even more, Newman has written many books about lesbian- or gay-parented families, and *Heather Has Two Mommies* has been revised and reissued many times. The same cannot be said for *Too Far Away to Touch*. Ford writes: "A chasm separates the presentations and concepts of Newman's two picture books for children; a chasm separates their implied audiences" (205). To be less grandiose and more specific: six years separate the publication of the two picture books that Ford compares. Newman published other books between the two Ford highlights: *Gloria Goes to Pride* (1991), *Belinda's Bouquet* (1991), and *Saturday Is Patty Day* (1993). All three of these books feature lesbian-parented families and *Heather Has Two Mommies* remains, by far, the most popular and, I imagine, lucrative.

Even more, the themes of her 1995 text, *Too Far Away to Touch*, AIDS and death, are hardly "safe." Still, Ford argues that in *Too Far Away to Touch* Newman "abandons danger for relative safety" (206). This is because, according to Ford: "Heather provokes the fear that gay or lesbian parents will produce gay or lesbian children because her clothing, her features, her body, signal androgynous child, not boy or girl" (205). Ford's reading hinges on the gender expression of the focalizing child character.

Perhaps it will come as no surprise that in addition to her reasoning, I take issue with the size of Ford's archive. The article only considers two of Newman's readily available LGBTQ+ children's picture books, and Ford's reading is problematic because of it. Ford's critique is constrained by assumptions about author motivation and contorted by an investment in anchoring her critical reading in a critique of capitalism's influence on creators.

A Name on the Quilt (1999), written by Jeannine Atkins and illustrated by Tad Hills, focuses on mourning the loss of an uncle who has died. Additionally, this book subtly gestures to queer community while relegating its clearest articulations to back matter. In the book, Lauren has lost her uncle, Ron. The text's action pivots around Lauren, her parents, her grandmother, her little brother, and several of Ron's friends gathering to make a memorial quilt in his honor. While working on the quilt, Lauren recalls the close relationship she had with her uncle. She remembers swimming, ice skating, dancing, and laughing with him. Like other uncles depicted in HIV/AIDS-themed children's books, and in LGBTQ+ children's books that employ the gay uncle trope more explicitly, Ron is more playful and likely to engage children's interests than his straight counterparts. This story of love and loss beautifully captures the pain of mourning and does a wonderful job making the important work of memorializing present in image and text. However, although Ron's family and friends are participating in a queer community ritual by creating a quilt, and although information about the AIDS Memorial Quilt is included in the back matter, the text does not directly address the project's queer history and politics. In fact, Ron's family and friends appear to be participating in a private memorialization, untethered to community, politics, and history.

It is significant that when more-or-less gay uncles appear in LGBTQ+ children's picture books before 2000, they are all dying or already dead. This does problematically link queerness to death, especially when it isn't tethered to the family unit through parenthood. One notable exception is *My Two Uncles* (1995), which is written and illustrated by Judith Vigna. Like many early representations of gay, or possibly gay, uncles, this book identifies Uncle Ned and his "friend" Phil as "favorite uncles." Told in the first person, from the point of view of a young girl, Elly, this is one of very few picture books to depict homophobia within families as the text's central problem. Elly adores her two uncles, especially making crafts with them, which she does at their home. Elly lives in a multigenerational house with her parents and her grandparents, which allows Vigna to explore intergenerational family challenges.

At the start of the text, everyone is preparing to celebrate Elly's grandparents' fiftieth wedding anniversary by throwing a big party in the backyard. When Elly asks if she can sit between her uncles, her grandfather announces that Ned's "friend" is not welcome at his home or party. The reader learns, along with Elly, that Phil and Ned have lived together for five years, but her grandfather has never met Phil. Elly wants to understand why, so she asks her father. The two are depicted sitting on the porch stairs as her father explains. Elly's grandfather stands behind them watering plants. Although not participating in the conversation, he is present for it. Elly's father explains that Phil and Ned are gay. He then explains what it means to be gay by letting her know that some men love men and some women love women. The problem, as he identifies it, is that not all people accept their love. He makes it clear that her grandfather is one of those people.

Perhaps this description of his bigotry forces Elly's grandfather to see it as a problem, since it is homophobia that Elly's dad identifies as a problem in their heartfelt talk. Although Elly's uncles do not attend her grandparents' anniversary party, in the last two-page spread Elly, her uncles, and her grandmother are illustrated standing together at a window in Phil and Ned's apartment as they wave down at Elly's grandfather. He leans against his car, finally "meeting" Phil, albeit from a distance. Importantly, this image, which concludes the text, depicts Elly's grandfather as the outsider, which is represented by real spatial distance.

Representations of gay uncles change radically post-2000. Instead of dying from an AIDS-related illness or being seen as outsiders within the family, gay uncles are often depicted in relationships, frequently getting married. Some things don't change. Gay uncles, and to a lesser extend gay dads, are still depicted as playful and pleasure seeking. They are rarely characterized as workers with jobs, quite unlike lesbian mothers, who are frequently identified with careers. These texts are explored in the next chapter.

Family Diversity and a Little Racial/Ethnic Diversity

A smattering of LGBTQ+ children's picture books that focalized children and families of color were published in the 1990s, often by small, mission-oriented presses invested in multicultural representations.[3] For instance, written by Lois Abramchik and illustrated by Alaiyo Bradshaw, *Is Your Family Like Mine?* was published in 1993 by Open Heart Open Mind Press. In the book, Armetha, a young girl with loose, dark curls and brown skin, becomes self-conscious about not having a father after she starts kindergarten. She asks her racially and ethnically diverse classmates about their families and realizes that some have stepparents, some have single parents, some are in foster care, and some live with a mom and a dad. The message is that all families are different, but all families are centered on love. Although she accepts the lesson that she learns from her friends, Armetha is still curious and asks her moms why she doesn't have a daddy. They explain: "One kind of Daddy helps create babies and another kind helps raise them. You have the first kind of Daddy, who helped create you and you have two mommies who love you and will help you grow up." Armetha is quite satisfied with this response. This is an example of the family diversity trope introduced in Lesléa Newman's *Heather Has Two Mommies*, but not really centered in picture books and popularized until after 2000, when self-published books that engage this trope increased in number.

The bilingual picture book *Best Best Colors/Los Mejores Colores* (1999) was written by Eric Hoffman, illustrated by Celeste Henriquez, and published by Redleaf Press, a nonprofit publisher focused on antibias education materials. *Best Best Colors/Los Mejores Colores* is the story of a young boy named Nate, who has recently decided that only one color, one friend, and one mom can be his "best best." Henriquez depicts Nate with glowing light-brown skin, chubby cheeks, and a head of curls. His moms appear Latinx. The short story takes readers through a day in Nate's life. He goes shopping for shoes, picnics in the park, and spends time with friends. During every event, he discovers a new "best best" color. Nate's moms help him understand that choosing between people and colors isn't always necessary. To reinforce this message, they show Nate a rainbow flag they've created for the Pride parade. Nate gets excited and wants to make a Pride flag to show all his best friends. This sweet picture book avoids representing lesbian parents as a problem while subtly weaving aspects of queer culture into the story.

Queer Youth Desire

None of the youth characters in the various texts identified seem to have sexual awareness or desire. This makes the few picture books that do explore queer youth desires especially significant. One early example is Eric Jon Nones's *Caleb's Friend* (1993), published by Farrar, Straus and Giroux, which offers a queerly seductive representation of same-gender, interspecies desire. Caleb, a tan-skinned boy of about twelve, is an orphan who works on a boat. One day an icy-blue-skinned merboy approaches the ship to return a harmonica Caleb has accidently dropped into the sea. The human boy and merboy continue to meet, but they exchange objects like shells and flowers instead of kisses. These scenes are gorgeously rendered, often lingering on the merboy's slim form. One day, the merboy is caught in the fishers' net and the ship's captain sells him to a merchant, who profits off of putting him on display. Caleb saves the merboy and reunites him with the sea. The merboy reciprocates the favor, saving Caleb and his shipmates during rough weather. The boys eventually part ways, although the text ends by noting that every year Caleb returns to the village near his adventure with the merboy to throw armfuls of flowers into the sea. This dabbles in the trope of doomed queer love that appears frequently in LGBTQ+ young adult literature and LGBTQ+ cinema.

Read in the context of LGBTQ+ children's picture books, I am reminded of a recent controversial and award-winning book by Jessica Love: *Julián Is a Mermaid* (2014). In an extended fantasy framed as a daydream, the protagonist of Love's text is depicted transforming from a boy to a mermaid. Some have suggested that Julián's body is eroticized in these images of transformation, much like the merboy in *Caleb's Friend*. Notably, in a blog post on *Booktoss*, Laura M. Jimenez critiques the book, particularly its eroticization of a young brown and, as she reads it, trans body. Jimenez writes that there is "no where in the book where I am not aware that this is another book about looking AT a trans body. The transformation of the body is a huge fixation, almost a fetish, for cis folks" (L. Jimenez, "Trans People Aren't Mythical Creatures"). I agree with Jimenez's critique of the fetishization of the trans body and her characterization of the author as a "White, cis, woman." Both these things are facts and necessary truths to bring to a robust reading of the text. Additionally, Jimenez references a tweet by a Children of the Glades contributor named Indigo. Jimenez writes, "Indigo looked at the objectification of yet another 'brown femme' body and felt danger there." Indigo's experience being objectified as a young, brown-skinned queer framed her reading of Love's book as problematically objectifying. Indigo assumed an adult gaze perversely staring at the often scantily clad Julián and recognized that differential and hierarchal power dynamics often influence eroticization. I think this is an important and convincing interpretation of the text. According to Jimenez, Love's "outsider's gaze" seems to overdetermine interpretive possibilities and disallow readings that explore its transformative potential. I find Indigo's and Laura Jimenez's readings of Love's picture book compelling, but I don't think their interpretive analyses cancel the possibility of other readings. In fact, I explore alternative interpretive opportunities in chapter six. However, I think Jimenez and Indigo make an essential observation about the challenges of queer youth representation that accounts for the very real, very material vulnerability of queer youth of color.

Chapter Three

Virtually Normal

Lesbian and Gay Grown-Ups in Children's Picture Books

In previous work, I've referred to post-2000 LGBTQ+ children's picture books as "new queer children's literature" to distinguish them from picture books of the 1970s, 1980s, and 1990s, which almost exclusively focused on lesbian and gay parents, with the exception of a few gay uncles and the occasional sissy boy (Miller, "For the Little Queers"). It took until the 2000s for LGBTQ+ children's books to begin to be regularly published by established presses and for the total number to exceed a few dozen. Not surprisingly, the production quality of books improved immensely once presses like G. P. Putnam's Sons and Simon and Schuster started publishing LGBTQ+ children's picture books. However, since 2000, many LGBTQ+ children's picture books continue to be published by small presses or self-published, so traditional press interest expands rather than replaces publication options for LGBTQ+ content. Additionally, after 2010, the number of LGBTQ+ children's picture books published yearly saw another leap in growth.

As this chapter demonstrates, representations of lesbian and gay adults have changed the least in the past twenty years. That doesn't mean subtle shifts in representations and representational practices cannot be detected and analyzed. For instance, given the political context in the US post-2000, it should come as no surprise that politicized representations of lesbian and gay marriages are popular in LGBTQ+ children's picture books of this period, as seen in books like Cynthia Chin-Lee's 2011 *Operation Marriage,* which is about California's Proposition 8 and Jill Twiss's 2018 *A Day in the Life of Marlon Bundo*, which satirized Mike Pence's homophobia. These texts respond to contemporary politics while reframing them by focusing on the point of view of characters affected by homophobia.

Although the number of books featuring lesbian, gay, and even the occasional transgender adult has grown over the last two decades, with few exceptions, LGBTQ+ adult characters are only present in picture books if they have a familial relationship to children. The *Adventures of Rumplepimple*, a two-book series written by Suzanne DeWitt Hall and illustrated by Kevin Scott Gierman, is a notable exception. The series depicts two lesbians "parenting" a troublemaking dog (think *Garfield* or the more recent *Puppy Dog Pals*). Of course, the parenting dynamic is present even though the act of parenting is transposed to an animal. Additionally, in the past several years, biographies of notable LGBTQ+ figures have begun to be published. These are explored further in chapter seven.

I am optimistic that the field of LGBTQ+ biography will continue to grow. However, I am less optimistic, but still hopeful, that fictive picture books featuring queer adulthood will extend beyond a narrow vision of family life, which limits how queer futures are imagined. Most representations of adult LGBTQ+ persons secure queer adults to the family as mothers, fathers, and uncles, occasionally as grandparents. This fixes visions of the future to the familial and, by extension, limits representations of queer intimacy and sociality in children's picture books. The absence of diverse adult queer representation is concerning, since so many LGBTQ+ young people grow up isolated from queer adults. If we continue to limit LGBTQ+ adult representations available to children to those exceptional enough to be featured in a biography or those anchored to children in some way, we limit the ability of queer youth to imagine expansive queer futures.

Homonormativity and Critical Optimism

Founded in 1980, the Human Rights Campaign (HRC) is the United States' preeminent LGBTQ+ organization. At its start, the HRC's mission was to "provide financial support on behalf of the gay and lesbian community to political candidates who supported gay civil rights legislation" (Human Rights Campaign, "HRC Foundation"; Human Rights Campaign, "Our Victories at HRC"; Human Rights Campaign, "About Us"). However, the HRC has since expanded its work to include hashtag campaigns that reframe LGBTQ+ social justice issues, data collection and analysis of LGBTQ+ experiences, and educational campaigns to support LGBTQ+ youth. The HRC currently boasts over three million members and is the largest US-based LGBTQ+ organization (Human Rights Campaign, "HRC Foundation").

Because of its size, success, and prominence, the HRC is convincingly critiqued for amplifying and throwing its substantial resources behind issues of primary concern to white, middle-class lesbians and gays, while failing to acknowledge the needs of the most vulnerable queers, particularly people of color, transgender, and lower-income queers (Human Rights Campaign, "HRC Foundation"; Marks; Meronek). For example, in a 2017 article, Jadyn Marks suggests that the political issues the HRC magnifies are

> an indication of their privilege as middle and upper-class white people. Because of this privilege, their concentrations are on problems that middle and upper-class white LGBTQIA+ people face. They lack a comprehension of intersectionality: the awareness that different identities intersect in complicated ways and cause each person's experience of oppression to be unique.

The liberal politics espoused by the organization seek to secure the "basic human rights" of LGBTQ+ persons within existing social institutions from marriage to the military. It is the group's liberalism and one-dimensional understanding of social identity that are most often critiqued for not going far enough to identify and demand meaningful political change. Others are frustrated that the HRC is the media's LGBTQ+ darling. For instance, in 2015 Toshio Meronek of Truthout described the HRC as "the de facto organization journalists call when they need an "LGBT viewpoint" on a topic." This critique identifies the HRC as controlling the LGBTQ+ political narrative while creating a false sense of community cohesion.

Mainstream LGBTQ+ political and cultural representations often reify liberal, assimilationist ideals that foreground inclusion of LGBTQ+ persons in already existing, and arguably oppressive, social institutions. Indeed, the majority of LGBTQ+ children's picture books reject queerness in their overt clamoring for normalcy defined vis-à-vis participation in marriage. In his 2005 book, *In a Queer Time and Place: Transgender Bodies, Subcultural Lives*, Jack Halberstam writes: "Queer uses of time and space develop, at least in part, in opposition to the institutions of family, heterosexuality, and reproduction" (1). Since the vast majority of LGBTQ+ representations in children's picture books pivot around the family, it is not surprising that queer cultures, identifications, and desires are rarely present. However, LGBTQ+ children's books show lived realities that anti-equality voters, organizers, and politicians want to keep children from seeing and adults from sympathizing with, and, in doing so, they demonstrate the reality, livability, and desirability of LGBTQ+ lives, even as they also conform to raced and classed homonormative social expectations of family values and forms.

It is essential to maintain a commitment to critical optimism when exploring adult LGBTQ+ representations in children's picture books. This is because, as I note, the available representations *are* limited and *do* capitulate to and reinforce narrow versions of the good life that are tethered to oppressive regimes of normativity. However, seeing lesbian and gay adults in children's literature can help young readers imagine a reality that is still all too often denied publicness. As a result, to again reference Rudine Sims Bishop, LGBTQ+ children's picture books about lesbian and gay parents are an important window for children who do not have lesbian and gay adults in their lives and an important mirror for those who do. Additionally, these representations can help young LGBTQ+ readers imagine growing up, which can still be a challenge in a heteronormative media landscape that fails to fully and meaningfully embrace LGBTQ+ identities and expressions. Because of this, I appreciate the important visibility work that even the most homonormative children's picture books accomplish. This doesn't keep me from wanting to see child-free queer futures represented, utopian communities imagined, existing subcultures explored, or queer desire present in LGBTQ+ children's picture books. I'm hopeful we'll get this content one day, but for now my project focuses on the books that do exist.

In this chapter, I continue to use the framework of critical optimism to consider the transformative potential of LGBTQ+ children's picture books while simultaneously acknowledging their frequent acquiescence to ideas, institutions, and identities that reproduce inequality. To do this I place two ideas, that of normalizing queerness and that of normalizing queers, in tension. I argue that LGBTQ+ children's picture books have transformative potential insofar as they trouble the ubiquity of heterosexuality in children's culture, making new ways of loving and living available to young readers. I also argue that LGBTQ+ visibility is troubling when the queer futures made imaginable are tethered to heterosexual familial norms. In other words, I concede to claims that many LGBTQ+ children's picture books are homo-normative, but I also search for moments that reveal the limits of assimilation into oppressive social institutions. Much of this work is carried into subsequent chapters, which focus on queer children and the failure of straight families to adequately meet their needs. I suggest that even though most creators do not represent a queerly transformed world in their books, in the gap between wished for acceptance and the much more complex reality that continues to confront LGBTQ+ persons, the truth of the radical work that needs to be done to create the just world desired haunts the text.

Becoming Virtually Normal: The Gay Uncle Now

As mentioned, after 2000, the legalization of same-sex marriage became hotly contested in the public sphere *and* representations of same-sex marriage in LGBTQ+ children's picture books quickly multiplied. My research shows that most same-sex marriages represented in children's picture books were between men, and that gay uncles of a child focalizer were most frequently depicted. After 2000, euphemisms, like "friend" and "roommate," that coded gay and lesbian relationships in the 1970s, 1980s, and 1990s were slowly retired. Gay uncles find love and, some might suggest, even grow up (a little).[1]

Shifts in representations of gay uncles, from peripheral figures marked for death in the late 1980s and 1990s, to warmly accepted characters preparing for marriage after 2000, reflect changes in social perceptions of homosexuality. These shifts also show that the distance between straight and queer worlds began to collapse post-2000 as some gays and lesbians were normalized vis-à-vis participation in one of the straightest institutions: marriage. Whereas pre-2000 LGBTQ+ children's picture books featuring gay uncles most often ended with their literal deaths, children's picture books that engage the trope now give gay men a familial future.

Of course, it is important to always bear in mind that when we are talking about LGBTQ+ children's picture books, we are generalizing from a small archive. Because the archive of LGBTQ+ children's picture books is so small, individual authors and presses play a substantial role in shaping the field. However, even though there are few titles, taken together, more recent picture books representing gay uncles do notably different cultural work than their predecessors. Most significantly, instead of helping children reconcile

Uncle Bobby's Wedding

SARAH S. BRANNEN

Figure 2 *Uncle Bobby's Wedding* (2008), written and illustrated by Sarah S. Brannen, published by G. P. Putnam's Sons

with queer death, new picture books show children's acceptance of semi-queer life. Now, the gay uncle trope is most often mobilized to represent gays and lesbians as virtually normal, not as peripheral subjects with contingent invitations into straight society. For instance, *Uncle Bobby's Wedding* (2008), written and illustrated by Sarah S. Brannen, is about a little girl, Chloe, who is worried that her favorite uncle, Bobby, will have less time for her once he marries his partner, Jaime.[2] As shown in the cover image (see figure 2), the characters are depicted as guinea pigs.

Chloe shares her concerns with her mom and later her uncle. Uncle Bobby comforts his niece by explaining she isn't losing an uncle, she's gaining one. Interestingly, it is her uncle's marriage to his partner that will legitimize their relationship enough for Jaime to become part of the family, which suggests that queer acquiescence to heterosexual markers of relationship legitimacy is needed for queer acceptance in state society. In other words, in this picture book, marriage serves as a marker of belonging in the straight world and pulls Jaime into Chloe's life as a family member instead of an outsider. Similar dynamics are repeated in *My Uncle's Wedding* (2011), written by Eric Ross and illustrated by Tracy K. Greene. This self-published picture book focuses on a young boy helping plan his uncle's wedding. Marriage provides gay men and lesbians (although there is no lesbian aunt trope that corresponds to the gay uncle) a path to maturity that is conceptualized as "settling down" and settling for marriage and monogamy.

Whereas in the 1990s the gay uncle trope was used to simultaneously reveal and conceal queerness, post-2000, the gay uncle's gayness is no longer an open secret, but instead a celebrated part of life that need not be obscured by euphemisms. This also represents the expanded possibilities for some gay men and lesbians to claim "virtual normalcy" by foregrounding their sameness to their straight counterparts. However, the consistent infantilization of adult gay men, their construction as loved by children because they are childlike, remains present in picture books depicting gay uncles. This has the, quite likely unintended, effect of subordinating gay men's desire to the whims and desires of the children in their lives, children who they are, importantly, not tasked with parenting. This also positions gay men as heterosexual helpmates who are loved for swooping in and entertaining the children of straight couples when those couples are off doing the serious work of being grown-ups.

Another example of the infantilization of gay men and their subordination to the whims of children can be found in author/illustrator Pija Lindenbaum's *Mini Mia and Her Darling Uncle* (2007), which was originally written in Swedish and later translated to English by Elisabeth Kallick Dyssegaard. The picture book follows Mia's introduction to her favored uncle's new boyfriend, her jealous reaction, and her ultimate acceptance of the relationship. Mia's obstinance is comically present in each illustration, including the quirky cover, which depicts a scowling Mia, framed by the long, thin legs of two men, kneeling on a dirty restaurant floor as she dumps sugar onto one of the men's shoes. Mia's over-the-top disdain for her uncle's boyfriend provides the comic relief missing from many LGBTQ+ children's picture books, which forgo quirkiness for heartfelt realism. Mia is a brat, but she is quite amusing.

Mia's parents are not present in the text. They appear to be on a trip, so she is staying with her grandmother. Mia's three presumably heterosexual, suit-wearing, meatloaf-eating uncles either live with Mia's grandmother or take all their meals at her home. In contradistinction to the dull portrayal of her straight uncles, Mia's gay uncle, Tommy, dresses with flair and is more of a silly friend than a serious grown-up. Uncle Tommy is bright colors and exotic cuisine, play-filled days and surprises, as opposed to the monotony and seriousness of straight adults. This book, more than any other, creates a strong opposition between straight and gay uncles, further establishing the link between gay uncles, pleasure, and play.

All is well between Tommy and Mia, until Tommy introduces her to Fergus, his new boyfriend. Mia is terribly jealous of Fergus and terrible to him.

She treats him like a child stealing her best friend and is never reprimanded for her behavior; after all, chastising his niece would be a decidedly grown-up activity. Mia's relationship to Fergus changes when her uncle spends the day sick in bed and Fergus entertains her by playing soccer—in other words, subordinating himself to her whims and entertaining her as a good gay uncle or uncle proxy should.

Like most books that engage the gay uncle trope, and many that represent gay fathers, this one depicts gay men with no responsibilities. Uncle Tommy can stay home with his niece when her presumably straight uncles are at work. A critical reading might suggest that this reiterates the position of acceptable homosexuals as heterosexual helpmates, since it is Tommy, not Mia's grandmother, who entertains her while her parents are away, even though he is not entrusted with feeding and sheltering his niece. In the case of gay uncles and gay men generally, by infantilizing and trivializing potentially subversive characters, and therefore constraining their transformative potential, gay men are rendered "harmless" and seem to do little more than have fun. Fun and pleasure could be subversive, but in LGBTQ+ children's picture books, queer adult pleasure doesn't make its way into the story and adult queer men are at the whim of their nieces and nephews.

I want to be clear: I am not taking issue with the existence of playful gay uncles who are beloved by their nieces and nephews. Instead, I'm concerned that dominant representational strategies, particularly child focalization, leave out LGBTQ+ adults in LGBTQ+ communities by representing LGBTQ+ adults extracted from queer culture and community and plunged into the straight world of their heterosexual-parented nieces and nephews. This, like infantilization as a representational strategy, coheres into a subtrope through repetition and neutralizes the queer potential of LGBTQ+ children's picture books by focusing on assimilation into straightness rather than transformation of straightness. Even as I write this, I want to reiterate the size of the archive I am analyzing. The overall archive I've identified and engage throughout this book consists of approximately two hundred titles, and the "gay uncle" trope is present in about a dozen texts. That is, however, a substantial percentage of available LGBTQ+ children's picture book titles. The size of the general archive demonstrates the influence of a handful of authors and presses in shaping the field of queer visibility. The creation of more LGBTQ+ children's picture books will potentially "trouble" the trope so that the gay uncle becomes a far more dimensional, nuanced, and diverse representation that doesn't create a narrow expectation for "gay uncleness."

Indeed, there are already a couple of LGBTQ+ children's picture books that "trouble" the gay uncle trope. Written and illustrated by Laurel Dykstra, *Uncle Aiden* (2005) is a first-person narrative told from the point of view of a young girl named Anna Maria Flannigan Cruz. Anna Maria's Uncle Aiden has bright red hair and piercings. Like most gay uncles, he is his niece's favorite. Uncle Aiden plays pirate and tea party with Anna Maria, gracefully entering her world. Unlike most gay uncles in the archive, Uncle Aiden also invites his niece into his world. He introduces her to boyfriends, subtly presenting the possibility of polyamory. He also takes her to Pride. The book represents a mode of reciprocity rarely found in LGBTQ+ children's books, which tend to reinforce the idea of queer characters visiting the straight world, instead of vice versa. Here, queer culture is made accessible to the child. Additionally, adult-child hierarchies are unsettled in the text. Uncle Aiden learns Spanish from his niece, subtly upsetting the typical adult-child hierarchy and introducing an intersectional understanding of cultural diversity as she introduces him to one of her heritage languages. This book gestures toward the transformative power of LGBTQ+ children's picture books by modeling reciprocal relationships between adults and children as well as the possibility of learning from differences, be they linguistic or cultural.

Additionally, *Love Is in the Hair*, a 2015 Flamingo Rampant publication written and illustrated by Syrus Marcus Ware, provides young readers with dimensional gay uncle characters. The story focuses on a light brown–skinned little girl named Carter who is about to become a big sister. Her uncles are taking care of her when her mom and dad are at the hospital waiting for her new sibling to be born. Carter is having trouble sleeping and wakes her uncles up. One prepares warm milk while the other tells her stories about his life, stories represented by the beads and strings woven through his long dreadlocks. One bead is a memento from the day she was born; a long thread reminds him of the day he met his partner. After listening to the comfortable personal stories about familial love, Carter is sleepy enough to head back to bed and have sweet dreams about the baby she'll meet the next day. This story is unique in that queer romance is part of the bedtime story, normalized without losing its specificity. Even more, this is one of very few representations that does not infantilize gay uncles by representing them only as playmates. These uncles are caretakers who, through storytelling, collapse distinctions between straight and queer worlds.

Love and Marriage

Currently, there are quite a few LGBTQ+ children's picture books about marriage. These fall into two categories: 1) first-person narratives that focalize a presumably heterosexual child witnessing a queer adult relationship, and 2) third-person narratives that focalize queer young adult characters and encourage readers to identify with queer desire. According to Maria José Botelho and Masha Kabakow Rudman, "Stories are social constructs offering a selective version of reality, told from a particular focalization of viewpoint. Authors position readers to respond in particular ways through the decisions they make about choice of genre, language use, point of view, and other literary devices" (8–9). LGBTQ+ children's picture books that employ child narrators usually focus less on adult romance than on children securing or formalizing a normative family for themselves through their adult caretakers' marriage. On the other hand, books that mirror popular fairy tales, as well as those featuring nonhuman characters in love, position young readers to identify with queerness and perhaps encourage them to see themselves as desiring subjects. I return to these latter representations in chapter six as I suggest they do very different cultural work than the first set of representations.

Marrying Moms

Telling the story of marriage from the perspective of the child or children raised in a lesbian-parented family amplifies the significant role marriage plays in creating a secure environment for children as well as the virtual normalcy of the lesbian couple. This is the case in two 2011 publications: Lesléa Newman's *Donavan's Big Day* and Cynthia Chin-Lee's *Operation Marriage*. Both texts incorporate child focalizers and appear to be creative responses to arguments in support of marriage equality that emerged in political discourse during the early 1990s and that suggested marriage equality was good for children, families, and the nation. For example, in 1991, three gay couples in Hawaii argued it was unconstitutional to discriminate against lesbian and gay couples by denying them access to marriage. The case, *Baehr v. Miike*, appealed to child-protection rhetoric to support an argument for the state's investment in marriage as an institution intimately bound to having and raising children. In *Baehr v. Miike*, many experts were called to the stand to describe the influence same-sex parenting had on the social and psychological development of children. Almost all the experts claimed that same-sex couples were fit to raise children. Even more, several experts suggested that children were being denied benefits, including access to health care, because same-sex couples were unable to marry. Some went so far as to suggest that the state was denying children economically stable homes by denying gays and lesbians access to the institution of marriage (Chang). By constructing themselves as caring parents, early lesbian and gay activists sought inclusion into the institution of marriage by politicizing not their sexuality but their family status. Books like these, which predate the 2015 Supreme Court decision to legalize marriage equality, also make creative arguments of their own about the validity of lesbian and gay families.

Donovan's Big Day (2011), written by Newman and illustrated by Mike Dutton, is a third-person narrative that ends with a young boy's moms getting married. The child is centered throughout the text, as suggested by the title of the book as well as the cover illustration, which depicts a boy with scruffy hair and pale skin whose beaming face is framed by an oversized bowtie (see figure 3). Readers are not sure what Donovan is excited about until the end of the book. Instead, readers visually track Donovan hurriedly getting ready for his big day as illustrations are reinforced by text that reads, "He had to race downstairs / and give Sheba her breakfast / and gobble up all the pancakes. . . ." The quick rhythm of Newman's prose conveys the controlled frenzy and excitement of the day. Although the reader knows the day is important, it is not until Donovan delivers two gold rings to his moms that the reader learns why. It's Donovan's big day because he is the ring bearer at his moms' wedding. Because Donovan doesn't see his mothers as desiring beings, romance is left out of the story. Instead, Donovan's big day appears to be a celebration of family, not romantic love. It's unlikely that Newman was responding directly to legal arguments in support of marriage equality while penning the story, but the logics and warrants in support of marriage equality that dominate the historical moment of the book's creation are embedded in the text just the same.

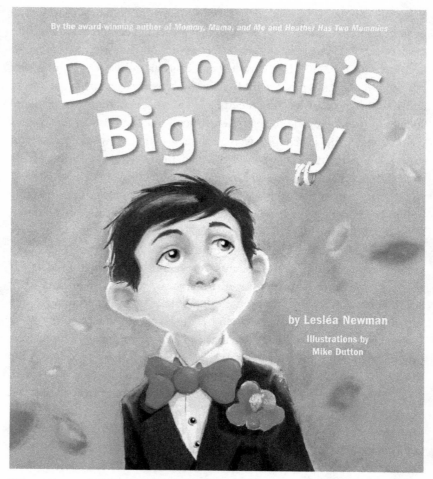

Figure 3 *Donavan's Big Day* (2011), written by Lesléa Newman, illustrated by Mike Dutton, published by Tricycle Press

Operation Marriage (2011), written by Cynthia Chin-Lee and illustrated by Lea Lyon, is more directly political than Newman's picture book. It takes place in California in 2008, when Proposition 8 was on the ballot. The theme of family legitimacy and state-recognized marriage is personalized and given a sense of immediacy at the very start of the book. The first two-page spread depicts an elementary school with several upper elementary–age students. A girl, perhaps nine years old, explains that her good friend, Zack, told her they can no longer be friends because her parents, a lesbian couple, aren't really married. The girl, Alex, responds that they are, but Zack continues to challenge her. She angrily leaves the school with her younger brother, Nicky, in tow. At home, she learns that her parents' commitment ceremony isn't recognized by the state. Alex and Nicky's parents show them videos of the ceremony, which both children enjoy. Afterward, a confused Alex asks her parents if the state will let them get married now. Her parents explain that, although they can, people are fighting to take that hard-won right away. Both children want their parents to have a state-recognized marriage. Their parents are resistant to getting married and explain that it is a lot of work. Nicky comes up with "Operation Marriage," a mission to convince their parents to get married. The children's parents, encouraged by their enthusiasm and the looming threat that Prop 8 will pass, decide to get married. In text that faces an image of the informal wedding, Alex notes: "It was the happiest day of my life to see Pastor Rob marry our parents." Alex's happiness is linked to the social acceptance she expects to experience now that her parents' relationship has been legitimated by the state. The focus on Alex and her feelings reflects that of some pro–marriage equality arguments that, like this picture book, focus on benefits to children and, by extension, the potential harm caused to children by limiting marriage equality.

The story doesn't end at the wedding, with its close-up of the sweet family of four. Instead, it jumps forward a month. Proposition 8 has passed, and Alex is "glad our parents married before that happened." The image facing this information focuses on Zack and his mother, who have appeared at the family's home with a plate of cookies and an apology. They stand on one side of the door, while Alex and one of her parents stands on the other. The text reads, "We invited them in." The ending of the book seems to suggest that life goes on regardless of the laws that constrain legal aspects of our lives. It is quite interesting that *Operation Marriage* depicts the homophobic bully and his mother, although not his father, changing their minds about the lesbian-parented family *after* they participate in a state-sanctioned wedding. Zack and his mother appear at Alex's home, cookies in hand, not to welcome the family to the neighborhood they've lived in for quite a while, but to recognize their acceptability and normalcy.

Both books, although quite different, offer normative visions of queer adulthood. Additionally, they further the connection between marriage and relationship legitimacy found in books about gay uncles getting married. Once available to gays and lesbians, marriage becomes a marker of relation-ship validation and a vehicle for respectability and inclusion in the national imaginary as an adult community member. Marriage represents that the lesbian or gay couple accepts a version of institutional and interpersonal being and belonging previously reserved for heterosexuals.

Incidental Queerness

Whereas prior to 2000 many LGBTQ+ children's picture books were published by niche presses like Lollipop Power Inc. and Alyson Wonderland, after 2000, the accessibility of digital publishing programs prompted many LGBTQ+ parents to write their own stories. These books are often "diversity vehicles" with the express intent of providing "mirrors" for the children of gays and lesbians by showing them families like their own. Additionally, Canada-based micro press Flamingo Rampant Press has published about six books a year since 2015. Flamingo Rampant's mission is "producing feminist, racially-diverse, LGBTQ+ positive children's books, in an effort to bring visibility and positivity to the reading landscape of children everywhere" ("Flamingo Rampant"). Although these books cover a variety of experiences, including family formation and snapshots of daily life, they all share the common desire to affirm LGBTQ+ families by expanding the field of children's picture books to include more nuanced representations of families. The fact that the families are headed by same-sex parents is clear but not a theme explored. Instead, the books serve as portals into the lives of lesbian and gay families. Additionally, at least in the case of Flamingo Rampant Press, there is a deliberate and successful attempt to represent diverse intersectional identities authentically and expansively.

I use the term *incidental queerness*, a term already in circulation, to describe LGBTQ+ children's picture books that represent queer identities and expressions without thematizing them. After 2000, several picture books for very young readers that depicted incidental queerness and introduced basic concepts ranging from colors and opposites to queer families and culture were published. Early examples include *Monicka's Papa Is Tall* (2006) and *Ryan's Mom Is Tall* (2006); both picture books were written by Heather Jopling and illustrated by Allyson Demoe. After serving as a surrogate for a gay couple, Jopling noticed that there were "very few children's stories that dealt with non-traditional families in a down-to-earth manner" (Nickname Press). Like many creators of LGBTQ+ children's picture books, Joplin identified gaps in children's picture books and created content to fill those gaps.

Other texts that represent incidental queerness and respond to perceived absences in the field of children's literature include those published by the small press My Family!/Dodi Press, which specializes in reading material featuring racially and ethnically diverse, lesbian- and gay-parented families swimming, vacationing, and preparing for science fairs with their happy children. In fact, Cheril N. Clarke and her wife and business partner, Monica Bey-Clarke, started the press after deciding to foster children in their home. In a July 2019 correspondence, they said that they wanted their books to represent "settings that lean upper-middle class instead of urban/inner-city, which is typical when you finally do get a book or see media representation of African American families." By representing a Black lesbian couple with plentiful financial resources parenting a young Black child in a suburban setting, Bey-Clarke and Clarke trouble two representational fields: 1) the depiction of lesbian and gay families as white and 2) the depiction of Black families as working class and living in urban areas. This does significant work expanding the "windows and mirrors" available in children's picture books. The repeated conflation of whiteness with queerness as well as blackness with poverty begins to function as a controlling image affecting how we perceive ourselves and each other (Collins).

Bey-Clarke and Clarke created two books featuring a Black family and one featuring a multiracial Latinx and white family. Their first book, *Keesha and Her Two Moms Go Swimming* (2011), is a simple snapshot of a family's day at a public pool. The family's class status is signaled on the front cover (see figure 4). Keesha stands between her parents, towel over one arm, ready to jump in the pool. A two-story home set back on a large, well-manicured lawn is in the background. Although the cover image signifies material comfort, the illustration's low quality and amateurish design reveal the material challenge small start-up presses often have both identifying and paying for talent. Additionally, the very existence of the press is evidence of the real challenge LGBTQ+ families of color experience when trying to find books that represent families that look like theirs. Although the books published by MyFamily!/Dodi Press will surely be critiqued as homonormative, the abiding reality is that we all live in and negotiate oppressive norms. Perhaps complacency and resistance can coexist. The books certainly resist narrow representations of Black families, even though doing so necessitates capitulation to white capitalist norms. Realist texts depict the world as it is, and a more robust and inclusive depiction of the actually existing world is a

Figure 4 *Keesha and Her Two Moms Go Swimming* (2011), written by Monica Bey-Clarke and Cheril N. Clarke, illustrated by Aiswarya Mukherjee, published by Dodi Press

political project, even if the queer transformative potential of these texts is lacking. Even more, *Keesha and Her Two Moms Go Swimming* is one of very few LGBTQ+ children's picture books that doesn't depict gay- and lesbian-parented families either in isolation or surrounded by heterosexual families. Keesha's best friend, Trevor, is at the pool with his two dads.

Published five years later, *Keesha's South African Adventure* (2016) reintroduces Trevor, who is in Keesha's class. In school they learn about South Africa, and Keesha is so excited that she tells her parents all about it, exclaiming that she wants to go on an African safari. A few weeks later, Keesha's moms surprise her with the best birthday present ever—a trip to South Africa. The impromptu and inevitably quite costly trip to South Africa does work like the large home conspicuously placed on the cover of *Keesha and Her Two Moms Go Swimming*—both deliberately signify upper-middle-class privilege in order to uncouple representations of race from financial hardship. The family's trip is depicted in the ensuing pages, and upon their return, Keesha shares her experience with her peers in class.

Monica Bey-Clarke and Cheril N. Clarke's third book, *Lopez Family: Science Fair Day*, features a multiracial, gay-parented household. One of the men appears Latinx and the other white. The child is racially ambiguous, but his skin tone appears more similar to his Latinx father (2011). The protagonist is a young boy named Felix Lopez, and, like the title suggests, the plot pivots around his school's science fair. His parents help him build a remote-control airplane to enter. Although they clearly support him, much of the story is about Felix problem solving on his own. The story's central conflict is Felix's experience being bullied by Buzz the Bully, who calls him "Nerd Boy." Right before the science fair, Buzz the Bully ends up tripping Felix, which causes his plane to break. Although Felix is upset, he quickly composes himself, explains what happened to his teacher, and fixes his plane. Felix's teacher, Mrs. Sanchez, gives him a gold star for telling the truth, and he wins the science fair. When he tells his dads about his day, they are very proud. Like Keesha, Felix is surrounded by material comforts that signify middle- to upper-middle-class status. And, as is typical of most "snapshot" of everyday life LGBTQ+ children's picture books, this one represents gay-parented families as unexceptional. This is set in relief by the existence of a bully who doesn't find the fact that Felix's fathers are gay men compelling material and instead focuses on the boy's interest in science for bantering inspiration.

Although, as mentioned, work by Bey-Clarke and Clarke can certainly be described as normalizing lesbian and gay familial experiences, and even more, as reifying middle-class values of mobility and materialism, an intersectional reading must account for how their picture books *also* trouble conflations of people of color with poverty by celebrating the trappings of middle-class family life. Reading children's picture books through the framework of critical optimism isn't meant to absolve picture books of their role in reinforcing oppressive values. Instead, this interpretive strategy seeks to identify the dream underneath the representation. I suggest that these authors are attempting to write into being a future for Black queer families, even as their vision capitulates to a version of the good life that needs to be reimagined to really do justice to queer individuals, families, and communities. As is, these picture books show families enjoying the benefits of contingent and precarious access to a dominant version of success that is anchored to capitalist logics. Ironically, in challenging prevalent representations that code people of color as poor, Bey-Clarke and Clarke face the same issue they experience in representing lesbian and gay families as normal: how best to represent queerness as normal without normalizing and standardizing LGBTQ+ identities so that they fall in line with heteronormative expectations, which are influenced by race and class values. This problematic permeates the archive of LGBTQ+ children's picture books, often leading to representations that disappointingly demonstrate allegiance to institutions and ideals that reproduce systems of privilege and oppression. Perhaps we need more speculative LGBTQ+ children's picture books?

Incidental queerness also appears in recent picture books geared toward babies and young toddlers, like *Pride Colors* (2019) by Robin Stevenson; *Rainbow: A First Book of Pride* (2019), written by Michael Genhart and illustrated by Anne Passchier; and M. L. Webb's *GayBCs* (2019). Although hardly radical calls for political revolution, these books do the important and potentially transformative work of interrupting a visual field dominated by visions of heterosexual families. In doing so, they render queer families and cultures possible and desirable. Even more, LGBTQ+-parented families that may be cut off from queer community can imagine themselves as part of a virtual network of same-sex families. In my introduction, I discuss the importance that *Spawning Generations'* editors, Epstein-Fine and Zook, placed on the lack of children's picture books about LGBTQ+ families in the 1980s. The editors, both raised by queer parents, note the ability of texts to help readers envision themselves as part of a community of strangers à la Benedict Anderson. In reading children's literature, importantly, child readers both see themselves in characters and see someone else, so they can form an identification with an imagined network of children sharing a common, although nonidentical, experience. This is particularly important in LGBTQ+-parented families who may have little access to queer community.

I would suggest that one practice constraining current LGBTQ+ children's picture books from reaching their transformative potential is the focus on nuclear families in isolation. This reproduces white, middle-class heteronormative logics that themselves emerge from and entwine with capitalist logics. The nuclear family, as the smallest self-reliant entity responsible for its own members, devalues community and justifies the neoliberal rollback of state welfare programs (Duggan, *Twilight of Equality?*; Duggan, "New Homonormativity"; Duggan, "After Neoliberalism?"; Grady et al.; Frow).

Radical transformation requires a new way of imagining our relationship to one another and our commitment to community.

j wallace skelton is the author behind one of Flamingo Rampant's first children's picture books, *The Newspaper Pirates* (2015), which is illustrated by Ketch Wehr. This book gestures toward "new" ways of envisioning community care, ways many people experience every day, but that are devalued through lack of dominant cultural representations. The book's narrator-protagonist, Anthony Bartholomew, is a young boy with pale white skin, red hair, and big glasses. Anthony has an admirable sense of style, often boasting long scarves, pearl bracelets, and large rings. His fathers, Papa and Abba, are as perplexed as he is when their newspapers go missing from in front of their apartment. The story pivots around Anthony trying to solve the mystery of the missing newspapers. Like all of Flamingo Rampant Press's publications, this one deliberately incorporates multiple modes of diversity, including race and age. Additionally, skelton pays attention to how characters and relationships between characters are represented. Anthony's family is multiracial, and his genderqueer aesthetic goes against the grain of LGBTQ+ children's picture books that tend to represent children raised by lesbian and gay parents as cisgender and presumably straight. Additionally, whereas much children's literature takes place in single-family homes, this story takes place in an apartment, and the setting is important to the plot. An older couple who live in the building take care of Anthony when he arrives home from school, demonstrating a community of caring adults beyond the queered nuclear family unit. Even more, it is in the apartment building's recycling room that Anthony (perhaps) discovers clues about the newspaper thief. Like many snapshots of everyday life in LGBTQ+ children's picture books, this one is purposefully lighthearted. In fact, the "About" section of Flamingo Rampant Press's website explains its founders' motivation: "When traditional publishing produced mostly difficult stories of harassment or bullying and insipid books whose proud 'message' was that gay parents aren't necessarily bad, Flamingo Rampant went . . . a different way. We show LGBT2Q+ kids, families, and communities that are full of fun, celebration, adventure, shenanigans and lots of love" (Flamingo Rampant, "About Flamingo Rampant"). In these books, queer gender and sexual identities are present, but not thematized. Instead of gender or sexual expression and identity being "problems" negotiated in Flamingo Rampant Press creations, gender and sexual diversity are matter-of-factly treated as part of everyday life, normal, without needing to conform to norms.

Although the vast majority of books featuring LGBTQ+ adults position them in relation to children, Suzanne DeWitt Hall's *Rumplepimple* (2015) and *Rumplepimple Goes to Jail* (2017), both illustrated by Kevin Scott Gierman, are rare exceptions that do not portray queer adults as parents of human children. These books focus on the exploits of Rumplepimple, a wire fox terrier with lots of energy; his cat sister, Chicken; and their two moms. The Rumplepimple series is reminiscent of other children's cultural texts starring adventurous pets who are quasi-anthropomorphized, like the recent Disney program *Puppy Dog Pals* or well-known cultural icons like *Garfield*.

In the first book, Rumplepimple won't leave one of his moms alone, so his other mom takes him on a trip. He enjoys the car ride but isn't excited when she starts leaving him in the car to go shopping. Right before the door slams shut, Rumplepimple hears a cry for help and leaps out of the car. It turns out that the scream came from a little girl being bullied by a mean kid. Rumplepimple saves the day, but instead of seeing him as a hero, his mom sees him as a runaway dog. The second book in the series, *Rumplepimple Goes to Jail*, introduces readers to a single dad raising his son and their tutu-wearing boy cat named Mr. Noodles. Rumplepimple's cat sister, Chicken, has an unrequited crush on Mr. Noodles. This adventure begins when Rumplepimple notices his new friend sneaking off to a street festival. Worried his buddy might get hurt, he chases after him, busting through his screen door to save the day. But Rumplepimple's heroism is again misinterpreted. He is discovered by a police officer and taken to jail but is soon reunited with his moms. Rumplepimple is positioned like a child with limited agency and is misunderstood by the adults in his world. Like Flamingo Rampant Press publications, this series deliberately depicts a diverse cast of characters of varying sizes and with multiple skin tones.

The only fictional adult gay and lesbian characters I have identified who are not represented through their relationship to a child (or pet) appear in Daniel Kibblesmith's *Santa's Husband* (2017). The book reimagines Santa and his partner as an interracial gay couple. Santa Claus, a Black man, and his white partner, David, live in the North Pole, check the naughty/nice list twice, and take care of all the reindeer. The idea that some people don't approve of a gay, Black Santa is introduced but is quickly dismissed with a note that people have always imagined Santa in different ways. Like most of the books discussed in this section, *Santa's Husband* disrupts the persistent heteronormativity that permeates children's culture generally. This book does so by reimagining one of the most idolized fictional figures in many children's lives: Santa Claus.

Almost all of the books discussed in this section were created as a response to a gap in representation that their creators identified and sought to fill. They function as both mirrors and windows to the children reading them and in doing so transform the field of visibility available and accessible to children in meaningful ways. However, as noted in my discussion of Bey-Clarke and Clarke's work, they also tend to demonstrate attachments to ideas and institutions that reproduce inequality—for instance, by celebrating representations of marriage, mobility, and money that reify ways of life that sustain inequality and justify a social world that cannot do justice to the most vulnerable queers.

Family Formation

A handful of LGBTQ+ children's picture books depict queer family origin stories, either through donor conception, as is the case in Lesléa Newman's *Heather Has Two Mommies* as well as Christy Tyner's more recent *Zak's Safari: A Story about Donor-Conceived Kids of Two-Mom Families* (2014), or through adoption stories, which are far more frequent. These stories thematize the desire to be parents that many LGBTQ+ adults experience, as well as the specificity of queer family formation. On the other hand, they are penned to celebrate queer families and the real challenges, material constraints, and social contexts negotiated to become a parent are relegated to back matter if present at all.

In Tyner's *Zak's Safari*, illustrated by Ciaee, the young narrator speaks directly to the reader as he tells the story of his conception. Zak explains that his parents met, fell in love, and wanted more than anything to have a baby— so they decided to make one. In simple but accurate language, the young narrator explains terms like sperm and egg cells, known donors, donors from sperm banks, and genes. The second half of the book celebrates Zak's family, echoing books that depict snapshots of everyday life. Zak and his moms are shown eating meals together, playing at the beach, going for nature hikes, and hanging out with friends and family.

As mentioned, there are far more stories about same-sex couples adopting children, including Lesléa Newman's *Felicia's Favorite Story* (2002), Jean Davies Okimoto and Elaine M. Aoki's *The White Swan Express: A Story About Adoption* (2002), Andrew R. Aldrich's *How My Family Came to Be—Daddy,*

Papa and Me (2003), Kyme Fox-Lee and Susan Fox-Lee's *What Are Parents?* (2004), Jarko De Witte van Leeuwen's *Arwen and Her Daddies* (2009), and Stephanie Burks' *While You Were Sleeping* (2004). Many of these are tales of international adoption, as in the case of Lesléa Newman's *Felicia's Favorite Story* (2002), illustrated by Adriana Romo, which tells the family's origin story as a favorite bedtime story. At the story's opening, two moms clean the kitchen of a single-family home as their daughter makes a puzzle. Soon it is the little girl's bedtime. Mama Linda tells her she'll read her a book if she gets ready for bed quickly, and Mama Nessa promises to join them soon. Felicia decides she doesn't want Mama Linda to read a book; instead she wants to hear her favorite story about being adopted by her parents. Mama Linda tells the story of going with Mama Nessa to Guatemala to adopt their little girl. As in most of these stories, what would be an emotionally, financially, and politically fraught experience is removed from any social framework and represented as a family origin story. As a result, this and most other family formation stories function as funhouse mirrors, distorting reality in order to make a sanitized version of personal history palpable. This limits the possibility that readers will think about family formation critically and understand it as a social justice issue. But the possibility, slim as it may be, is still present. Recognition that forming families is a strong desire of many LGBTQ+ persons hindered by legal, financial, and cultural issues lingers below the surface.

Jean Davies Okimoto and Elaine M. Aoki's *The White Swan Express: A Story About Adoption* (2002) is another tale of international adoption, but this one works to make the adoption process plainer by focusing on four different families as they journey from North America to China to meet their daughters. One family, the Suzukis, is likely Japanese, but the other families appear white. One is a heterosexual couple, one a lesbian couple, and one a single woman. The soon-to-be parents come together in Guangzhou, where they board the "White Swan Express" to meet their children for the first time. The political and cultural context, particularly China's former one-child policy, is discussed in informative back matter. Reasons singles or lesbian couples might go all the way to China to adopt, or the financial resources each family would need to feasibly adopt, are not part of the back matter.

Another example of international and interracial adoption is Jarko De Witte van Leeuwen's *Arwen and Her Daddies* (2009), which is based on the author's adoption experience. Unlike *The White Swan Express: A Story About Adoption*, in which North Americans travel to China to adopt, this book features European men, one white, one Black, who travel to the US from Europe to adopt. This picture book is brilliantly critiqued by Cedric Essi in his groundbreaking analysis of international and interracial adoption in LGBTQ+ children's literature. Essi convincingly argues that picture books tend to center whiteness and produce queer progress narratives that ignore the race and class power hierarchies at play in adoption. He writes:

> I understand the reluctance to address race as a subconscious maneuver to repress the preconditions of interracial adoption. White couples are often matched with non-white adoptees because racial profiling in the state's practices in penalization and incarceration particularly undercuts the custody rights of parents of color and especially those of African Americans, which ultimately leads to a disproportionate number of black children in the adoption system. (7)

In addition, Essi notes that white couples in Europe may adopt Black American babies because: "Until recently, laws in most European countries either officially or unofficially denied or limited adoption rights to LGBT couples while policies against gay adoption remain intact in the majority of countries across the globe" (Essi 17). I agree with Essi's understanding of the complex contexts both enabling and constraining adoption practices. Additionally, I see the shared experience of being deemed "unfit" by the state as an unexplored opportunity for envisioning and developing models for racial and sexual minority coalition building within and across identities and experiences that could prompt imagining reproductive and family justice more inclusively by accounting for intersectional identities. Of course, this opportunity is buried far below the surface of actually existing children's picture books, which abandon concrete origin stories in favor of bland, although occasionally charming, bedtime stories that create a distorted mirror of queer family becoming.

Essi is also critical of first-person narrative strategies in many adoption narratives, which tend to be written by adoptive parents and told in the voice of the adoptee. Essi suggests that this "reveals more about adult desires of queers for familial recognition than about the needs of their adopted children" (2). In other words, Essi sees these texts as performing what I've been referring to as "virtual normalcy" by demonstrating the similarities between straight and queer families. He suggests the adoptee as narrator embodies

Figure 5 *How My Family Came to Be—Daddy, Papa and Me* (2003), written by Andrew R. Aldrich, illustrated by Mike Motz, published by New Family Press

"the trope of the child as a savior figure by which queerness is redeemed from cultural stigma and converted into a nuclear family" (Essi 10). The destigmatization of queerness through demonstrated acquiescence to heterosexual norms, like marriage and nuclear family formation, is something I make note of in my discussions of shifts in the gay uncle trope as well as some texts about lesbian- and gay-parented families, most notably Cynthia Chin-Lee's *Operation Marriage* (2011). LGBTQ+ picture book creators seem to recognize, even if they don't explicitly comment on, the legitimizing function of marriage and parenting.

The need to textually perform exceptionalism in order to avoid stigma is present, although often subtly depicted and never critically explored, in many LGBTQ+ children's picture books. Essi considers the demand for exceptionalism through a reading of another tale of adoption, Andrew Aldrich's *How My Family Came to Be—Daddy, Papa, and Me* (2003). This story is narrated by a child adoptee who describes the family origin story in what Essi refers to as "the de-stigmatizing innocence of a child's rhyming voice" (8). Essi does not dismiss this strategy, but instead connects it to the residual stigmatization of gay men in the cultural imaginary by noting that gay men have to "perform as uber-fathers" (10). This is a point I've noted in my discussions of queer exceptionalism as well as descriptions of early depictions of gay-parented families that represent gay fathers as better than heterosexual fathers because they are more involved in the lives of their children. The familial intimacy of the gay-parented family at the center of Aldrich's text permeates every page. The cover of the picture book is an ode to family togetherness (see figure 5). Two white men sit together on a large blue chair. A young Black child sits on the shoulders of one man as his chubby arm points to a book titled *Classic Tales* that the other man holds. All smile broadly. The scene is reminiscent of peaceful notions of family time, and the title of the book shared by this family further connects their queer family to other families, disavowing difference in the performance of idealized family togetherness.

Although issues of social justice are never the theme of LGBTQ+ children's adoption stories, social justice issues do appear in discourses surrounding LGBTQ+ children's picture books, although, as suggested by Essi, they are rarely intersectional and most frequently fail to account for race and class privilege. For instance, in a podcast interview with Charlotte Robinson, De Witte van Leeuwen explained the lengthy struggle that occurred before he and his partner could adopt internationally. Robinson summarizes:

> Jarko and Jos were married in 2001, the year when gay marriage was legalized in the Netherlands. After returning from their honeymoon their dream was to start a family. They soon discovered that joint adoption only applied to children born in the Netherlands where very few children are available. In order to adopt jointly internationally Jarko and Jos fought for 7 years to gain joint international adoption rights. (C. Robinson)

The reality of the LGBTQ+ struggle for equal rights, although erased in the picture book, is present in the story told about it. However, the reasons children are available to adopt in the US, particularly Black children, are not addressed in the interview, nor is the financial cost of both a seven-year battle to adopt and the cost of international adoption itself. As a result, the potential to really envision possibilities for reproductive and familial justice inclusively, and perhaps even queerly, are curtailed.

Family Diversity

The family diversity trope represents lesbian- and gay-parented families alongside other families, including single-parented families, foster families, or intergenerational families, as similar because they are based on love. Exemplary titles include *What Are Parents?* (2004), written by Kyme Fox-Lee and Susan Fox-Lee and illustrated by Randy Jennings, as well as *Dear Child* (2008), written by John Farrell and illustrated by Maurie J. Manning. Many books featuring family diversity are by small, mission-oriented independent presses that feature multicultural titles. These texts represent race and ethnicity with different degrees of specificity. Some represent race through illustrations only and lack racial and ethnic specificity. Others take a more inclusive relationship to race and ethnic differences, producing rich representations at the intersection of multiple identities.

Families (2017), cowritten by Jesse Unaapik Mike and Kerry McCluskey and illustrated by Lenny Lishchenko, is a more recent example. It was published by Inhabit Media, an Inuit-owned press that was founded in 2006 to help "Nunavut kids to see their culture accurately represented in the books they read in schools" (Inhabit Media). The picture book introduces readers to family diversity through the lives of students at a school in Iqaluit, the capital city of Nunavut, a Canadian territory, which is majority Inuit. The lesson that all families are different is deftly introduced as the protagonist, a child named Talittuq, moves through his first day of year two at school. It opens with Talittuq and his anaana (Inuktitut for mother) sitting companionably at their kitchen table eating breakfast. Talittuq asks his anaana why his dad does not live with them. She matter-of-factly responds that his father lives in Mittimatalik and they live in Iqaluit. Talittuq's mother assures him that all families are different and reminds him that although their family consists of only two members it is full of love and happiness.

Although the story focuses on multiple family forms, Talittuq's growing independence is also explored, which creates depth and allows the authors to develop Talittuq's character nicely. For instance, this is the first year "his anaana had agreed to let him ride his bike to school all by himself." Once he arrives at school, Talittuq begins to play on the monkey bars. While swinging wildly, he startles his much younger friend, Qaukkai, who begins to cry. A concerned Talittuq finds his young friend's anaana and mom to help comfort the child. Interestingly, although Talittuq reflects on not wanting his family to be "different," he does not seem to apply the same judgment to his friend's lesbian-parented family, a family that gets more "different" when, on the next page, Talittuq discovers that the third woman Qaukkai's mothers were speaking with was Qaukkai's puukuluk (Inuktitut for birth mother).

Qaukkai is quickly comforted, and the bell soon rings, sending all children to the door where they line up to enter their classes. Today will be Talittuq's first day in his new class. His new teacher introduces himself and explains that he recently moved to Iqaluit with his husband and son. His teacher's homosexuality is effortlessly introduced with little comment, other than a side note that the teacher and his family are "awesome skateboarders." One student the reader is briefly introduced to is raised by divorced parents who share custody, and another by her grandmother. The text ends like it begins: Talittuq has returned home for lunch where his anaana waits for him. Anaana and son sit at the kitchen table as Talittuq absorbs the lesson his anaana offered that morning: "every family is different." I've noted before that many LGBTQ+ children's picture books miss opportunities to imagine community building across difference. This text does a wonderful job envisioning family outside a hetero-/homonormative binary. Additionally, it explores feeling "different" as a characteristic of being in the world that is not the property of queerness but instead a shared experience across identities.

Children as Change Makers

In general, I've found that community and coalition across difference are far more likely to be present in work by creators of color than in work by white creators, which tends to focus on the isolated family unit and perhaps on schools. Texts by Indigenous and queer creators of color are also far more likely to present children as dimensional characters with agency and the ability to reflect on oppressive social systems. One example, *The Zero Dads*

Figure 6 *The Zero Dads Club* (2015), written by Angel Adeyoha, illustrated by Aubrey Williams, published by Flamingo Rampant

Club (2015), written by Angel Adeyoha and illustrated by Aubrey Williams, is similar to picture books mentioned in the previous section insofar as it focuses on family diversity. However, this text offers a critique of heteronormativity that isn't present in most books that focus on family diversity.

The story unfolds around Father's Day. Two dark brown–skinned children sit next to each other at a desk. One, Akilah, complains to her friend Kai about painting an image of a tie. She is upset because neither of them has a father. The activist-minded Akilah suggests they protest Father's Day, but after some discussion they decide that instead of a protest they will start a club, which they name the Moms Only Club. They quickly change the name to the Zero Dads Club to account for the growing membership of children with diverse families including abuelas and tías instead of, or in addition to, moms. The group of first graders meets to make cards for the grown-ups they love, and what ensues is a celebration of the many women in their lives, including a transgender mom, lesbian moms, and single moms. As mentioned in previous discussions of Flamingo Rampant Press, careful attention is paid to representing diverse characters, and this is extended to include different races, religions, and abilities as represented in the picture book's cover (see figure 6).

A subtler representation of child agency is presented in Rigoberto González's bilingual children's picture book *Antonio's Card* (2005), which is illustrated by Cecilia Concepcion Alvarez and published by Children's Book Press, a nonprofit publisher of multicultural children's literature. The protagonist, a Latinx boy named Antonio, lives with his mother and her partner, Leslie. Antonio's peers make fun of Leslie, a tall woman with a masculine haircut and penchant for paint-splattered overalls, which are described as making her look "like a box of crayons exploded all over her" or "like a rodeo clown." As Mother's Day approaches, Antonio's class begins to honor the important women in their lives by creating cards. Although Antonio includes Leslie in a picture of his family, he hides the drawing from his schoolmates, aware that his family likely looks different from theirs. Antonio is very uncomfortable when he finds out the cards will be displayed at an upcoming school event. He eventually confides his feelings to his mom. Although she doesn't tell him what to do, she does help him understand the situation. She explains that he needs to risk being mocked by inviting Leslie into his school to see the display or risk hurting Leslie's feelings by not inviting her. When he begins to think about how important Leslie is to him, his anxiety about being mocked dissipates. He would be sad and lonely without her, and because he loves her, he won't meet his classmates' mockery with shame.

When reading LGBTQ+ children's picture books to identify transformative potential, I consider how various relationships are represented and how they change. Here, for instance, Antonio's relationship to shame changes as the text progresses, and as he reflects on the importance of his relationship with Leslie. The book ends with an image of Leslie and Antonio making eye contact as they stand in front of their front door. They are about to go see the school Mother's Day display, where Antonio will greet the image of his family with pride. Books like this can be significant tools to help children growing up in rainbow families develop strategies of resistance and resilience.

Chapter Four

Beyond the Sissy Boy

Pink Boys and Tomboys

The sissy boy trope resurfaces in the 2000s, but a lot has changed. "Sissiness" is not explained away as it is in earlier texts like *William's Doll* but is a central part of characters' identities; in other words, "sissiness" prevails. Not only does sissiness prevail, on occasion it saves the day. In other words, characteristics associated with the sissy, those most often associated with femininity like being nurturing and appreciating beauty, are seen as valuable, not embarrassing, at least not to the sissy boy himself. For example, *Max: The Stubborn Little Wolf* (2001), written by Marie-Odile Judes and illustrated by Martine Bourre, is the story of a young wolf who wants to be a florist when he grows up. His father, a hypermasculine wolf, attempts to change Max's mind by making a "man" of him. First, Max's father takes him hunting, but Max hates hunting and warns a rabbit of his father's intentions. Second, Max's father assumes his son is a coward and tries to convince him that being a florist is dangerous. Although Max appreciates his father's concern, he assures him he will be careful. Finally, Max's father sprays flower-scented perfume all over his sleeping son's bedroom, hoping he will become disgusted with the scent. Although this does prompt Max to choose a new career path, as a perfumer, it is hardly the masculine career change his father envisioned. Max is portrayed as appreciating beautiful flowers and fine scents. He demonstrates compassion and care for the rabbit his father plans to shoot, and he doesn't appear to notice or respond to his father's frustrations. In this book, gender policing fails quite miserably, and the unhappy character isn't the queer child, it is his hypermasculine father. Judes's sissy departs from past representations of sissy boys and ushers in a new wave of post-2000 sissy boys, marking a change from sissiness as a problem to the precarious acceptance of diverse gender expressions. This time, the joke is on the hypermasculine father who only succeeds at redirecting his child's queer desires, not straightening him out. Additionally, the queer child doesn't need to be exceptional to be accepted, since acceptance isn't on his mind. Post-2000 sissy boys don't seek validation or acceptance. In fact, the table is turned, and it's the bully who is represented as unenlightened and unhappy.

Introducing the Pink Boy

In chapter two, I introduced the boy-meets-skirt trope to separate the desire for feminized attire and its representation from the sissy boy, illustrating early recognition and representation of boys who desire objects associated with girls while maintaining masculine gender expression. Bruce Mack's *Jesse's Dream Skirt* (1979) is the earliest example of this representation and a harbinger of the post-2000 pink boy, a category that advocates introduced to destigmatize boys who desire femininized objects like dresses. In Mack's picture book, the title character, Jesse, lives with a single mom who is happy to help him make the skirt of his dreams. When he goes to school wearing it, his teacher is supportive and kind. Even more, other children are inspired by Jesse to create makeshift skirts of their own. This book serves as an urtext for affirming children's picture book about skirt-wearing boys. In fact, its relevance was affirmed when the text was rereleased in 2019 in celebration of its fortieth anniversary.

Ten years after the rerelease of *Jesse's Dream Skirt*, half a dozen "pink boy" books were published in a five-year period, beginning with Cheryl Kilodavis's *My Princess Boy* in 2009. Kilodavis is the mother of a gender-creative son, and she wrote the book "to explain her son's fondness for pretty things to teachers and fellow students" (Kilodavis). This book was followed a few years later by *Roland Humphrey Is Wearing a WHAT?* (2013), which was also written by the mother of a "pink boy." Then, parent-advocates Sarah and Ian Hoffman wrote *Jacob's New Dress* (2014), which was recently followed by

Jacob's Room to Choose (2019). *Jacob's Room to Choose* reintroduces readers to Jacob. In this book, he is several years older, still wearing dresses, and struggling with being bullied, especially when he uses the school bathroom. The last picture book I've identified as representing a pink boy is by Christine Baldacchino, a former preschool teacher who published *Morris Micklewhite and the Tangerine Dress* (2014) the same year the Hoffmans published their pink boy story. These books are part of a political-cultural project to provide boys with destigmatized access to femininity and to recast feminized objects, like dresses, as gender neutral. Even more, they are all authored by advocates, most often parents, who are deeply invested in the well-being of pink boys.

One of these authors, Sarah Hoffman, coined the term *pink boy* to insert a new way of thinking about gender expression into discussions about gender. Hoffman suggests that instead of trying to fit "pink boys" into a binary gender category, we should focus on changing the sociocultural landscape that forces children to conform to a gender binary (Hoffman, "My Son"). She proposes that the pink boy category could function similarly to the tomboy category. Of course, the idea that a pink boy category that parallels the tomboy category would be destigmatizing and affirming assumes that tomboys are socially accepted. This reading of the tomboy is not without its critics, a point I return to at the end of this chapter through a brief genealogy of the tomboy in children's picture books.

Importantly, Hoffman's understanding of pink boys has proven quite influential. She even successfully challenged gender theorist Alice Dreger for reproducing a cisgender/transgender binary in her treatment models for gender-nonconforming youth. Hoffman took to task the scholar's 2009 *Hastings Center Report* publication "Gender Identity Disorder in Childhood: Inconclusive Advice to Parents" for outlining two medical models for "treating" gender-creative children. One, a "therapeutic" model, sought to eliminate gender-nonconforming behaviors. A second "accommodating" model sought to prepare gender-nonconforming children for transition into a binary gender category (Dreger, "Gender Identity Disorder in Childhood"). Both models identify gender nonconformity as a "problem" to be solved through medical intervention, and both models reproduce a binary gender system even as they unlink gender from the sexed body as a determinant. Hoffman suggested that a more nuanced understanding of gender and a more complex model of care were needed.

Dreger published a response to Hoffman's evaluation that thoughtfully engages the parent-advocate's observations of her own child's gender expression and identity. She began by summarizing Hoffman's critique:

"You've done a good job of outlining the warring factions," Sarah told me. But, she added, "I think that there is a third, quieter point of view—the perspective that, sure, transgender kids exist, but really, most of these gender-nonconforming kids are just kids who don't fall to the most-masculine or most-feminine ends of the spectrum, and that's okay. They don't need treatment, they don't need sexual reassignment, they just need a supportive home life, schools with anti-bullying protocols, and therapy for any harassment they face for being different. (Hoffman qtd. in Dreger, "Pink Boys")

Dreger ended up agreeing with Hoffman. She even appropriated the phrase *pink boy* in her description of types of care that might benefit gender-expansive boys. Dreger writes: "Some pink boys may benefit simply from meeting a swishy gay man—or better yet, two or three such men who can show them you can grow from being a pink boy to a pink man and have (dare I say it?) a fabulous life." After considering Hoffman's argument, Dreger revised her thinking and concluded that boyhood femininities may be signs of proto-gay identities that will manifest as flamboyance.

None of this is to say that people aren't transgender and that children do not need emotional and medical support, including puberty blockers, to live their best life. Instead, reading gender within a cisgender/transgender binary forecloses gender differences that may unsettle binary gender expressions and identifications. Dreger also notes the homophobia that appears in many discussions of youth and gender identity. She writes: "It's worth keeping in mind that in North America, some of the advocates of the 'therapeutic' approach to childhood gender dysphoria have had a very negative view of sexual minorities, and so they've sought to 'cure' children who might otherwise turn out gay, lesbian, bi, or transgender." Of course, this collapse of queer genders and queer sexualities is problematic. Feminine boys can grow up to be feminine men who are exclusively attracted to cisgender women. Increasingly, gender theory and LGBTQ+ children's picture books are accounting for nuance in meaningful ways that challenge rather than reproduce innumerable binaries so that our understandings and representations of gender and sexuality better reflect how we live them.

Children's picture books about pink boys are queer worldmaking projects, most often by parent-advocates who understand that it is necessary to challenge the sociocultural imperative to conform to binary gender identities and expectations. The advocate-authors responsible for pink boy books are rewriting the sissy boy script by rejecting both the desirability and inevitability of boyhood masculinity as well as untangling masculinity as a mode of gender expression from both gender identity and genitals.[1] In these books, "sissiness" is not something to overcome but instead something to accept and embrace as new narratives that refuse gender shame are created.

As urgent as this work is, and as thrilled as I am that parent-advocates like the Hoffmans are supporting their queer children, the fact that cisgender, heterosexual adults are at the center of new queer worldmaking projects must be addressed. In a recent book chapter about Lori Duron's mommy blog *Raising My Rainbow*, I note the limits as well as the potential of this kind of advocacy work. Lori Duron is the mother of a gender-creative child whose early gender expression and identity was similar to that of pink boys. *Raising My Rainbow* is Duron's reflection on raising a gender-creative child. My critical engagement with the blog identifies Duron's attachments to normative mothering scripts as well as her failure to identify her race and class privilege. I argue that it is her raced and classed performance of motherhood that legitimizes her advocacy work on behalf of the queer child (Miller, "Queering the Straight World?"). This isn't to say that Duron isn't doing significant advocacy work. I read my case study of Duron's blog through the framework of critical optimism to identify her nascent recognition that her child cannot experience lasting justice in the existing social world. Instead, the world must be radically transformed and our attachments to regimes of gender and sexual normativity released for queer youth and adults to experience life without discrimination based on gender and sexual identities and identifications. In other words, like many LGBTQ+ children's picture books, Duron's blog, a queer cultural text in its own right, gestures toward an understanding of the radical changes needed to do justice to the queer child while revealing problematic attachments to the existing world.

Similarly, in this chapter, I use critical optimism as a reading strategy to identify the pull of normativity present in pink boy books as well as the parent-advocate-led rejection of a binary gender system. I am particularly critical of attempts to render queer gender expressions banal. For instance, in pink boy books, gender-creative expressions are often discussed as "play" or

Figure 7 *My Princess Boy* (2009), written by Cheryl Kilodavis, illustrated by Suzanne DeSimone, published by KD Talent LLC

"fantasy," which diminishes the important social and political work accomplished by rejecting binarized gender roles. I have noticed that, like Duron, the authors of pink boy books are queered through proximity to the queer child and that, also like Duron, these authors tend to demonstrate psychic investments in heteronormative, and ultimately harmful, ways of imagining self, other, and social world. The following interpretive readings of these texts elucidate the tension between desire for a transformed world and attachments to regimes of normativity.

Cheryl Kilodavis's *My Princess Boy* (2009), illustrated by Suzanne DeSimone, is a nonfiction picture book based on her experiences raising her gender-creative son. Unlike other pink boy books discussed in this section,

Kilodavis's book is narrated by and focalized through the position of the pink boy's mother. It also takes a more didactic approach than other texts discussed and appears geared to a younger and predominantly cisgender audience. In fact, the text begins by noting Princess Boy is four years old, quite a bit younger than other characters in this subfield. Additionally, instead of foregrounding the affective experience of being a pink boy, the book is focused on helping other children process cognitive dissonance, so they can practice affirming responses to gender-creative boy children. Kilodavis's narrative strategy and assumed audience forecloses identification with queerness by positioning readers as "normals" encountering queerness in the form of a gender-creative child. More optimistically, it attempts to normalize gender creativity instead of requiring the gender-creative child to conform to gender norms.

Suzanne DeSimone depicts the cast of faceless, brown-skinned family members frolicking on rambling green hills over a cotton candy–pink background (see figure 7). A sense of whimsy and play characterizes the illustrations, which are likely to appeal to young readers. The facelessness of the characters is echoed in their namelessness, which amplifies the abstraction and unreality of the text. The protagonist is referred to by the narrator-mother as my Princess Boy, a seeming contradiction, like pink boy, that captures the character's essence, but not his specificity.

Throughout the text, Princess Boy is depicted interacting with several characters. These characters model affirmative ways of interacting with gender-creative boys. The first character Princess Boy interacts with is his brother, a cisgender boy who appears unbothered while twirling his tiara-wearing younger brother in circles. Princess Boy's brother's masculinity is signified by the blue baseball uniform he wears in one illustration, bat hanging from his arm, like the unconscious interjection of a phallic symbol. Princess Boy is also shown with his traditionally masculine, khakis-wearing father who holds his hand and tells him he is pretty. In addition to family members, the reader meets two of Princess Boy's friends, a boy and a girl. In the illustration, Princess Boy's boy friend wears a blue T-shirt and dark pants, and his girl friend wears a red dress accessorized with a purple bow. In stark relief to their subdued, albeit normatively gendered clothing, Princess Boy wears a green leotard, pink skirt, and pink shoes accessorized with a wand and tiara.

Kilodavis, like many writers of pink boy books, characterizes her protagonist's gender expression in terms of fantasy and play. Even more, Princess

Boy's gender expression doesn't influence the gender expressions or identities of his family or friends. In this text, as in other pink boy picture books, gender creativity is rendered banal and, I would argue, deliberately so. The pink boy trope, after all, is about constructing gender expression as harmless, not as a radical act of self-love that can encourage social transformation by undoing oppositional gender constructs. Although the book seems to celebrate the queer child's gender expression, it also seeks to depoliticize it by rendering queer gender a banal difference. However, gender creativity *is* disruptive. It disrupts a visual field based on binary genders as well as a dominant cultural logic that suggests gender expression and identity are naturally linked to the sexed body. I propose that the gender expressions of pink boys and other gender-nonconforming children are politically transformative on a few fronts. First, gender-nonconforming children demonstrate that gender is an achievement, not an essence (Butler, *Gender Trouble*; Newton). This brings much social-constructionist work in gender and sexuality studies home, quite literally, to families who haven't thought about gender critically. Second, the issues that gender-nonconforming children experience, from bullying to challenges accessing public spaces, show the extent to which binary gender logics permeate social institutions and practices, similarly to Lois Gould's *X: A Fabulous Child's Story*. Third, gender-nonconforming children have the potential to queer the straightest of institutions—the family. Finally, queer and straight distinction, as well as distinctions between self and other, potentially collapse as cisgender heterosexuals are brought into proximity with queerness through their love for queer kids. For instance, Princess Boy's mother is very protective of him. When he is ridiculed, she shares his emotional pain. She doesn't just sympathize with him or even empathize with him; she identifies with him and is queered in proximity to him. In the text, Princess Boy's mother recollects adults making fun of her son when he purchased "girl" things at a store and, on a separate occasion, when he went trick-or-treating in a "girl" costume. She hurts *with* him. No other book in this field centers the parent of a pink boy to the extent that Kilodavis's does, even as most are by mothers of gender-nonconforming boys.

One such book, *Roland Humphrey Is Wearing a WHAT?* (2013), was penned by Eileen Kiernan-Johnson and illustrated by Katrina Revenaugh. In an interview about the picture book and the child that inspired it, Kiernan-Johnson describes her son as a little boy who "loves butterflies, flowers, and the color pink" (Riesco). In the same interview, Kiernan-Johnson shares her hope that the book will encourage questions about why children are forced to conform to binary gender norms (Riesco). As mentioned, unlike *My Princess Boy*, *Roland Humphrey Is Wearing a WHAT?*'s omniscient narration focalizes the queer child, not his mother. Readers are positioned to identify and empathize with Roland, not to witness and accept him, as in Kilodavis's text. Roland's fashion choices mix traditionally feminine as well as traditionally masculine items, which is the case in most books depicting pink boys. Also, like other books about pink boys, this one shows Roland negotiating just two social institutions: home and school. In this book, gender is policed by other children, and school becomes a site of trauma, which introduces yet another characteristic of pink boy texts. In these books, written by supportive parents, home is unsurprisingly portrayed as a safe space.

At the beginning of the story, Roland is shown waiting for the school bus with several other students. Two of his peers wield clipboards, representing the monitoring and managing labor of school children as they police their peers' gender. These students use bullying techniques to encourage normative gender expression. For instance, the clipboard-wielding girls mock Roland for wearing a pink and yellow striped shirt. One of the girls, Lucy, chants: "Since you're a boy, pink isn't allowed— / not if you want to be in with the crowd." A dejected Roland is shown frowning with downcast eyes as he sits alone. Although he is free to wear whatever he wants, he is not free of consequences. The tension between personal desire, manifested as being true to oneself, and social pressure, which most often takes the form of peer-aged bullies, permeates the pages of LGBTQ+ children's picture books, especially those about gender-nonconforming children.

In stark opposition to his school, Roland's home is free of gender management. For instance, in a two-page spread that follows the initial episode of peer rejection, readers are invited into Roland's home, where he is illustrated sitting between his mother and father on a couch. His younger sister stands in front of them, directly underneath a family portrait. The illustrated scene and the family portrait on the wall both reinforce this straight family's lack of investment in normative gender expression. While standing in front of the couch, Roland's sister is shown wearing a pink dress, white wings, a hard hat, and a tool belt. In the family portrait hanging on the wall above her head, Roland wears a purple tutu and a blue baseball cap. His sister again wears a pink dress. In this book, as in others explored in this section, clothing is stripped of gender connotations, at least to some people. In other words, one's essential boyness or girlness isn't compromised by clothing choices even as these choices position their wearers as antinormative, queer even. The mixing and matching of gendered objects is meant to degender traditionally gendered objects. For instance, the tool belt wrapped around the hips of a tutu-wearing girl no longer connotes masculinity. Instead, these objects are simultaneously degendered and queered by their wearers who affirm their gender identities without attaching any particular meaning to them.

Roland wants to be accepted by his peers, but he appears unable to grasp gender rules and seemingly quite obtusely breaks them. For example, after being bullied, Roland tries to follow gendered fashion norms as communicated to him by his classmates, but he fails. On one occasion, he wears blue jeans and "a manly dark green shirt" but accessorizes with glitter and butterflies. Of course, his gender-policing peers, Ella and Lucy, are quite bothered when they see him and quickly take out their clipboards. They explain that boys can like footballs and basketballs, but certainly not butterflies. Roland's insistence on being a boy *and* liking butterflies is a compelling and convincing challenge to the conventionally accepted "truth" about boys that his friends spout.

One of the reasons Roland is confused about how to "do" gender is related in the text to the gender flexibility seemingly afforded girls. In dialogue with his mother, Roland proclaims: "The girls at my school dress in all sorts of hues, / but for boys there's so much less we can choose." For Roland, the tomboy is both a model and warrant for gender-nonconforming boys who can demand access to the same destigmatized gender flexibility boyish girls are allowed. After Roland's before-bed chat with his mother, he goes to bed thinking about what to wear the next day. In the morning, he shows up at the bus stop wearing a pink dress, a tiara, necklaces, and a butterfly pin. Roland is empowered to confront his bullies with a show of unflinching self-acceptance, because he thinks boys should have the same access to free gender expression as girls. At the bus stop, Roland waves to the half dozen peers waiting for their ride to school and gives a speech:

You need to know that I'm no longer scared. / [. . .] I'm so much more than what colors or clothes I choose. / And if you judge me on just that, I've got some sad news: / You're the one who misses out. / It's what's inside that really counts. / [. . .] So if based on my clothing for me you feel loathing, / then too bad for you because I choose to be the me that is true.

Roland's peers are moved by his performance of self-acceptance as demonstrated in an illustration of the clipboard-wielding girls, minus their clipboards, embracing him and assuring him: "It's cool that you're confident in who you are, / that you choose to follow your own north star." The girls hold his hands and drag him to the playground, replacing disdain with unqualified acceptance, bordering on adoration, as they note: "We like you for you, whatever you wear. / You're brave and you're funny. You're sensitive and rare." With these words, the text ends with celebration of the queer child; uniqueness becomes a virtue, not a vice, and pursuit of an authentic self, along with kindness, wins over even the most ardent gender police.

Like other pink boy titles, *Morris Micklewhite and the Tangerine Dress* (2014), written by Christine Baldacchino and illustrated by Isabelle Malenfant, is about a young boy who falls in love with a dress. The "boy-meets-skirt" trope appears in all of these texts, representing a queer object of desire and vehicle for rendering the boy child's difference visible to others. In the case of pink boy books, I suggest that repetition of the boy-meets-skirt trope is put to work rendering the pink boy category visible and viable as a mode of identifying oneself and perceiving others based on a destigmatized attachment to feminine objects. These titles share several commonalities beyond a queer attachment to skirts and dresses: namely, affirming relationships to the family as a social institution and troubled relationships to school as a social institution. The representation of school as a site of oppression in post-2000 pink boy books stands in stark opposition to Bruce Mack's *Jesse's Dream Skirt* (1979), the urtext for the boy-meets-skirt representation, in which Jesse's schoolteacher quickly embraces his dress-wearing, as do his peers. This is one reason it is necessary to distinguish pink boy picture books as a subfield of LGBTQ+ children's books from the use of the boy-meets-skirt trope.

Pink boy picture books are also distinguishable from texts that employ the sissy boy trope, since familial support is constant in pink boy books. Unlike pink boys, sissies negotiate stigma and must perform acts of queer exceptionalism to fit in, whereas being true to oneself is a catalyst for the pink boy's self, familial, and social acceptance. For instance, Morris's mother, who appears to be single, is shown as consummately loving and nurturing. To demonstrate familial support, families are shown together as a unit, as opposed to separately as individuals. Even more, dialogue between parents and children, as well as among siblings, is often represented. In literature that engages the sissy boy trope, parents, especially fathers, are most frequently positioned managing and policing gender identity. They have a clear investment in cisgender identities and are far more interested in conforming to normative expectations than getting to know their children as autonomous individuals with unique identities. This doesn't mean that children do not have dimension and specificity in early LGBTQ+ children's picture books but instead that adults and children tend to inhabit different worlds, and this division is evidenced by the relatively little amount of time adults and children spend talking as well as their spatial proximity as represented in illustrations.

In pink boy picture books, families are frequently shown in spatial proximity within the home, especially in kitchens, which demonstrates their emotional connectedness. Importantly, bedrooms also appear as a site of familial connection in many pink boy books, which isn't the case in the broader field of LGBTQ+ children's picture books. As Katie Sciurba notes in "Flowers, Dancing, Dresses, and Dolls," gender-nonconforming children's private sense of self is challenged in the outside world when gender expectations are not met. She observes that gender nonconforming children are often depicted in "virtual or literal solitude as they express their true selves" (283). In other words, bedrooms and dreams are safe spaces for the queer child's imagination to wander, but these are often lonely spaces. However, in pink boy books, the queer child often invites his mother into his bedroom or his dreams.

Kitchens, bedrooms, and dreams are all essential sites of family connection in *Morris Micklewhite and the Tangerine Dress*, as is the negotiation of school. The text opens with a close-up of the protagonist, Morris, and his mother, Moira, sitting at a kitchen table enjoying a breakfast of pancakes. Morris and his mother share the same tangerine-colored hair, which is similar in hue to their cat's orange fur. Morris, wearing boyish blue pajamas with airplanes scattered over them, plays at the table with animal figurines as his mother and cat watch him.

Early in the text, Morris is also depicted at school playing with paints and puzzles, eating, and singing. He especially loves the dress-up corner. A dreamy illustration of Morris swathed in orange material and juxtaposed with an orange tiger is accompanied by text: "Morris likes the dress-up center. / And the tangerine dress. / Morris likes the color of the dress. / It reminds him of tigers, the sun and his mother's hair." The dress is seen, through Morris's eyes, as connoting warmth, power, and love. It is not a feminine object of desire per se. This is not how dresses tend to be described. Morris is making his own queer meaning that gestures toward queer possibilities beyond gender binaries. The text elaborates on Morris's embodied experience of wearing the dress as well as the meaning it has for him: "He likes the noises the dress makes—swish, swish, swish when he walks / and crinkle, crinkle, crinkle when he sits down. / He takes turns wearing all the different shoes, / but his favorite ones go click, click, click across the floor." Visual image and textual description of Morris's dress-wearing complement each other and work together to destabilize the gendering of cultural artifacts like dresses. This, by extension, troubles simplistic readings of Morris's desire for a dress as an easily recognizable desire to be feminine.

The next several pages represent the consequences of dress-wearing in the often-repressive environment of school. Morris experiences waves of rejection. In one instance, a group of children point and laugh as Morris, wearing the tangerine dress, walks by, eyes downcast, arms pulled tightly behind his back, pretending not to hear. In another instance, a girl named Becky tries to pull the dress off him. Finally, a group of boys refuse to play with him. Peer rejection affects Morris. He pretends to be sick so he can stay home from school. Importantly, school is not just a site of oppression; it is also where Morris was introduced to the dress, which makes it a site of queer possibility as well as gender policing.

Morris's mom, Moira, allows him to stay home from school. While at home, Morris is depicted in his bedroom reading a book while cuddling with his cat. As mentioned, bedrooms are particularly important when exploring gender-expansive subjectivities. Children often lack language to describe gender identity and expression, so bedrooms show what children are unable to tell. Morris's room is depicted as typically boyish. A blue-striped comforter covers his bed, a soccer ball and dinosaur drawings are the only decorations, and Morris wears the blue airplane pajamas he sported at the text's opening. The only marker of femininity is the tangerine dress, which is at the foot of the bed.

After time passes, and here time is marked by the turning of a page, Morris's mother joins him in his bedroom and watches him play. They never discuss the stigma and rejection he is experiencing at school, but her silent support and witnessing seem to impart strength. After all, Morris's tangerine dress reminds him of several warm orange things he associates with strength: a tiger, the sun, and his mother. Morris continues to feel better in the comfort of his home, and on Sunday morning, he wakes from a vivid and joyful dream about a space adventure; in the dream, wild animals make the sounds he associates with the tangerine dress: "elephants swish, swish, swish," "elephants ate giant leaves that crinkle, crinkle, crinkle, crinkled," and "the buttons on the spaceship click, click, clicked." The masculine images of wild animals and spaceships that swirl through Morris's dream further disrupt assumptions about gender binaries as well as readings of the dress as a clear signifier of femininity. The text presents the idea that there are not boy and girl things: boys can like objects associated with girls and femininity without challenging or even thinking much about their gender identity. This introduces femininity and masculinity as precarious categories contingent on specific social and cultural norms that are being strained in the contemporary moment. I address this point further in the next chapter, through a discussion of recent sociological and anthropological work about transgender children as well as engagement with LGBTQ+ children's picture books that represent nonbinary and transgender youth characters.

As suggested above, Morris doesn't appear to think in binary terms of masculinity and femininity; he doesn't see embracing a feminine object as necessitating abandoning masculine objects. When Morris awakes from his dream, he commits it to paper. Morris paints a portrait of himself in which he is smiling broadly while wearing his tangerine dress and riding a large blue elephant. The dress represents the heat of the sun, familiarity of his mother, and fierceness of a tiger. These things are, for him, beyond or before gender; they do not reflect gender, even as they allow us to reflect on gender.

Morris uses this self-portrait to communicate an understanding of gender expression and identification he doesn't have words for. In fact, as close as he is to his mother, their understanding and intimacy is communicated through comfortable silences and physical proximity, not dialogue. Morris's self-portrait allows him to quite literally show his feelings to the world, and he starts the process of sharing with his mother. Morris lets his mother take in the image he has created as he explains that the "little boy in the tangerine dress / riding atop the big blue elephant" is how he sees himself. This can be read as an empowering moment when the queer child, unable to find mirrors that reflect their sense of self, creates one (Bishop).

Whereas Kilodavis's *My Princess Boy* assumes an audience of cisgender youth and is primarily motivated by the didactic goal of teaching acceptance of the queer other, many pink boy books assume a split audience and work to impart a dual message that includes self-acceptance and respect for the queer other. In fact, in these books, self-acceptance is represented as the key to peer acceptance. In other words, by accepting one's queer difference, others will learn to accept, perhaps even to appreciate and be inspired by, queerness. This is exemplified in *Morris Micklewhite and the Tangerine Dress*. The day after Morris has his transformative dream and draws a picture to show how the tangerine dress makes him feel, he goes to school. Morris brings the painting and the tangerine dress in his book bag. The cycle of social rejection begins again, but Morris brings a new confidence and self-understanding to the situation. Although he wants to play with his peers, he also wants to wear the tangerine dress. Queer desire is persistent and encourages resistance to regimes of normativity reproduced by bullies. This time when the boys in Morris's class tell him that he cannot play with their spaceship, he builds his own and hangs the dreamscape he painted in front of it. The boys, after looking at the picture, ask if there are elephants and tigers in space, and Morris invites them in to find out. The boys follow him into the make-believe rocket as the fantasy world of children transforms the classroom environment in very real ways. Concurrent with this event, Becky, the bully who previously tried to tear the dress off Morris, reiterates the rule that boys don't wear dresses, but this time Morris cleverly responds: "This one does." This concludes the text with the establishment of a new social order: the bully is put in her place, and Morris has made a place for himself among the boys, tangerine dress and all.

Unlike other creators of pink boy picture books that engage the boy-meets-skirt trope, Christine Baldacchino is not the parent of a gender-creative child. She wrote *Morris Micklewhite and the Tangerine Dress* in response to a situation she observed while teaching in a preschool classroom. In an interview with Mark Joseph Stern for *Slate*, Baldacchino shared her motivation for drafting the picture book:

> I worked at a prekindergarten program, and there was one 4-year-old boy who liked to wear this gold dress from the dress-up center with little red shoes. One day, his mother came to pick him up for a dentist appointment and saw him wearing the dress. She told the director that she didn't want to him wearing the dress because he looked "ridiculous." Every day after that, for several weeks, the boy asked me where the dress was. Was it getting fixed? Cleaned? Eventually he figured out that the director had removed the dress on purpose so he wouldn't be able to wear it. Then he told me, "If you bring back the dress, I promise I'll never wear it again." (Stern)

In the same interview, Baldacchino describes writing *Morris Micklewhite and the Tangerine Dress* to share with her class. She says she had no intentions of publishing it. However, the director of the school refused to let her share the story. Interestingly, like parent-advocates crafting tales of pink boy acceptance to remove the stigma attached to feminine boys, Baldacchino creates a loving and supporting mother, a mother radically different from the one who entered her classroom and demanded her child not be allowed to wear dresses.

As much as I love the book, and I do love the book, I want the story of the mother who fails her queer child too. Post-2000 LGBTQ+ children's picture books that focalize queer children frequently represent the heterosexual family unit as a bastion of queer affirmation, which is simply not always the case.

The reality of queer children's experience is more complex and varied than negotiating school bullies, but negotiating isolation and bullying at school are the central problem in pink boy picture books. In these books, the heteronormative nuclear family maintains meaning and value as a state-sanctioned unit of care tasked with meeting the needs of children and capable of doing it without institutional support or the help of the queer community. In pink boy picture books, queer dignity and doing justice to the queer child are not related to institutional change but instead culminate in some mean children seeing the error of their ways and being nicer. This demonstrates a failure to imagine a queerly transformed world, one that can truly account for queerness, celebrate it, and be changed by it.

Sarah and Ian Hoffman's coauthored *Jacob's New Dress* (2014), illustrated by Chris Case, was published at the tail end of the pink boy picture book trend, which is ironic as Sarah Hoffman both coined and popularized the term. Hoffman's journalistic writing and interviews about children and gender were critical to the little mainstream attention given to the pink boy category (Hoffman and Hoffman). At the start of the Hoffmans' pink boy picture book, Jacob, a blond, white boy, is playing dress-up at school with his brown-skinned best friend, Emily. Jacob likes dressing up in a fancy princess costume. As in most other pink boy books, conflict emerges in the form of a bully with a mandate to police the queer child's gender expression. Jacob's bully, Christopher, confronts him for failing to meet gendered social expectations, but his friend Emily is quick to leap to his defense. Jacob's friendship with Emily offers a refreshing alternative to the lone and lonely queer child written into both *Morris Micklewhite and the Tangerine Dress* and *Roland Humphrey Is Wearing a WHAT?*

No one, other than the requisite bully, is bothered when Jacob wears the princess costume. After all, dress-up connotes play, so the dress-up corner functions as a space-off, a term feminist film theorist Teresa de Lauretis uses to describe "spaces in the margins of hegemonic discourses" (*Technologies of Gender* 25). In the dress-up corner, children can pretend to be what they are not, including dinosaurs and princesses. In these spaces, play can have real effects, manifesting new ideas in the ignored cracks and corners of conceptual and material social worlds. The inability of dominant cultural forces to contain and control the crevices of the most normative institutions, in this case school, permits queerness to seep in. Disguised as play and easily dismissed, queerness, understood here as an antinormative social force, does serious work. When queerness inserts itself into the straight world, it proves to be anything but banal.

Relegating queerness to the realm of play is a central dynamic in *Jacob's New Dress* and other pink boy books that seek to render boyhood femininities innocuous. This tactic is motivated by a desire to protect and is one outcome of the ventriloquism that informs the texts, which are most often written by parent-advocates for queers, not queers themselves. The desire to protect permeates the pages of pink boy books. For instance, Jacob's mother initially draws a line between appropriate and inappropriate times and spaces for "dress-up." She identifies his bedroom as a safe space where he can dress up, and she identifies his Halloween costume, a witch's gown, as appropriate dress-up material.

As previously discussed, in LGBTQ+ picture books, bedrooms often work as windows into the queer child's psyche. Jacob can embrace and exteriorize his desires in his bedroom. Like Morris's bedroom, Jacob's depicts a masculine sense of self beneath the feminizing desire for a dress. Airplanes, cars, a soccer ball, and blue and green crayons are strewn around his room. Jacob dances around his bedroom in his witch costume, striking poses with a big smile on his face. Empowered by the pleasure he feels, Jason informs his mother that he wants to wear his dress to school. She rejects the idea, suggesting the costume is for playing dress-up at home and might get dirty at school. The excuse protects Jacob from identifying dress-wearing with stigma or shame while also shielding him from the consequences of public displays of queerness. However, an unperturbed Jacob requests a regular dress. Again, his mother hesitates before telling him she needs to think about it.

Despite his mother's hesitation, Jacob's queer desire persists. In *Bouncing Back: Queer Resilience in Twentieth- and Twenty-First-Century English*

Literature and Culture, Susanne Jung references recent scholarship about youth and resilience. She characterizes resilience as "bouncing back," "elasticity," and "flexibility" (14–15). Additionally, she cites scholarship that suggests resilience is about more than survival. It's about living a fulfilling life (16). Jung notes that most queer affect theory, including work by Heather Love and Ann Cvetkovich, has focused on queer trauma. By entering an ongoing conversation about queer affect and bringing it into conversation with sociological and psychological discussions of resilience, Jung hopes to shift the focus to agency, away from being damaged and toward being whole (20). I introduce Jung's work here because I find that it helps me articulate something I've noticed in LGBTQ+ children's picture books, and even discussed, albeit rather clumsily, in an earlier publication (Miller, "A Little Queer").

In my first publication about LGBTQ+ children's picture books, I discuss Marcus Ewert's *10,000 Dresses* and Cheryl Kilodavis's *My Princess Boy.* I'm particularly interested in the repetition of events in *10,000 Dresses,* which I discuss at length in the next chapter. This picture book is about a transgender child named Bailey who dreams of dresses every night. In the morning she shares her dream with family members and they "dismiss her desire, affirm her sex assignment, and tell her to go away and never mention dresses again" ("A Little Queer" 38). In my analysis I write: "The repetition of rejection is an important feature of the text; it demonstrates the persistence of queer pleasure-seeking in the face of staunch familial resistance, representing desire for a dress as far more important than familial recognition and acceptance" ("A Little Queer" 38). Of course, from the vantage point of Jung's work, Ewert's character is demonstrating queer resilience. Instead of reading the queer child's ability to "bounce back" as resilience, I read it as naivety, and wrote that Bailey is "failing to anticipate rejection" ("A Little Queer" 40). In truth, there is no good reason to suggest that Bailey does not expect rejection, and my own reading implies another possibility, namely that Bailey desires a dress more than familial acceptance. In my conclusion, I wrote:

> The protagonists of *10,000 Dresses* and *My Princess Boy* have not learned to expect pain and so they have not created barriers to avoid it, Bailey's resilience, continuing to out her gender identification and desire to family members who each in turn reject her, demonstrates the pleasure-seeking pull of queer desire even as it remains tethered to the uniquely circumscribed agency of youth. ("A Little Queer" 48)

One could convincingly argue that Bailey does in fact anticipate the possibility of rejection, but, encouraged by a commitment to her queer desires, she hopes for acceptance and "bounces back." Perhaps Bailey's fulfilling life includes a wardrobe full of dresses. I interject this here because pink boy picture books offer a lesson in queer resilience by modeling it.

Jung's work on resilience is a useful framework through which to read *Jacob's New Dress* and so many other picture books featuring queer children. After Jacob's mother denies him permission to wear a dress to school, Jacob takes matters into his own hands and creates a makeshift dress with a towel he ties with a pink bow. When his father sees him, he tells Jacob that he cannot wear a towel to school. Contradicting his father, Jacob's mother grants permission, but makes him put the towel over a t-shirt and pants. This scene depicts a parental struggle to simultaneously meet the needs of the queer child and meet social expectations. At school, Christopher, the bully, is portrayed with his arms crossed. Christopher immediately challenges Jacob, asking him what he is wearing. It is Jacob's mother who responds, stepping into the role of protector: "Jacob's wearing something new he invented. Isn't it nice?" By not referring to the towel as a dress, but instead a new invention, Jacob's mother attempts to remove gender from the equation. Emily asks Jacob to help her make one and he agrees. Both his mother and friend validate him and work to shield him from Christopher.

Later that day, while the children play outside, Christopher pulls the towel off Jacob, who responds by crying. An angry Emily is shown glaring at Christopher. Emily supports Jacob at school where his mom's love can't reach. But later that day when Jacob is back home, he recollects his experience with Christopher and his mother engulfs him in a warm embrace. Instead of desiring to stop wearing dresses, he asks his mother to help him make a real dress. Again, Jacob's mother hesitates, a clear gatekeeper who is unclear what to do. The Hoffmans quite beautifully present the mother's silence from Jacob's perspective: "Mom didn't answer. The longer she didn't answer, the less Jacob could breathe." This also demonstrates the Hoffmans' attempt to understand and represent the gender-creative child's subjectivity. His mother does agree to help him make a dress, noting that there are many ways to be a boy. The reassertion of gender identity is another theme that runs through pink boy picture books, which emphasize the queer child's identity as a "boy" even as he strains against the characteristics that tend to define the category.

The next day, Jacob shows up to school in the dress he made with his mother. Emily accepts his outfit, noting that they are both wearing pink and white. The pair continue with their day. During circle time, Jacob shows off his dress while surrounded by a dozen of his peers. Unsurprisingly, Christopher interrupts Jacob, asking why he is wearing a dress. The teacher quickly defends Jacob, stating: "I think Jacob wears what he's comfortable in. Just like you do. Not very long-ago little girls couldn't wear pants," a comment that explicitly connects boy dress-wearing to girl pants-wearing—pink boy culture to tomboy culture. However, the school bully isn't convinced. On the playground, Christopher stands with a group of boys who appear to mock Jacob, and when the children play tag, Christopher suggests that Jacob belongs on the girls' team.

Christopher is the clear antagonist in this pink boy picture book. However, bullies aren't all bad; they force the queer child to reflect on the persistence of their queer desire, value queerness over social acceptance, and persevere in rejecting straight gender and sexual norms. Prompted by Christopher's bullying, Jacob undergoes a metamorphosis on the playground. The Hoffmans write: "Jacob felt his dress surrounding him. / Like armor. / Soft, cottony, magic armor." For this dress-wearing boy, much like Morris, dresses connote strength and are associatively linked to things like armor, tigers, the sun, and moms. In fact, the book ends with a depiction of Jacob and Emily running from a perplexed-looking Christopher, who Jacob has marked as "it" in their game of tag. The text reads: "Jacob sprinted across the playground, his dress spreading out like wings." Here, the dress represents mobility, flight, the opposite of its usual connotation of restriction; in a dress the girl child must sit like a lady, but the boy child flies like a bird.

Where Is the Pink Boy Now?

Pink boy picture books comprise a fascinating historical archive that reveals a contemporary pressure in our understanding of gender. The importance of normative gender expression is fading, even as gender identity is constantly reaffirmed. To be clear, the gender identity that is affirmed in pink boy books, at least through 2020, is not neutral but instead confirms natal sex assignment. However, gender expression is allowed more fluidity and flexibility. This textual ambivalence, namely a commitment to gender that reinforces sex assignment, may relate to authorship. After all, most of these books are written by cisgender heterosexuals and demonstrate attachments to the normative sex-gender system even as they clamor for the acceptance of queer kids.

I'm interested in charting the distance between the hope of acceptance manifest in the pedagogical mission of pink boy books and the real constraints on imaging queer futures also evident in these texts. As I read these sweet picture books, I keep thinking: You can't get there from here. You can't get to the world these advocates desire, one in which queer kids are celebrated, without imaging and enacting a queer new world. That work isn't done in these books. Instead, the imperative of books like Kilodavis's *My Princess Boy*, Kiernan-Johnson's *Roland Humphrey Is Wearing a WHAT?*, Baldacchino's *Morris Micklewhite and the Tangerine Dress*, and the Hoffmans' *Jacob's New Dress* is to destigmatize boyhood femininities by constructing them as harmless variations of gender expression. The "problem" of queerness is resolved when dress-wearing boys are no longer bullied. The straight world isn't transformed or even critiqued, since all the oppressive and regulating power of society is consolidated into the form of a little school bully who is easily dismissed.

I think the pink boy had a relatively short shelf life because the construct itself betrayed attachments to regimes of gender normativity that must topple for the queer child to truly thrive. The pink boy had an uneasy birth and throughout its brief existence remained secured to the protective maternal arms of the mother-advocates who created it. These parent-author-advocates wanted the world to accept their sons, and their strategy was to render the queer child's queerness banal, but queerness isn't banal. Queerness is a world-making pulsion that rejects to create. My theory is that when the pink boy started to grow up, the limits of acceptance became clear. Queer kids cannot fit into existing social structures; those structures need to be queered to account for the queer kid.

I note this because the experiences and feelings described in pink boy books are not fictionalized from firsthand experience but are instead the product of imagining the "other," who, in the case of most of these books, is a much-loved child. Imagined feelings and experiences are then narrated as if they were one's own, an act of ventriloquism similar to that described by Cedric Essi in his work on transnational adoptees. For parent-advocate-authors, this is a labor of love and, I suggest, a powerful exercise in empathy that could work to collapse distinctions between self and other so that the straight self is queered as a result of proximity to the queer child. This possibility is never actualized in these texts, texts that represent the queer child as different but not destructive, in need of understanding, but not imitation.

Five years after publishing *Jacob's New Dress*, the Hoffmans published *Jacob's Room to Choose* (2019), also illustrated by Chris Case. In this picture book, Jacob is joined in his gender-creative exploits by brown-skinned, curly-haired Sophie, who prefers plaid shirts and khakis to dresses, which pale-skinned, wavy-haired Jacob likes best. The two seem confident with their gender presentations as they enjoy learning time in their school library. However, Sophie and Jacob both experience anxiety when it's time to go to the bathroom. An illustration depicts Jacob, in a dress, standing in front of a bathroom door that is marked as the boys' bathroom through the presence of a pants-wearing stick figure. Sophie stands next to him, in jeans and a plaid shirt, looking concernedly at the dress-wearing stick figure marking it the girls' room. Neither child ends up using the bathroom.

When their teacher finds out, she prompts the class to think more critically about gender expression. Working together and reflecting on their own gender expressions, the children realize there are lots of ways to be a girl or boy and that everyone should be able to use the bathroom regardless of how they look. The students decide to desegregate the school bathrooms, and they make signs to replace the boy and girl stick figures that previously adorned their school's bathroom doors. Unlike *Jacob's New Dress*, *Jacob's Room to Choose* engages structural changes that need to occur to accommodate the "pink boy." Far from being a banal difference, gender nonconforming children challenge conventional notions of masculinity and femininity as well as the relationship between gender identity and expression and the sexed body. In the next chapter, I discuss picture books that explore transgender and nonbinary identities, but before moving on, I turn to children's picture books about tomboys to challenge the suggestion that the tomboy category provides girls with a destigmatized way of embodying masculinity, which is an ever-present assumption in much pink boy fiction.

Seeing the Tomboy: A Brief Genealogy of a Persistent Cultural Form

Many of the parent-advocate-authors mentioned above seek to provide boys with more flexible options for gender expression than those currently afforded within our binary sex-gender system. In fact, the pink boy is envisioned as a conceptual parallel to the tomboy, and, as seen in several of the pink boy books discussed above, it is assumed that girls have the freedom to play with masculinity in ways unavailable to boys. However, in *Female Masculinity*, Jack Halberstam suggests that girlhood masculinities are not without consequences. He writes: "If we are to believe general accounts of childhood behavior, tomboyism is quite common for girls and does not generally give rise to parental fears" (5). Halberstam challenges the idea that female masculinity is not policed and argues that if masculine identifications are intense or extend to adolescence tomboyism stops being tolerated (6). Halberstam taxonomizes female masculinities to make them visible for analysis, which he describes as an attempt to intervene in hegemonic processes of naming and defining. Halberstam appeals to Eve Sedgwick's theorization of "nonce taxonomies" to do this work; nonce taxonomies are "categories that we use daily to make sense of our worlds but that work so well that we actually fail to recognize them" (8). By taxonomizing various expressions and experiences of female masculinity, Halberstam hopes to "challenge hegemonic models of gender conformity" (9). Even more, by recognizing embodied acts of resistance to regimes of gender normativity as challenges and refusals of existing gender categories, it becomes clear that existing gender concepts are inadequate. In this way, the embodied performances of children as well as cultural representations of children challenge the use of dominant gendered descriptions and demonstrate the need for more subtle and specific accounts of gender that work to render existing realities more plain instead of obscuring them behind oppositional norms.

Halberstam isn't the only scholar interested in articulating the subversive potential of the tomboy. Michelle Ann Abate's 2008 publication, "Trans/Forming Girlhood: Transgenderism, the Tomboy Formula, and Gender Identity Disorder in Sharon Dennis Wyeth's *Tomboy Trouble*," also claims the tomboy as a subversive figuration of gender that does the work of "calling into question the socially constructed nature of gender roles" (42). Through close readings of Wyeth's 1998 publication, Judith Butler's theory of gender performativity, and several editions of the *Diagnostic and Statistical Manual of Mental Disorders* (*DSM*), Abate convincingly claims that the tomboy presents gender as "fluid and malleable" (42). According to Abate, Georgia, the eight-year-old tomboy character at the center of Wyeth's book, experiences pressure to embody conventional femininity at school and home (44). This pressure isn't significantly different from the gender policing sissy boys and pink boys experience.

In *Tomboy Trouble* (1998), Wyeth employs the new school trope common to LGBTQ+ picture books, including Jane Severance's *Lots of Mommies* (1983) and Lesléa Newman's *Heather Has Two Mommies* (1989), to place Georgia, her child protagonist, in an environment with strangers. Unlike in Severance's and Newman's work, which focuses on lesbian-parented families as a "problem," in *Tomboy Trouble*, Georgia's gender presentation is the "problem." Abate writes: "Moving to a new school in the opening pages of the text, eight-year-old Georgia also gets a chance to move into an entirely new gender identity that falls outside of the boundaries of conventional notions of maleness and femaleness" (44). Georgia, an avid baseball player, cuts her hair short before starting at her new school. Short hair paired with boyish clothes prompt her new peers to read her as a boy. When Georgia corrects them, they are often angry, frustrated, and confused, but Georgia maintains that she is a girl throughout. This leads Abate to argue: "By frustrating the formerly rigid distinctions between male and female, masculine and feminine, boy and girl, Georgia and her tomboyish gender identity are iconoclastic, non-normative or, simply, queer" (48). Like Abate, I identify the tomboy as queer insofar as she troubles conventional notions of femininity and embraces embodied modes of masculinity. There are meaningful similarities between the pink boy, as articulated by parent-advocates, and the tomboy, a cultural figure with a far longer history.

Abate's cultural study of the tomboy, specifically her readings of various editions of the *DSM*, demonstrate that both the "sissy" boy and the tomboy were increasingly pathologized beginning in the 1980s when the American Psychiatric Association redirected its moralistic pathologizing of homosexuality onto nonnormative gender expressions by introducing the term *gender identity disorder* (50). In her now canonical 1991 publication, "How to Bring Your Kids Up Gay," mother of queer theory Eve Kosofsky Sedgwick theorized the cultural logic and continued wish for gay annihilation anchoring the 1980 removal of homosexuality and subsequent inclusion of "gender identity disorder of children" in the *DSM III*. According to Sedgwick, the seeming depathologization of homosexuality is contingent on masculine gender expression and codifies the effeminacy of boys as pathological. She sees this shift as part of a move to "theorize gender and sexuality as distinct though intimately entangled axes of analysis" ("How to Bring Your Kids Up Gay"

20). At its core, this surface-level shift in social stigmatization via medical pathologization reveals a wish that gay men did not exist. Sedgwick suggests this needs to be combated not just by destigmatizing and depathologizing effeminate boys and the gay men many grow up to be but instead by desiring "gay people in the immediate world" ("How to Bring Your Kids Up Gay" 26). Although Sedgwick focuses on boyhood femininities, both Halberstam and Abate convincingly argue that girlhood masculinities were increasingly stigmatized throughout the 1980s and 1990s. I introduce this scholarship to demonstrate the sociocultural significance of the tomboy as a disruptive figure that resists gender conventions. Of course, gender and sexuality should not be conflated, but they certainly have a complex relationship and, I would suggest, mutually constitutive relationship. Gayle Rubin's now canonical scholarship about the sex-gender system suggests that heterosexuality demands binary gender. When the social imperative to perform conventional gender is refused, heterosexuality's naturalness and inevitability are troubled in addition to normative gender.

I want to take the cultural trouble that tomboys make seriously through a brief and certainly nonexhaustive look at the trope of the tomboy in children's picture books. Even in a small archive, the figure of the tomboy changes over time. For instance, early iterations of the tomboy have less to do with gender expressions or stylizations and more to do with assertive attitudes and desires for access to experiences and opportunities reserved for boys. On the other hand, more recent representations are likely to identify tomboys visually through boyish clothing and a general disregard for appearance as well as an interest in more boyish activities. This shift can be attributed to more general cultural changes that disassociate the pursuit of physical adventure or intellectual curiosity with men as demonstrated by Mattel's new "You Can Be Anything" Barbie (Mattel). Girl children are now sanctioned, even supported, in imagining themselves as firefighters, veterinarians, and even fashionable presidents through creative play with career-branded Barbies. This was not the case in the 1970s when the desire for a career other than teaching or nursing was enough for a girl to disrupt socially prescribed gender roles. In fact, Lollipop Power Inc.'s 1972 publication *Exactly Like Me*, written and illustrated by Lynn Phillips, features a rambunctious little girl confident enough to challenge social norms about what little girls can and should want, do, and be. She rejects the idea of being a nurse or a teacher, instead imagining herself growing up to be an astronaut or politician. Unlike the majority of tomboys depicted in picture books, the protagonist's long hair marks her as embracing some aspects of femininity, even as she rejects restrictive gender role expectations.

Elizabeth Levy's 1974 publication *Nice Little Girls*, illustrated by Mordicai Gerstein, takes a different approach. Instead of celebrating resistance in a consequence-free environment, Levy explores the challenges of being a tomboy, particularly when boyish behaviors are paired with short hair, overalls, and sneakers. When Jackie begins her first day at a new school, her teacher, Mrs. James, introduces her as a boy, only to be loudly corrected by the energetic girl. Of course, the class erupts in laughter at the expense of both Jackie and her teacher. On the playground, her new classmates continue to make fun of her gender expression, telling her she's really a boy, not a girl. Jackie is so upset that she holds back tears while mulling over what it would mean to agree with them and just be a boy. This idea cheers Jackie up, and she begins to march around the playground shouting, "I'm a boy." Although her peers first think she's weird, they quickly follow her lead. Levy writes: "Jackie felt good for the first time that day." Jackie doesn't seem to have any allegiance to a gender identity, and her peers do not seem bothered when she identifies herself as a boy. In fact, Jackie's teacher is her biggest obstacle and gender critic. Whenever Mrs. James asks for volunteers to help her use the projector or build a box, Jackie enthusiastically waves her hand in the air, only to be told those are boy jobs. Even more, Jackie's teacher dismisses her when she claims she is a boy.

Continuing to play with her new gender identification, a sullen Jackie decides to use the boys' room. However, she is confused and disturbed by urinals and quickly runs to the girls' room. This is one of the few moments that Levy provides readers access to Jackie's thoughts: "She knew she couldn't really be a boy, but she wasn't going to be the kind of girl Mrs. James liked, either." This moment of self-reflection, although somewhat empowering, is ultimately disappointing insofar as it locates the truth of gender on the sexed body, a point reinforced by its connection to the bathroom and Jackie's confusion about urinals. Even more, this stray opportunity to access Jackie's thoughts suggests that being a boy may be what she really desires—a possibility that goes unexplored once mentioned. Jackie continues to reject gender stereotypes and "pretend" she is a boy until her frustrated teacher complains to her parents. Jackie's supportive parents assure her they love her and explain that Mrs. James has a narrow idea of what girls can and should do.

Back at school, Mrs. James continues to police Jackie's gender, but with the support of her parents, Jackie begins to reclaim being a girl, even though she continues to be a girl who loves to build things. One of the popular pretty girls, Susie, who bullied her when she started at her new school, soon befriends Jackie. It turns out feminine Susie is also a budding gender outlaw. She has an epic train set in her attic bedroom. Shortly thereafter, Susie invites Jackie to her birthday party, much to the chagrin of her friend and fellow sometimes-bully, Barbara. When Barbara complains about Susie inviting a "boy" to her party, Susie paints a mustache on Barbara and calls her a boy. This quickly ends in giggles and all three girls sporting painted mustaches. Mrs. James ends up with a painted mustache of her own.

The body as the ultimate marker of gender truth is less taken for granted in postmillennial children's picture books, which are beginning to depict transgender and nonbinary characters, but in the 1970s, the sex-gender system remained a firm constraint on visions of gender, even in the most radical children's picture books and, frankly, in most of the gender theory of the time. Instead, it is gender roles and norms that are questioned in these early decades of gender trouble in children's picture books, not gender itself.

Annie's Plaid Shirt (2015), written by Stacy B. Davids and illustrated by Rachel Balsaitis, is a more recent tomboy picture book that, like Levy's, depicts a young girl who enjoys wearing boyish clothes and participating in physical activities. Annie is a racially ambiguous, plaid shirt–wearing tomboy (see figure 8). Several images of Annie dressed boyishly in red high tops and a flannel shirt while participating in physical activities—like hitting a piñata, to the applause of boys and chagrin of girls—represent Annie as the quintessential tomboy. The conflict in the text does not center on winning the approval of schoolyard bullies as it does in several other picture books; in fact, Annie appears oblivious to the stares of her peers. This is highlighted on the book's cover, which depicts Annie zooming alongside a school bus on her skateboard. Although the students on the bus peer at her incredulously from inside the bus, Annie doesn't notice. Her thick, curly hair flies behind her and a smile beams on her face. The image introduces readers to Annie as a young girl who embraces freedom of motion and doesn't care what her peers think of her. Throughout the text, Annie appears uninterested in social conventions. She is desire-driven to wear clothes and participate in activities that she likes, regardless of anyone's opinion.

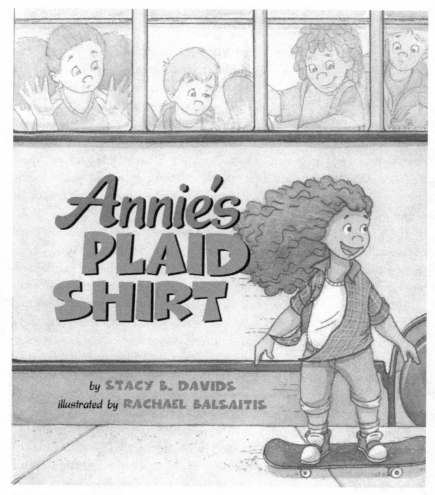

Figure 8 *Annie's Plaid Shirt* (2015), written by Stacy B. Davids, illustrated by Rachael Balsaitis, published by Upswing Press

The text's conflict emerges within the family when Annie's typically supportive single mother expects her to wear a dress to a wedding the family will attend. This reveals the limits of parental acceptance of the tomboy, who is expected to dress appropriately for the event. Annie and her brother are sitting at the kitchen table painting pictures when their mother mentions that they need to buy outfits for an upcoming wedding. Annie declares that she will wear her plaid shirt, but her mother dismisses the idea. She takes the children to a mall, and Annie tries on several dresses. Subsequent illustrations of Annie trying on dresses clearly reflect her discomfort: scrunched eyes, crossed arms, tight lips. Her mother is thrilled with her appearance in the final dress, but when the family returns home with their purchases Annie escapes to her room, angrily slamming the door behind her.

As mentioned, bedrooms often provide access to young characters' interiority, a window into their psychic life, as they are one of the few spaces children tend to have relative control over. In Annie's room, pictures of hand-drawn dinosaurs, horses, and giraffes decorate the walls, and a stuffed koala bear and unicorn, a doll, and a baseball bat litter the room. Stereotypical girl colors are missing. Her bedspread is blue; a throw rug is green, as are a pair of slippers that lie discarded by her bed. While in her room, readers are also provided with rare access to Annie's inner thoughts: "She wished her mom understood her. / Annie felt weird in dresses. She was happiest / when she wore her plaid shirt. / Why couldn't her mom see that?" The bedroom décor as well as Annie's commitment to not wearing a dress work together to create a sense of unconventional gender identity that is essential to Annie's sense of self. The child feels "weird" in dresses, a fact her mother appears unaware of as she dismisses Annie's suggestion that she wear her flannel shirt to the wedding.

In this book it is Annie's brother, Albert, who is portrayed as a consummate and effortless ally. He is depicted asking their mother why Annie must wear a dress to the wedding. Their mother answers that she is concerned about what people will think. Whereas Annie appears unaffected by social conventions, she is vulnerable to the whims of her mother, who, as in many texts about gender-nonconforming children, functions as a gatekeeper able to constrain the queer child's gender expression. Annie's mother must reconcile social expectations with her daughter's wishes. If she allows Annie to attend a wedding in informal and masculine attire, she runs the risk of being queered by proximity to her boyish daughter. Even more, her parenting will likely be called into question. Despite these challenges, she does listen to her children, which demonstrates a parent-child relationship that challenges hierarchal patterns of relating. This mother is willing to learn, and her transformation is centered even as it is focalized through her daughter. The next day while the family prepares to go to the wedding, Annie and Albert conspire behind their mother's back. When the children come downstairs, Annie is wearing her brother's old white suit. The siblings match, but instead of a dress shirt underneath her jacket, Annie wears a flannel shirt and bow tie. Her mother cheers at the sight of her beaming children.

Concluding Thoughts

This chapter describes the pink boy category as an extension and modification of the sissy boy category. Additionally, it traces the development of the tomboy category in children's picture books from the 1970s to the 2010s. Changing representations of boyhood femininities and girlhood masculinities both reflect and encourage transformations in gender expectations and expressions occurring at a societal level. Concerned parent-advocates of queer children who sought to destigmatize boyhood femininities created the pink boy classification to parallel the tomboy category, which they understood, perhaps incorrectly, as providing girls with consequence-free gender flexibility. In many pink boy picture books as well as other discourses about gender-creative boys, the tomboy category is viewed as stigma free, but that is not how many masculine girls experience being a tomboy. This is especially true if behaviors associated with masculinity are paired with ambiguous gender expressions. I argue that both tomboy and pink boy picture books also chronical changes in adult-child relationships, particularly shifts toward accepting and respecting children's gender expressions. Although I see this as progress and read these texts optimistically as harbingers of new modes of relating to children as well as new ways of understanding gender, perhaps as flexible identifications instead of hardened essences, children's play is constituted in these texts as a site of experiment separate from the real world of presumably normalized gender and sexual identities.

Chapter Five

Queer Youth and Gender

Representing Transgender, Nonbinary, Gender-Creative, and Gender-Free Youth

Something is happening to gender.

They was Merriam-Webster's 2019 word of the year (Merriam-Webster; Dwyer).

Nonbinary fashion is all over runways (Afanador; Krischer).

A recent study by the Trevor Project found that 25 percent of LGBTQ+ youth identify as nonbinary, with an additional 7 percent identifying as transgender (Trevor Project).

Something is happening to gender.

This chapter explores how the "something" happening to gender manifests in children's picture books. My last chapter explored representations of pink boys and tomboys in picture books. Both girlhood masculinities and boyhood femininities are examples of nonnormative gender expressions. However, both pink boys and tomboys identify with their natal sex assignment even as they disavow conventional expressions of femininity and masculinity. In other words, they resist normative gender expressions and roles while continuing to identify with their sex assignment. This chapter focuses specifically on representations of nonbinary and transgender children who often do not identify with their natal sex assignment.[1]

Nonbinary children may identify as agender or gender-free (terms meaning without gender), bigender (a term meaning more than one gender), or two-spirit (a Native/Indigenous term meaning both masculine and feminine genders). New language is always being developed to capture nuanced gender expressions and identifications. Terms like *genderqueer*, *gender fluid*, and *gender creative* are frequently used to describe genders that do not conform to the dominant sex-gender system. The term *transgender* is most frequently used to describe children who reject their natal sex assignment and socially transition to a gender that is readable within the existing sex-gender system. However, the term may also be used far more broadly to include gender expressions and identifications catalogued above. Importantly, gender identity has no determining relationship to sexuality.

Anthropologist David Valentine maintains that "since the 1970s (intensifying in the 1990s) there has been a radical transformation . . . in the possibilities of gender and sexual identification in the United States" (15). Valentine traces this shift through a case study of the emergence and development of transgender as a category of identification. His work demonstrates that the meanings attached to words can and do change, which has sociopolitical implications for self-identification, community making, and political activism. Shifts in the availability of language to describe gender expressions and identifications can be traced through many cultural texts, including LGBTQ+ children's picture books. Exploring representations of nonnormative gender expressions and identifications in LGBTQ+ children's picture books allows us to reflect on the sociocultural construction of gender, its historical constitution, and its malleability. Even more, it demonstrates that young people are agents with complex relationships to gender and the will to embody it as they see fit.

Indeed, recent children's books that support young people on their gender journey—most notably Maya Gonzalez's 2017 publication *The Gender Wheel: A Story about Bodies and Gender for Every Body*—position children as experts of their own desire and agents of social change able to challenge gender conventions. *The Gender Wheel: A Story about Bodies and Gender for Every Body* provides visual tools and reflection prompts that encourage readers to think about gender beyond Western patriarchal norms that demand binary identifications and expressions. Gonzalez's inspiring work is always inclusive of diverse body types, skin tones, abilities, and gender expressions (see figure 9).

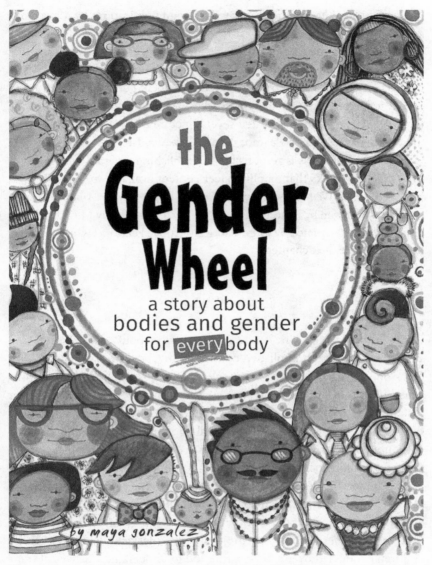

Figure 9 *The Gender Wheel* (2017), written and illustrated by Maya Gonzalez, published by Reflection Press

The Gender Wheel is one of many significant publications by Maya Gonzalez, who founded Reflection Press with Matthew SG in 2009 (Gonzalez). They use the platform to publish inclusive queer content for children that prompts personal reflection and social engagement. Gonzalez describes the press as a "POC queer and trans owned independent publisher of radical and revolutionary children's books and works that expand cultural and spiritual awareness." The pair have created several picture books together, including *They She He Me: Free to Be!* (2017) and *They, She, He Easy as ABC* (2020). Additionally, the press is responsible for publishing several LGBTQ+ children's picture books that amplify queer content available to young people, including *When We Love Someone We Sing to Them: Cuando Amamos Cantamos* (2018), written by Ernesto Javier Martínez, illustrated by Maya Christina Gonzalez, and translated by Jorge Gabriel Martínez Feliciano, which I discuss at length in the next chapter.

Knowing Gender Now

In the last couple of years, nearly a dozen books about queer children and childhood have been published by major university presses (Davis; Gill-Peterson; Travers; Robertson; Meadow). Much of this scholarship has a strong sense of political urgency and clear commitment to structural change. For instance, Heath Fogg Davis's *Beyond Trans: Does Gender Matter?* (2017) seeks to dismantle regimes of gender and sexual normativity by providing practical recommendations. Other scholarship uses queer theoretical interpretative frameworks and social science methods to understand transgender youth and create social policies and practices that affirm their existence. Others are interested in cataloging and theorizing the "gender revolution." For instance, Ann Travers's *The Trans Generation: How Trans Kids (and Their Parents) Are Creating a Gender Revolution* (2018) draws on interviews with transgender children conducted over a five-year period to understand the lives of trans youth and their families. Similarly, Tey Meadows's *Trans Kids: Being Gendered in the Twenty-First Century* catalogs experiences of growing up transgender through interviews with transgender children as well as their families and demonstrates that parents are often far more affirming of their transgender children than has previously been the case. Mary Robertson's *Growing Up Queer: Kids and the Remaking of LGBTQ Identity* (2019) also foregrounds the voices of LGBTQ+ youth to understand what makes growing up as a gendered and sexual being in the last decade so very different from the past. Still other scholars, most notably Julian Gill-Peterson, challenge the idea that transgender identities and expressions are new. Through critical readings of clinical archives, Gill-Peterson argues that gender-nonconforming children existed before the term *transgender* made its way into the mainstream.

I suggest that at this historical juncture, various social agents and social forces are coalescing and generating the potential to radically transform dominant social policies, practices, and, indeed, the social institution of gender itself. This is demonstrated by the normalization of affirming medical models of care for nonbinary and transgender youth, praxis-oriented scholarship, and creative work like children's picture books. It is also made clear by the backlash against sociocultural changes that seek to limit or deny transgender youth access to health care and safe schools as well as myriad other anti-child and anti-queer initiatives led by the radicalized Right in the US (Harris; Holmes; Vidal).

As these texts illustrate, a growing number of young people are disinvesting from rigid gender identities in favor of more flexible identifications. Robertson notes: "In addition to trans* awareness, increasingly more people—especially young people—are adopting 'genderqueer' and 'gender fluid' (along with fluid sexualities) as terms to describe gender that does not conform to the female/male, feminine/masculine binary" (72). Robertson attributes the abandonment of gender and sexual rigidity to transformation of the cultural texts available to youth and writes:

> Young people coming of age during the rise of trans* awareness have witnessed increasing exposure to trans* experience, including high-profile trans-identified celebrities and countless news stories about trans*-identified children and youth, and among their peers, they are experiencing a proliferation of gender identities beyond the binary male/female. The young people coming of age today are living with a different phenomenological experience of gender than those who came of age before them. (69)

For Robertson, the visibility of transgender and nonbinary identities introduces children to gender and sexual possibilities beyond cisgender heterosexuality.

Cultural representations certainly play a significant role in introducing young people to queer gender and sexual identities and expressions, but adult gatekeepers have an essential role to play supporting young people. In *The Trans Generation: How Trans Kids (and Their Parents) Are Creating a Gender Revolution* (2018), Ann Travers highlights parents' role in creating an affirming place for their children to explore gender identity. Travers writes:

> Since the mid-1990s . . . an increasing number of kids are finding it possible to openly resist the sex category assigned to them at birth and to identify themselves in unexpected ways. This agency has become possible as a result of adult transgender activism, the availability of information about LGBT people and identities via the Internet, and emerging social movements on behalf of trans kids consisting of parents, therapeutic/medical providers, and trans people of all ages. (5)

Along with culture, as noted by Robertson, Travers claims a variety of institutions, including medicine and the family, play a role in developing the context of possibility for more children to identify and express genders that disrupt the existing sex-gender system. Even though Travers attests that affirmation is an emerging social trend, they recognize "trans kids are incredibly vulnerable because of the way in which gender identities are imposed on children in general, with particular negative consequences for trans kids" (10). Although individual parents, schools, sports teams, and other groups are becoming more welcoming to and affirming of transgender youth, the fact remains that family, education, and athletics (to name only a few examples) remain deeply vested in monitoring and managing normative gender identity.

In the next section, I discuss picture books about transgender youth published between 2009 and 2018. Many of these books confront the reality of trans young people negotiating regimes of gender normativity that operate in various social institutions, notably school and family. I agree with both Robertson and Travers, who suggest that culture plays an essential role in the recent articulatable expansion of youth gender expressions and identifications. However, by taking a long view of nonnormative gender representations in LGBTQ+ children's picture books, I think we can see, as suggested by Gill-Peterson, that a multiplicity of gender subjectivities and performativities have always existed. Like Halberstam, who hopes to "challenge hegemonic models of gender conformity" by taxonomizing them in his study of female masculinities, I hope that my discussion of the archive of queer gender expressions and identifications in children's picture books demonstrates the field's documentary function and transformative potential.

Transgender Representations

Jody Norton published her now canonical essay "Transchildren [sic] and the Discipline of Children's Literature" in 1999, over twenty years ago. In this essay, she laments the lack of explicit transgender representations in children's picture books and theorizes ways of reading children's books that disrupt the logic of gender binaries. For Norton, barring the "creation of a substantial body of specifically transchildren's [sic] literature, we can intervene in the reproductive cycle of transphobia through strategies of transreading: intuiting/interpreting the gender of child characters as not necessarily perfectly aligned with their anatomies" (299). Now, more than twenty years after Norton first published her article, a "substantial body of specifically" transgender and nonbinary children's picture books does exist.[2] At their best, these books represent queerness as attractive and desirable as well as attainable, and provide avenues for identification with queerness. Some offer snapshots into queer sociality—for instance, Marcus Ewer's *10,000 Dresses*, briefly discussed in the previous chapter, introduces the idea of chosen families. Other picture books give rare peeks into queer adulthood and position grown-up characters as role models, as in Alice Reeves's *Vincent the Vixen* (2018). Still others, for example Jo Hirst's *A House for Everyone* (2018), model queer community building. My favorite books provide straight-ish kids pathways to queerness, as in Kai Cheng Thom's *From the Stars in the Sky to the Fish in the Sea* (2017). Whether realistic or whimsical, recent LGBTQ+ children's literature is a creative archive that reflects shifting adult-child relationships as well as the magnification of queer gender expressions in embodied practice and cultural representation.

Marcus Ewert's 2008 publication, *10,000 Dresses*, illustrated by Rex Ray, is the first children's picture book to explicitly represent a transgender child. It was published by Triangle Square, the children's book imprint of the politically progressive Seven Stories Press. The press's investment in transforming young readers is apparent in its description of how it perceives its audience: "We see children and young adults as active readers and doers who will change the world for the better" (Seven Stories Press). The production quality

Figure 10 *10,000 Dresses* (2008), written by Marcus Ewert, illustrated by Rex Ray, published by Triangle Square

is high, and both the writing and illustrations are remarkable, which is rare in a subfield of children's literature dominated by books that are either self-published or published by politically motivated, low-budget presses.

Bailey, Ewert's protagonist, is a transgender girl who experiences repeated rejection from unsupportive family members. Every night, while comfortably tucked into her bed, Bailey dreams about special dresses. In the morning when she wakes up, she shares her dream with a family member. Each family member, in turn, dismisses her dream, ignores her attempt at self-definition, and tries to silence her. The repetition of rejection is an important part of the story. It illustrates the tenacity of queer desire and resilience of the queer child as well as the heteronormative family's failure to account for the needs of the queer child.

In Bailey's first dream, she tries on a dress made of crystals (see figure 10). She is delighted by the sparkle of the crystals and the gentle clinking sound they make. Bailey shares her dream with her mother, who is depicted clipping coupons in the kitchen. As Bailey describes the dream, her mother adds an occasional and distracted "uh-huh." However, she becomes animated when asked if she'll buy Bailey a dress. At this point, Bailey's mother declares that boys don't wear dresses. Bailey's response is hauntingly illustrated. Ray depicts her with slumped shoulders and downcast eyes.

Later that night, Bailey again dreams of the castle. This time she tries on a dress made of flowers. When she wakes up, Bailey shares her second dream with her father, who is depicted manicuring the lawn. Standing outside, in her father's domain, Bailey asks him to grow her a dress, but he refuses. Then, he goes even further, banishing her from the backyard and demanding she never speak about dresses again. Both of Bailey's parents are caricatures of cisgender heterosexuals performing their socially sanctioned gender roles. Readers never see their faces, and their monstrous bodies stretch off the page as they tower over Bailey, who appears small and vulnerable in comparison. In addition to representing straight parents as grotesque, the gendered division of labor and space within the home offers a subtle critique of heterosexual family life. Although on the surface the coupon-cutting mother and lawn-cutting father appear to represent an ideal vision of family life, the family itself lacks affective bonds and reciprocal feelings of care.

Whereas siblings are, occasionally, sources of support in LGBTQ+ children's picture books, that is not the case in this one. In her third dream, Bailey returns to the castle and tries on a dress made of windows. Instead of depicting the inside of a house, these windows open to the world. The next day, Bailey finds her knobby-kneed brother playing soccer with a small group of boys. She shares her dream with him. His response is similar to her parents. He calls her gross and threatens to kick her. At the threat of violence, Bailey turns from her brother, quickly running away from him and the family home.

At the end of the block, Bailey sees an older girl sitting on a porch with sewing needles, thread, and old sheets. Bailey approaches the older girl and learns that her name is Laurel. Unlike the characters who compose Bailey's nuclear family unit, Laurel is given not only a name but also a face. Laurel has all the materials she needs to make a dress, but no vision and no plan. Of course, Bailey's head is full of dresses. The two complement each other well, each having something the other needs. Although Laurel is older, there is no age-based power hierarchy. The relationship appears reciprocal and generative.

Bailey's relationship with Laurel stands in stark opposition to her relationship with her parents. Although Ewert depicts Bailey as an agent of her own desire, it is also clear that she is vulnerable, because of her age, and constrained by the will of her parents. Although Bailey must negotiate her parents' transphobia, by the end of the picture book, it seems clear she will persevere. With the help of Laurel, Bailey begins to manifest her dreams by making beautiful dresses. Ewert envisions a beautifully interdependent relationship between Bailey and Laurel, one tethered to queer worldmaking.

Marcus Ewert represents the heterosexual family unit as hostile to the queer child. Most other representations of transgender children in picture books offer a more sympathetic take on the heterosexual family. Further, like pink boy picture books, many are authored by the mothers of queer children. For instance, Jennifer Carr's 2010 publication, *Be Who You Are*, illustrated by Ben Rumback, follows a young transgender girl named Hope as she begins school for the first time. Carr, the mother of a transgender child, wrote the book to have an affirming story to share with her children.

In an article for the *Windy Times*, Kate Sosin describes the book as "the first children's book with a transgender character who transitions with the love and support of family and community. In transgender circles, that kind of narrative is ground-breaking. The lesson is as applicable to young people as it is their parents." Sosin interviewed Carr for the article and asked the author if she had read Ewert's *10,000 Dresses*. According to Sosin, "Carr and her kids disliked the book. Carr's son asked why Bailey's family rejected her just because she was trans. Her daughter said she 'didn't like Bailey's choices' to go play with an older stranger." The queer child in Carr's book is celebrated by her family; the title itself, *Be Who You Are*, is an affirmation.

The book's transgender protagonist, Hope, tells her parents she is a girl at a very young age, and they seem to effortlessly accept the information. As in many pink boy books, home is a safe space and parents are consummate allies. School, however, is a different matter. Hope doesn't initially choose to present herself as a girl at school. However, at one point, a still masculine-presenting Hope draws a picture of herself as a girl only to be corrected by her teacher. In another instance, Hope stands in line with other girls only to be told to move. These creative and performative acts of resistance also demonstrate Hope's investment in and construction of a transgender subjectivity. When Hope shares her discomfort at school with her parents, they become advocates. One of the first things they do is bring Hope to a therapist to share her feelings about gender. Hope's therapist, like her parents, affirms her gender identity. As a result, Hope has the confidence to grow her hair long and wear girl clothes more frequently. Her younger brother is also represented as an ally.

Most queer children will grow up in isolation from other LGBTQ+ children and adults, so it should come as no surprise that realist picture books about transgender youth experiences tend to focus on the isolated queer child within a heteronormative family. This is the case in the affirming *Be Who You Are* as well as the quite dismal *10,000 Dresses*, whose protagonist is devalued until meeting a friend outside of the family unit. Both of these texts, like most picture books about transgender youth, also focus on coming out, although *Be Who You Are* lingers on the often nonlinear process of social transitioning.

When Kayla Was Kyle (2013), written by Amy Fabrikant and illustrated by Jennifer Levine, represents the isolation of queer children in heteronormative families and schools. Kayla is an unhappy transgender child who is misgendered by the significant people in her life. At the start of the book, Kayla's father tries to get the child he sees as a son to play basketball with boys, even though Kayla is clearly uncomfortable with sports. Kayla's mother is loving, but she does not understand what Kayla is experiencing and is unable to provide support. Kayla does not have any friends at school and experiences peer- and self-alienation while presenting as a boy.

As in other books that focus on queer youth, readers are provided glimpses into Kayla's subjectivity through images she draws of herself. Her art allows Kayla to quietly assert her identity and bounce back from the trauma of being misgendered. Art is a strategy of resilience, as is the role of class clown she takes on at school to protect herself from isolation and bullying. Kayla uses these strategies to shield herself from the trauma of being misgendered and isolated (Jung). Although aware of her loneliness, Kayla's parents trivialize it, assuming she just needs to try harder to make friends. Her tenth birthday party is a breaking point. Kayla's mother has invited all her peers, and no one comes. After this, it is hard for her parents to dismiss Kayla's isolation. Things escalate quickly when Kayla confesses suicidal thoughts and explains that she is a girl. Her parents are surprisingly quick to accept her, and Kayla begins to transition.

The book does important work making plain the pain and vulnerability experienced by many transgender children, who are often provided inadequate support or met with open hostility at home and school. Although I was unable to identify Fabrikant as the parent of a transgender child, she does work as a gender diversity consultant in private and educational settings and appears to be a longtime youth advocate ("When Kayla Was Kyle"). I note this to make the motivation most authors have for beginning to write about transgender youth apparent. Hardly motivated by profit or fame, they are invested in putting age-appropriate transgender representations into the world to provide transgender youth with windows into lives that look like theirs (Bishop). This is a significant political-cultural project given the relative lack of cultural visibility and political vitriol shaping the life chances of many transgender youth.

Although representations of transgender youth remain relatively rare, it can be argued that transgender children in the US have a posterchild in Jazz Jennings. Jennings, now a young transgender woman with her own TLC show, first entered the spotlight in 2007 when she was featured on a *20/20* documentary about transgender children (*20/20*). That same year, she worked with her family to create a nonprofit that supports transgender and gender-nonconforming children (TransKids Purple Rainbow Foundation). Jennings is a social media personality and fierce advocate for transgender rights. While a young teenager, Jennings coauthored *I Am Jazz* (2014), an autobiographical children's picture book written with Jessica Herthel and illustrated by Shelagh McNicholas. *I Am Jazz* is similar to many of the picture books featuring transgender children already discussed. Jazz is isolated in her queerness and must negotiate school and family, where she is misgendered. Like Kayla, drawing is a strategy of resilience that helps Jazz rebound from being misgendered and misunderstood. In pictures, she is able to explore a sense of self she doesn't have the words to articulate.

On the cover of the picture book, a smiling Jazz is depicted with long, dark hair, rosy cheeks, and pale skin (see figure 11). She stands in front of a wall of family pictures and is smiling happily in all of them. Although her facial features remain the same across images, the length of her hair varies. She is alone in most of the pictures, although there is one with her siblings and one with her parents. It's impossible to tell why the book's title character is exceptional enough to warrant an autobiography by looking at the cover. The narrative strategy relies on the reader's ignorance, real or imagined, as details about Jazz are revealed.

Figure 11 *I Am Jazz* (2014), written by Jessica Herthel and Jazz Jennings, illustrated by Shelagh McNicholas, published by Dial Books

The story opens with an image of her sitting next to a stuffed mermaid on a pink bed. The text above the illustration announces: "I am Jazz!" On the facing page, Jazz is depicted in a silvery dress accessorized with a tiara—she's a girlie girl. Readers quickly learn that Jazz loves dancing, soccer, and makeup, but the thing she loves most are mermaids, a symbol many transgender children are drawn to (Hurley).

In image and text, Jazz is depicted as a typical girl. Readers don't learn she is transgender until her identity is well established. Unlike other stories of transgender youth discussed in this section, readers move backward through Jazz's transition. The mood of the text changes when images of Jazz smiling with her friends are replaced by a sullen girl who acknowledges that she is not exactly like other girls. In a two-page illustration, Jazz sits with her stuffed mermaid next to her, drawing a series of pictures. Jazz shares her transition and expresses what it meant to her through this series of drawings. The first drawing is of an androgynous child who grows more feminine in subsequent images. The final image in the series is of a little girl with long hair in pink bows. The accompanying text explains: "I have a girl brain but a boy body. / This is called transgender. / I was born this way." Young readers experience Jazz's gender journey as a move toward happiness. The creative decision to allow Jazz, the character, to share her story with readers through images readers watch her create constructs children as agents capable of self-knowledge and self-narration. Even more, Jazz can identify herself as transgender and explain what this means in a direct address to readers.

After readers learn that Jazz is transgender, they're provided with back-story through a set of illustrations similar to the ones Jazz has drawn. In these illustrations, an androgynous child is depicted in various everyday scenarios. In one, a young Jazz plays with dolls as her mother tries to redirect her attention to blocks. Other images express the same message of subtle gender policing. Eventually, Jazz's parents realize she is happier if they let her play with girls' toys and wear girls' clothes. However, they lack the vocabulary to identify their child as transgender. Eventually, Jazz's parents begin to develop a vocabulary to account for their daughter's gender expression and identification. Once they visit a knowledgeable and supportive doctor, they, in turn, can support their daughter. As in Jennifer Carr's book, parents need medical experts to verify what their children are showing them to understand and fully support their queer children. In both books, but especially this one, the medical establishment is consulted so the parents of a transgender child can be helped as they learn to celebrate and support their child. Jazz's parents and siblings are depicted as supportive but in need of knowledge, gesturing toward the importance of transgender visibility, a political project Jazz Jennings has participated in since she was a child. In fact, I would suggest that each book discussed in this section is doing the important political work of increasing the cultural visibility of transgender youth.

Once Jazz's parents develop a better understanding of how to support their daughter, Jazz begins her social transition at school. This is not represented as effortless, but the queer child is resilient and, in this text, at least, not without support. The authors write: "Even today, there are kids who tease me, or call me by a boy name, or ignore me altogether. This makes me feel crummy." *I Am Jazz* gives readers a happy, albeit not utopian, ending. Jazz still experiences transphobia outside of her supportive family unit. However, she is depicted throughout the text as having a cohort of close friends who validate her identity and help her rebound from the trauma of being misgendered. This is a significant message, as the desire to protect children from pain, instead of empowering them to rebound from it, is clearly present in many of the pink boy texts discussed in the previous chapter. Those writing about transgender experiences, in this case, a transgender child herself, create different affective universes. For Ewert's Bailey, Carr's Kayla, and Jennings's Jazz, the point isn't a life without negative affect. Each author appears to recognize the futility of such desires. Instead, the point is resilience in the face of trauma.

There are a couple picture books about transgender youth that gesture toward the importance of queer role models and community. *Goblinheart: A Fairy Tale* (2012), written by Brett Axel and illustrated by Terra Bidlespacher, is an allegory of transgender experience told through the story of a goblin named Julep who is identified by others as a fairy. Like Carr, Axel is the parent of a transgender child (Sadjadi). Sahar Sadjadi reports hearing Axel speak in New York City, where he "explained that he created Goblinheart to provide a tool for other children in a similar situation to make sense of their experience." Both Carr's and Axel's creative projects represent a labor of love undertaken on behalf of the queer child.

In Julep's community, fairies and goblins live in and care for a big, beautiful tree. Goblins grow claws when they come of age and use their claws to tend to tree roots. Fairies grow wings when they come of age and use their wings to tend to tree leaves. Fairies and goblins even have different diets. When Julep matures, they begin to grow wings like a fairy, but in their heart, Julep is a goblin. When training to tend the tree begins, Julep lines up with the other goblins. After some discussion, the elders agree to allow Julep to work with the goblins. Julep eventually binds their wings and creates a pair of gauntlets they use to tend tree roots. Even more, Julep is eventually able to help a fairy from a different community in a similar situation, serving as a role model. This allegory engages two themes rarely present in LGBTQ+ children's picture books. First, Julep grows up. This is the only text I have identified in which the queer child comes of age and negotiates the physical changes brought on by puberty. Second, Julep serves as a role model for a younger queer character, which is also very rare. As often stated, most characters in LGBTQ+ children's picture books only negotiate two spaces: home and school. Even more, they tend to be isolated in their queerness in both social environments. By positioning Julep in a larger community and representing a queer character who grows up, Axel signals the possibility and importance of intergenerational queer community.

The importance of queer community and queer role models is also subtly explored in one other picture book. *Vincent the Vixen* (2018), written by Alice Reeves and illustrated by Phoebe Kirk, tells the story of a fox who develops a queer relationship to gender identity while playing dress-up. The book is published by Truth and Tails, a small press created by Reeves and Kirk. They started the press "to create children's fiction that eliminates prejudice, encourages acceptance and aids understanding by addressing hard-to-deal-with concepts such as gender, disability, and self-worth through simple, sensitive and beautiful stories featuring loveable characters" ("About Us").

The story begins with several foxes playing together. The foxes, identified as siblings, are seen without any identifying gender markers such as clothes. They're depicted playing hide-and-seek, swimming, and annoying a grumpy cat. None of these activities are particularly gendered, so at the text's opening, gender is represented as a nonpresence and nonissue. This changes when the fox cubs go to Betty the Badger's house. Betty lets the young foxes play with a box of her old dresses. The foxes are depicted laughing while wearing Betty's brightly colored, out-of-style, but very fun clothes. The text reads: "Vincent loved dressing up more than anything in the world, because he could use his imagination to be anything he wanted to be." Vincent is seen pretending to be a queen and a witch, two images of strong, powerful femininity that harken back to the pink boys discussed in the previous chapter.

While playing dress-up at Betty's home, Vincent always "pretends" to be a girl. Vincent's brothers and sisters eventually notice their sibling's penchant for feminine attire, and they mention it to Vincent. Vincent is not sure how to respond when asked about preferring feminine costumes and goes off alone to think about what the behavior might mean. While reflecting deeply about gender identity, Vincent realizes she is happiest when she can look and act like a girl. Vincent does not immediately share her thoughts with anyone, but the next day Betty the Badger is able to coax her into conversation. Vincent confides that she thinks she is a girl. Betty calmly nods and shares a story with Vincent. Betty's story begins: "When I was a young badger I loved playing make-believe with my sisters, just like you. I was also a boy badger, just like you." An image of a young Betty the Badger in too-big heels reminds the reader of Vincent the Vixen's dress-up play, creating a queer continuum across time and introducing an openly transgender adult character as a role model for a transgender child. Betty explains that she knew she was a girl just like Vincent knows she's a girl. Betty then shares that when she told her siblings they were confused at first but grew to understand. Even more, Betty tells Vincent that she was and is happy with her decision. Later that night, Vincent tells her parents that when she dresses up she is not really playing make-believe, she is not pretending to be a girl, she just is one. Like Betty's siblings, Vincent's family is confused at first, but they quickly accept that she is a girl.

By narrativizing her gender journey, Betty provides Vincent with a path to adulthood that she can imagine and emulate. The connections Betty makes between her queer childhood and Vincent's encourage Vincent to identify with Betty and, by extension, with queerness. This identification, shaped through shared stories, concretizes the possibility of gender transition for Vincent. As a result, Vincent gains the confidence needed to narrate her own identity to her family. Even more, in this picture book, child's play does important work by allowing Vincent to explore gender identity and actively create a transgender identity.

Nonbinary Gender Identifications

Complex understandings of gender are explored in several recent publications, starting in 2015 with the publication of *Are You a Boy or a Girl?* (2015). The book, written by Sarah Savage and illustrated by Fox Fisher, introduces readers to a nonbinary character named Tiny and their family. Tiny remains one of the only characters in LGBTQ+ children's picture books to identify *they* as their pronoun; most books simply avoid using pronouns altogether. In the book, Tiny and their family have just moved to a new town. At their new school, Tiny runs into the requisite bully, but their new teacher is supportive. Additionally, Tiny is quick to make friends. When asked politely by a curious new classmate about their gender identity, Tiny refuses binary gender identification.

Jamie Is Jamie: A Book about Being Yourself and Playing Your Way (2018), written by Afsaneh Moradian and illustrated by Maria Bogade, offers another realist depiction of a nonbinary child. Like so very many LGBTQ+ picture books, this one opens on the first day a child attends a new school. *Jamie Is Jamie: A Book about Being Yourself and Playing Your Way* is the story of

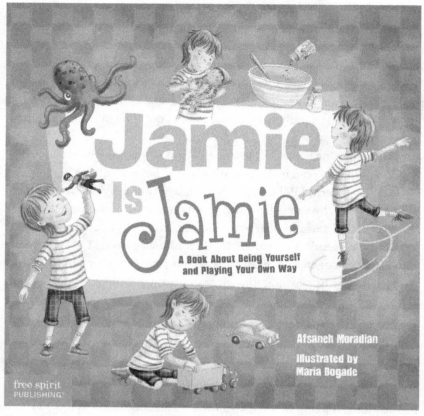

Figure 12 *Jamie Is Jamie: A Book About Being Yourself and Playing Your Way* (2018), written by
Afsaneh Moradian, illustrated by Maria Bogade, published by Free Spirit Publishing

a gender-free child named Jaime's first day at a new school. Jamie has an
ambiguous name, appearance, and choice in play (see figure 12). When Jamie
arrives at their new school wearing a red and white striped top with purple
pants and red shoes, their new peers end up reading Jaime's gender through
their play preferences. For instance, the little girl that Jamie plays dolls with
assumes Jaime is a girl. On the other hand, the boy that Jaime plays superhero
with assumes Jaime is a boy. Although the students cannot agree on Jamie's
gender, they all enjoy Jaime's company and appear to accept them. Even
more, Jamie's ability to step outside of binary gender expressions inspires
their peers, and the next day at school the boys and girls play together. This
harkens back to Gould's representation of X queering their classmates.

The subtle queering of straight kids is also explored in the delightfully whimsical picture book *From the Stars in the Sky to the Fish in the Sea* (2017), which is written by Kai Cheng Thom and illustrated by Li Kai Yun Ching. This book is about a young child named Miu Lan who cannot choose what to be: a boy or a girl, a bird or a fish. The multiplicity of options available to Miu is only limited by their expansive imagination, and the incorporation of nonhuman possibilities foregrounds fantasy as an important part of the text's reality. Miu's mother loves them unconditionally and lets them explore different expressions and identities. Miu's creative self-expression isn't constrained until it's time for them to attend school. As in many LGBTQ+ children's picture books, school is represented as a site of identity management and policing, a normalizing institution that stigmatizes and ostracizes the queer child as part of an overall strategy to produce gender conformity. Like other books about nonbinary youth, it is when Miu is confronted with strangers that the demand to identify within a binary sex-gender system emerges. Dressed in tiger stripes and peacock feathers, Miu appears confident the first day of school, unaware that their identity expression will confound their new classmates. At school, children refuse to play with Miu. The casual violence and violations experienced by queer children and frequently depicted in pink boy books are also present in *From the Stars in the Sky to the Fish in the Sea* as a classmate pulls Miu's peacock feathers. Subsequent days are just as bad.

Miu finally shares their experiences at school with their mother. She empathizes and explains that being different can be hard but is a livable choice. This appears to be the encouragement Miu needs. The pleasure of queer possibilities becomes a reward for resilience in the face of regimes of normativity. At school, Miu continues to bask in their queerness even though the consequences, including social isolation, are at first quite dire. Eventually, the children at Miu's school accept them in all their complexity and even begin to model themselves after the queer child.

Other books that explore the limits of binaries do so more conceptually than materially. By this I mean that they consider the absurdity of binaries, especially the idea that they are natural and inevitable without necessarily focusing on gender identity. One example, *Neither* (2018), by Airlie Anderson, is a study in collapsing binaries. The book opens like a fairy tale and reads like an allegory. Once upon a time, in a faraway place, the Land of This and That, there were blue bunnies and yellow birds. Then, something that was both, or neither, hatched. This creature had a bird body, bunny ears, and a bunny tale. Even more, instead of being yellow or blue, it was green. The birds and bunnies didn't know what to make of the new arrival, so they made fun of it, naming it Neither. They wouldn't let Neither play with them, eventually angrily telling Neither to go Somewhere Else. In their aimless journey, the exiled Neither stumbled upon an exciting new place—the Land of ALL. In the Land of ALL, a variety of animals who troubled easy classification lived together happily.

I am optimistic that the quantity of picture books featuring nonbinary youth characters, along with children's books that challenge binary and naturalized social sorting, will continue to grow. There were a very small number of books available by 2018, with a few added in 2019.[3] For instance, *Ogilvy* (2019) is a Henry Holt publication written by Deborah Underwood and illustrated by T. L. McBeth. The cartoonishly drawn title character, a white bunny with big eyes and rosy cheeks, has just moved to a new town and decides to explore a park. At the park, young bunnies, all wearing sweaters/dresses that fall to their waists, participate in a variety of activities, including drawing, knitting, and playing ball. Physically, the bunnies are indistinguishable, as is their attire, except for its color.

One of the young bunnies asks Ogilvy if their outfit is a sweater or a dress. It turns out that this is essential information because "bunnies in dresses play ball and knit socks, and bunnies in sweaters make art and climb rocks." Ogilvy decides to tell their new friends that their outfit is a sweater when they want to do sweater-wearer things and that it is a dress when they want to do dress-wearer things. Eventually, their new peers demand that Ogilvy choose. A fed-up Ogilvy loudly proclaims that they are wearing an ogilvy. Ogilvy's confidence and persistence encourages their peers to confront their taken-for-granted assumptions about dividing bunnies by clothing. One even notes that it is "silly for clothes to divide us." Underwood does a fantastic job demonstrating the absurdity of binary gender, even though the concept of gender is absent. It is by entering a world that defines and divides differently than our own that young readers can see the strangeness of our gender mandates.

Gender's Future

Whereas the books discussed in this chapter tend to focalize a single queer child who is either transgender or nonbinary, *A House for Everyone* (2018), written by Jo Hirst and illustrated by Naomi Bardoff, introduces children to a range of gender expressions and identities while shattering stereotypes about gender norms and showing queer children working collaboratively. Readers are introduced to the cast of characters enjoying various activities on their school playground. It is very difficult to "read" gender on the bodies of the joyfully playing children who soon decide to work together to "build a house for everyone." This is accomplished supportively and successfully by allowing each child's unique strengths and passions to guide the project. For instance, tan-skinned Ivy, a young girl with short, dark hair, is the fastest runner in the group. She runs all around the playground collecting sticks for the house. Ivy's hair and boyish clothes could mark her as a boy, but she is cisgender even though she does not conform to gender expectations. Another child, the pale-skinned Alex, prefers the pronoun *they* and does not identify as a girl or boy. Sam, a long-haired boy whose black hair contrasts with his light, pink-toned skin, collects plants and flowers. He decorates the house so it will look beautiful. The brown-skinned, curly-haired Jackson is a boy who likes to wear dresses. He is very strong and carries heavy rocks to put inside the house to "make comfortable seats for everyone." Tom, a deep-tan young boy, likes to spell and arranges rocks to create a "welcome" sign in front of the home. When he was born everyone thought he was a girl, but now they understand he was always a boy.

As these descriptions show, gender identity is not tied to gendered affinities for socially prescribed girl and boy clothes, toys, or activities. Ivy, Sam, and Jackson are cisgender; they identify with the gender they were assigned at birth, although they do not conform to gender stereotypes. The fast Ivy runs all over collecting sticks, the creative Sam decorates their home, and the strong, dress-wearing Jackson carries large rocks. Alex, a nonbinary child, has an able mind for engineering the building and Tom, a transgender child, enjoys the cerebral world of spelling over collecting materials and building.

We are finally beginning to see enough transgender and nonbinary representations to avoid the dangers of a single story, which is not to say we don't have a long way to go before the nuances of gender expression and identity are represented in LGBTQ+ children's picture books (Adichie). Taken together, the small but significant archive I've discussed in this chapter begins to offer varied and nuanced explorations of queer youth gender expressions and identifications building on earlier depictions of sissy boys, tomboys, and pink boys.

The existence of children's picture books about transgender and gender-nonbinary youth represents a shift in social awareness and understanding of gender identities. Additionally, this work represents a change in intimate and social relationships between adults and children. In these books as well as the pink boy books discussed in the previous chapter, most parents take their children seriously. They see them as agents of desire and respect them in ways that demonstrate their willingness to change for their children and change the world for their children. The shift in adult-child relationships depicted in LGBTQ+ children's picture books coincides with transformations in the visibility and social acceptability of LGBTQ+ identities that themselves represent a disinvestment in regimes of gender and sexual normativity.

Chapter Six

Queer Youth and Sexuality

Camp Flamboyance, Queer Fabulousness, and Even a Little Same-Gender Desire

Whereas the previous two chapters explored representations of queer youth genders in LGBTQ+ children's picture books, this chapter discusses strategies used to make same-gender youth desire, particularly gay desire, visible to young readers through depictions of camp, fabulousness, or explicit desire for someone of the same gender. Of course, exploring camp and fabulousness in picture books requires me to do the kind of queer decoding I may appear to criticize in my introduction. Here, I'll reiterate that my issue is not with scholarship that interprets picture books through queer frameworks. Instead, I am critical of work that dismisses explicit LGBTQ+ representations by suggesting that they are didactic, assimilatory, and antiqueer. For instance, in my introduction, I discuss Melynda Huskey's claim that popular children's books are more likely to represent queer challenges to regimes of normativity than explicitly LGBTQ+ children's books. Throughout this book, I've argued that LGBTQ+ children's picture books are, indeed, transgressive and transformative. Even more, I developed critical optimism as a reading strategy to explore both the radical possibilities and normative attachments embedded in LGBTQ+ children's picture books. This chapter continues this work while also identifying and analyzing the coded proto-gay affects and attachments that can be found in queer children's literature.

In her groundbreaking 1964 provocation "Notes on 'Camp'" Susan Sontag describes camp sensibility as, among other things, the conversion of seriousness into frivolity. I've always read this emphasis on pleasure over productivity, at least in part, as a rejection of capitalism's imperative to efficiency. Camp insinuates a different value hierarchy than the one we inherit and encourages investment in pleasure over production. Although Sontag's early theorization of camp identified the sensibility as apolitical, Madison Moore's recent discussion of Black queer eccentricity in *Fabulous* (2018) contends that the "pursuit of fun and pleasure are political gestures" (vii). Moore explores what he refers to as *fabulousness* as a queer aesthetic "that allows marginalized people and social outcasts to regain humanity and creativity" (vii). Although not to be conflated with camp, fabulousness shares a similar investment in artifice, creativity, and, above all else, pleasure. When present in children's picture books, both camp and fabulousness disrupt dominant hierarchies of value that I suggest are attached, if ever so subtly, to capitalist demands to repress desire in order to get down to business.

In addition to depictions of proto-gay child characters, a few picture books explicitly represent same-gender desire. Examples include *Caleb's Friend* (1993), *When We Love Someone We Sing to Them: Cuando Amamos Cantamos* (2018), and *Jerome by Heart* (2019). Although few in number, these texts introduce queerly desiring young boys to young readers. Far more common are depictions of characters who function as child proxies, allowing the veneer of sexual innocence to remain in place. This often occurs through the use of nonhuman characters, as in the case of *And Tango Makes Three* (2005), *Worm Loves Worm* (2016), and *Marlon Bundo* (2018). In other instances, it happens by queering fairy-tale conventions. Early examples include *King and King* (2002) and *King and Family* (2004). Unlike LGBTQ+ children's literature about lesbian and gay adults, which usually foregrounds the point of view of a child witnessing the romance of gay or lesbian adults, these texts encourage young audiences to identify with queer characters and, by extension, with queerness. Importantly, even at their most homonormative, these texts disrupt the field of compulsory heterosexuality that dominates children's literature by representing same-gender desire as a viable alternative to heterosexuality that is rich with possibilities for pleasure (Rich).

Figure 13 *Odd Bird Out* (2011), written and illustrated by Helga Bansch, published by Gecko Press

Camp Flamboyance (Birds and Boys)

As mentioned, camp is a decidedly gay affect, and when camp is present in LGBTQ+ children's literature, young campy characters can be read as proto-gay. Unlike the sissy boy trope, which frequently redeems effeminate behavior for heterosexuality, neutralizing possibilities for queer identification, campy characters are part of a gay genealogy. As early as the 1960s, Susan Sontag identified a "peculiar overlap" between camp taste and homosexual taste; noting that gay men were at the forefront of creating camp as a sensibility and aesthetic that centers playfulness and pleasure (117, 119). When the protagonists of LGBTQ+ children's picture books perform their identities and engage the social world through a camp sensibility, they enact pre-homosexual identities.

There is something about birds when it comes to depicting campy characters. *Odd Bird Out* (2011), written and illustrated by Helga Bansch, is the story of Robert, a "chirpy" raven, who enjoys dancing, singing, and dressing up. In one image, he is depicted in red heels, a pink skirt, a green-checkered jacket, and a red tie. He is coded as gay through his flamboyance, although neither sexuality nor gender is explicitly discussed in the text. Except for Robert, the ravens depicted in the book are illustrated wearing standard black clothing. They mock Robert before eventually forcing him out of town. His family is depicted as sympathetic but ineffective; they surround him, teary-eyed, as he departs.

Community rejection ends up being a valuable catalyst for Robert, who experiences career success in another tree with birds who can appreciate his queer sensibility and talent for entertainment. As Robert rises to stardom and begins to make a new home for himself, the community that rejected Robert realizes how boring life is without him. Apparently, the monotony of their conformity is no fun without an outsider-within to unite against. One night, Robert, reinvented as Bobby Raver, graces his old community with a performance. During the performance, the ravens "laughed and applauded," stirred from their boredom and, it turns out, inspired to emulate (i.e., appropriate) his style: "Ravens would dress-up for his concerts in the most outrageous, outlandish plumage." Queerness here is vaguely reminiscent of carnival as described by Mikhail Bakhtin in *Rabelais and His World*. Bakhtin suggests that carnival is a sort of space-off in which social norms and conventions are rejected, as the obscene, eccentric, and unfamiliar are embraced. This release from convention brings participants closer to the purely human (Bakhtin). Like carnival, Bobby Raver's performances allow a sanctioned release from convention for a period of time that can perhaps make the rest of the time more bearable. At the text's conclusion, Robert's identity remains concealed from his hometown's inhabitants, including his family, which prevents a true homecoming.

There are many similarities between Bansch's *Odd Bird Out* and *A Peacock Among Pigeons* (2016), written by Tyler Curry and illustrated by Clarione Gutierrez. This book is about a peacock named Peter who lives in a community of pigeons and doesn't fit in. Words like "flashy" and "flamboyant" are used to not so subtly queer Peter. Like Robert, Peter eventually flies the coop and creates a chosen family with an eclectic group of birds, including a "sassy" cardinal named Craig. Both books represent home as a site of queer oppression, and escape as a necessary, albeit painful, inconvenience for queer becoming and belonging.

The Boy Who Cried Fabulous (2004), written by Lesléa Newman and illustrated by Peter Ferguson, is pure camp pleasure-seeking fun with a generous dash of queer resilience tossed in. The text follows a young boy named Roger whose enthusiasm for life often distracts him from his tasks. The nostalgic illustrations present formally clad women and men strolling down the street in attire typical of the 1930s. The book opens with Roger waving goodbye to his mother as he heads to school. The text accompanying the image reads: "When Roger started out for school, / his mother set a simple rule. She said, "now Roger, you go straight—straight to class, and don't be late. / Roger tried hard to obey, he knew that he should not delay." The repetition of the word *straight* spoken by his mother represents the policing function of the heteronormative nuclear family and its investment in maintaining regimes of normativity. Additionally, Roger's clearly queer resistance to going "straight," and his investment in seeking and finding pleasure, gestures toward the perseverance of queerness and the resilience of the queer child.

The pleasure-seeking queer child in *The Boy Who Cried Fabulous* does not go straight to class, despite recognizing the importance of obeying his mother. His attention is diverted by a storefront featuring a man's red suit accented by purple buttons with a matching tie and handkerchief. The fabulous ensemble is itself an expression of camp that exceeds conventions in its flashy flamboyance. Roger enters the store and proceeds to use the word *fabulous* to describe everything in it. His boundless joy expresses the commitment to pleasure that Sontag identifies as essential to camp sensibility. However, reactions to and consequences for campiness are serious. When he finally gets to school, his teacher angrily orders him to sit and reminds him not to "gad about" on his way home from school. The term *gad* refers explicitly to seeking pleasure, which further reinforces the text's commitment to campiness and serves to queer Roger by associating him with camp.

Repetition is an element of children's picture books generally, and Newman's book is no exception. On his way home, Roger is again distracted by a fabulous world that offers so many exciting things to explore. The smell of pie, a woman's beautiful purse, and even a book all draw him in. Time passes quickly, and he realizes it is getting dark. He has gadded about.

When he finally arrives home, Roger is confronted by his sad mother and angry father, who send him to his room. Roger's parents debate how best to discipline their son, again showcasing the policing and managing function of the family. They decide regulating his vocabulary will help him channel his energy toward the productive and away from the pleasurable. Interestingly, their scheme to "straighten" out their son requires him to cease using the word *fabulous*.

While walking with his parents, Roger attempts to feel no pleasure, but the pull of queerness is strong. In one image, Roger is depicted, eyes wide, as he passes Marv's Diner. His mother and father look at him suspiciously as his mother holds his hand. The sign gave him an idea. He replaces the forbidden word *fabulous* with the word *marvelous*. While at lunch, he describes everything that he sees as marvelous. After they leave the diner, the family stumbles upon a parade. Of course, it is marvelous, but beyond marvelous it is "luscious," "scrumptious," "stunning," "thrilling," "brilliant," "magnificent," and, finally, "fabulous." After the forbidden word is spoken, Roger looks at his parents nervously. But, to his surprise, they smile and celebrate with him, queered by the child, able to see the world around them through pleasure-seeking, queer eyes.

The book ends with an image of Roger, balancing on his parents' shoulders as they tell him how much fun they had on their walk, referring to him as fabulous. Roger's family is meaningfully transformed through their love for him. Even more, their proximity to queerness allows them to see the world queerly. The text performs the kind of queer transformation I suggest is enabled by reading LGBTQ+ children's picture books, which, at their best, encourage identification with queerness. Of course, the ravens of *Odd Bird Out* eventually seem to be similarly transformed by queerness, but I would suggest Bansch's text represents surface-level appropriations of queer style, not affective and transformative engagement with queer pleasure.

Queer Fabulousness

In *Fabulous: The Rise and Fall of the Beautiful Eccentric* (2018), Madison Moore argues that fabulously deviant fashion choices are a form of aesthetic resistance to normativity. Although this resistance to norms is present in camp aesthetics, such as those discussed above, there is a political edge to Moore's theorization as well as a race and class dimension that distinguishes fabulousness from camp. Moore suggests that fabulousness embraces both pleasure and politics through publicly defying norms and expectations. Moore writes:

> With all its pomp and circumstance, fabulousness sees norms and resists them, twists them and makes them abstract, taking them on face-to-face, no holds barred. Perhaps one of the greatest creative gifts of marginalized people and

social outcasts is that power of abstraction—the ability to see through the here and now and to live dangerously through radical style, art, music, and ideas. (5)

Moore sees fabulousness as a strategy that emerges from social margins and associates it and its politics with marginalized groups who refuse to be invisible and undervalued. I bring in Moore for two reasons. First, I want to push back against Sontag's suggestion that campy pleasure seeking is apolitical by suggesting, alongside Moore, that embracing pleasure and refusing queer invisibility through conformity to conventions is political. Second, Moore's book influences my reading of Jessica Love's award-winning, but quite controversial, picture book *Julián Is a Mermaid*, which celebrates gender-expansive youth, femininity, intergenerational love and support, and Brooklyn's Mermaid Parade.

Every page of the text is laden with meaning, including the copyright and title pages, which depict Julián and his abuela walking toward a subway, while three women wearing mermaid attire trail behind. The next spread shows Julián, his abuela, and the mermaid women on the subway. Accompanying text introduces readers to the characters: "This is a boy named Julián. And this is his abuela. And those are some mermaids." Once on the subway, Julián and his abuela sit close and lock eyes. They hold each other's gaze throughout the text, communicating through eye contact and facial expressions, which sets a tone of quiet intimacy. A book about mermaids sits open in Julián's lap. As Julián stares at the real-life mermaids in front of him, his abuela watches him. One of the three brown-skinned mermaids, finding pleasure in performing femininity, tosses her long black hair over her shoulder, another twirls her tail, and the third, a pink-haired mermaid, waves at Julián.

Next, readers are invited on a journey into Julián's dreamscape. As in many LGBTQ+ children's picture books, dreams provide access to the queer child's psychic life. Julián's daydream is an imaginative space unconstrained by conventions. In Julián's daydream, a wave laps at him as fish swirl around him. His hair grows in a series of underwater vignettes that move readers deeper into his fantasy. Julián tumbles out of his clothes, changing into a mermaid with a soft pink and glowing orange tail. In subsequent images, a transformed Julián enjoys his body, admiring his tail as he does backflips in the water.

In his daydream, Julián confronts a large blue fish. They lock eyes, his expression imploring. Julián stretches his arms toward the fish, who has a necklace dangling from its mouth. At that moment, Julián is pulled back into reality by his abuela who says: "Vamonos, mijo. This is our stop." On the next page, they are depicted walking away from the subway car. Julián glances back at the mermaids, who smile and wave at their young admirer. When Julián and his abuela reach their doorstep, they lock eyes. Julián has his mermaid book open in one hand as he says: "Abuela, I am also a mermaid." His abuela doesn't respond to his announcement. Instead, she says: "I'm going to take a bath. You be good." His abuela's response appears dismissive and emotionally detached, but she doesn't avert her gaze during Julián's revelation. She continues to see him.

The next several pages explore Julián's fantasy of becoming a mermaid while acknowledging the constraints of reality. Echoing his daydream while on the subway car, Julián tosses off his clothes before making himself a crown of plants that creatively imitates the long girlish locks of his mermaid fantasy. He finds inspiration for a mermaid's tail in a flowing curtain that he wraps around his waist. When his abuela appears after her bath, enveloped in white towels, Julián presents himself to her as he presented himself to the fish in his previous fantasy. Abuela silently exits the room, leaving a dejected Julián behind.

Abuela soon returns, wearing a blue dress with the same markings as the fish that Julián confronted in his subway mermaid fantasy. Also, like the fish in his mermaid fantasy, she presents him with a necklace. This silent, but significant, gesture of support reproduces the quiet intimacy found throughout the text. In this moment, Julián's abuela becomes a collaborator in his queer performance—acknowledging and accepting that he is, at least for now, a mermaid. Even more, Julián's abuela takes his hand, gently leading him out of the house. Julián asks her where they are going, and she responds: "You'll see." On their walk, they turn a corner and stumble upon more mermaids. An awestruck Julián whispers, "Mermaids." Abuela's response is simple and deliberate: "Like you, mijo. Let's join them." Although her verbal response is quite matter of fact, her actions are unabashedly affirming as they join the parade together.

In this short, image-driven book, femininity is represented as artfully achieved and desirable, a little boy's dream of becoming a mermaid is represented as acceptable and possible, and the line between fantasy and reality is depicted as fluid, like the waves that carry us through the text's action. The truth of Julián's gender identity is unresolved in the text, but his fabulousness appears quite clearly. It can be found in the way Julián puts his ensemble together, pulling from found objects to make himself into the stuff of myth, quietly resisting masculinity to celebrate the feminine and claim it for himself. This is a significant rejection of normative gender roles. Even more, with the help of his abuela, Julián makes a spectacle of his desire, claiming queerness for youth, particularly Latinx youth.

Moore suggests that demanding space and embracing desire are political acts in a dominant heterosexist culture that privileges productivity over pleasure and tries to deny marginalized people cultural visibility. The queer-affirming intergenerational relationship that Love depicts renders being an ally possible in ways rarely seen in LGBTQ+ children's picture books. I also appreciate the ambivalence of the text. Julián can be interpreted as transgender, nonbinary, or, as I do in this reading, fabulous (and, perhaps, proto-gay). A definitive reading isn't possible; the text is too slippery. Instead, and directly related to the scarcity of meaning-anchoring text, the reader becomes an active participant in meaning-making. Regardless of how one reads Julián, he is a queer inspiration.

However, as mentioned, this text is surrounded by controversy. Love is a cisgender, white woman who some have criticized because of her treatment of Julián, her brown-skinned, Latinx, gender-creative protagonist. For instance, children's literature scholar Laura Jimenez, herself a Mexican American lesbian, contacted a Dominican American colleague for help evaluating Love's ability to capture authentic ethnic experience. Both scholars concluded: "The ease in which Julián's abuela accepts and encourages him to show his whole self might be something the author put into the book as a wish or hope. But, by creating this almost immediate acceptance, Jessica Love negated the real struggle so many Latinx LGBTQ people must go through" (L. Jimenez, "Trans People Aren't Mythical Creatures"). Although this is a compelling point, assessing authenticity is constrained by a number of factors, notably the varied experience within groups. Not all abuelas are unsupportive of queer affect and desire, although I can certainly concede that most are not likely to hand over their pearls, as occurs in *Julián Is a Mermaid*. Additionally, although Jimenez reads Julián's abuela's acceptance as rushed, my reading of the picture book suggests that Julián's queer desire was present for some time before he fully embraced his fabulousness. My interpretation suggests Julián's gender is an open secret à la Eve Sedgwick, not a surprise coming out moment (Sedgwick, *Epistemology of the Closet*).

Sexing Childhood: Animals (and Other Creatures) in Love

As mentioned, most stories about gay and lesbian adults in love are told from the point of view of children who are parented by or otherwise related to queer adults. This is such a popular representation that I devote my third chapter to it. I argue that these books position children as witnesses to queerness, but not as themselves queer. On the other hand, stories that anthropomorphize queer animals in love provide young readers with opportunities to identify with queer desire, since the focalizing character is most often experiencing romantic love. Young children can find pleasure and perhaps identify with the queer penguins, bunnies, or worms centered in the story. Importantly, I'm not suggesting that the nonhumanness of these characters makes identification with queerness more likely. I contend that the focalization of characters experiencing queer romantic love, instead of witnessing it, opens up the possibility to identify with queerness.

And Tango Makes Three (2005), cowritten by Justin Richardson and Peter Parnell and illustrated by Henry Cole, is the least queer and most controversial of the handful of queer animal love stories currently available. It's based on an event that took place at the Central Park Zoo. With the assistance of a zookeeper, two male penguins, Roy and Silo, raised a chick together. *And Tango Makes Three* has made the American Library Association's most banned book list eight times between 2006 and 20017 (Gomez; Machlin).

Richardson and Parnell paint a vivid love story that conforms quite neatly to heteronormative courting and family formation. Early in the text, the penguins are depicted bowing, singing, and swimming together, mimicking human dating. After some time passes, they even built a nest to house an egg, just like mating penguin couples. After witnessing their intimate relationship, the zookeeper, Mr. Gramzay, assumed the penguins were in love and placed an abandoned egg in their nest. Eventually, the well-cared-for egg cracked, and a chick with "fuzzy white feathers and a funny black beak" emerged. Mr. Gramzay named the chick Tango. Roy and Silo continued to care for Tango, making sure she was fed and warm.

Roy and Silo's love story is told by an omniscient narrator. Neither character is focalized; instead an observer interprets and shares their story. This positions readers as onlookers, much as if they were in a zoo observing confined animals in gloomy echoes of their natural habitat. Although the story denaturalizes heterosexuality, it doesn't allow for identifications with queerness as other books in this section do.

A Day in the Life of Marlon Bundo (2018), written by Jill Twiss and illustrated by EG (Gerald Kelley) Keller, parodies Marlon Bundo's A Day in the Life of the Vice President (2018), which was written by Vice President Mike Pence's oldest daughter, Charlotte Pence, and illustrated by his wife, Karen Pence. Twiss pokes fun at Pence's known homophobia by writing a charming and accessible children's picture book from the point of view of the Pence family's pet bunny. At the time of the book's publication, Twiss was a writer for Last Week Tonight with John Oliver, and the host promoted the book on his program. In A Day in the Life of Marlon Bundo, Pence is represented as a boring and mean stink bug who doesn't want Marlon Bundo to marry the boy bunny of his dreams.

Early in the text, readers are introduced to Marlon Bundo, who explains that he lives in an "old, stuffy house on the grounds of the U.S. Naval Observatory." He also shares that Mike Pence is his grandfather. However, the story isn't about Pence the man, although, as mentioned, his presence permeates the pages in spirit and caricature. Instead, this story is about a bunny falling in love. Marlon Bundo spends most of his time in the garden, which is where he meets Wesley. According to Marlon Bundo, Wesley is "bunny-beautiful." Marlon Bundo and Wesley explore the property together before deciding, later the same day, that they want to hop together forever. Children can delight in the text's silliness, while also taking the romance seriously.

The next day, the bunnies, with linked arms, tell their friends they plan to get married. Everyone, including a badger named Pumpernickel, a turtle named Scooter, and a hedgehog named Dill Pickle, greet them with enthusiasm. However, the mean stink bug is in charge and insists that boy bunnies can't marry boy bunnies. No one in the garden, including a very smart dog named Mr. Paws, understood why the stink bug was in charge, and Mr. Paws suggested they vote for a new leader. When they do, the stink bug is voted out. After the stink bug leaves office, Wesley and Marlon Bundo are free to marry. Although there are many sly cultural references young readers won't be able to identify, Twiss never abandons her young readers. They will surely be able to recognize the generic bully who somehow runs everything for no good reason. Importantly, the story offers a model of resistance, allyship, and queer love that children can see themselves inhabiting. In "Rabbit Weddings,

Animal Collectives, and the Potentialities of Perverse Reading: Children's Literature and Queer Worldmaking in *A Day in the Life of Marlon Bundo*," Angel Daniel Matos compellingly argues that despite the normative focus on marriage, the text serves as a queer worldmaking project by modeling affective ties that transcend species and age distinctions. Picture books that offer nonnormative templates for being together across difference, particularly those that evidence comradery and collective action, gesture toward queer possibilities alive in the present, potentially dominant in the future.

The love story that centers J. J. Austrian's *Worm Loves Worm* (2016), illustrated by Mike Curato, is similar to the romance at the center of *A Day in the Life of Marlon Bundo*, although it lacks satirical bite. Two gender-ambiguous worms fall in love, and their insect and arachnid friends demand they jump through all the traditional hoops to demonstrate it. This involves getting rings, even though they don't have fingers, and eating cake, even though they prefer dirt. The inclusion of these traditions, as well as the worms' critique of them, prompts critical thinking like that encouraged by Marlon Bundo's friends on realizing they have a choice about who is in charge. Both books position children to question what is taken for granted as right and true. However, in *A Day in the Life of Marlon Bundo*, Marlon Bundo and Wesley fully embrace marriage norms, whereas the worm couple at the center of *Worm Loves Worm* demonstrate general apathy toward marriage. Still, they go along with everything their friends suggest until it comes to choosing who will wear the white wedding dress and who will wear the tuxedo. At this point, the worms queer gender expectations. One pairs a traditional wedding dress with a top hat and the other wears a tuxedo with a veil. The book suggests queerness can disrupt even the straightest of institutions—marriage—by showing the worms embracing useful aspects of the institution while discarding what can't be queered.

The trope of gay exceptionalism resurfaces in Jase Peeples's *Square Zair Pair* (2015), illustrated by Christine Knopp. This quirky picture book gives off a Dr. Seuss vibe. The story takes place in Hanamandoo, a fantasy world inhabited by Zairs. Zairs hatch from eggs that grow from vines, which collapses distinctions between animal and plant life by queering Zairs' origin story. Some are tall and square; others are short and round. Round and square Zairs always form a pair by attaching tails. One day, two square Zairs pair. The community is outraged and demands they leave the group. The queered and exiled square Zairs leave town and build a hut. Exile from straight society isn't frequently found in LGBTQ+ children's literature, but its appearance is significant in books ranging from Marcus Ewert's *10,000 Dresses* to Fierstein's *The Sissy Duckling* and Bansch's *Odd Bird Out*.

As in Ewert's and Bansch's takes on queer exile, in Peeples's text, exile encourages the character's queerness to develop. Through resistance to normativity, new ways of being in the world are imagined and performed. For instance, when the queer Zairs run out of easily attainable berries, they work together and discover that they can climb trees to reach the better tasting berries at the top because of the unique way their bodies work together. As a result, when a storm comes, causing their old community to suffer, the queer Zairs stay safe and eat. Even more, they generously help the community that banished them by reaching berries at the top of trees. After their demonstration of queer exceptionalism, the moralistic Zairs who thought they were better than the paired square Zairs begin to feel ashamed. They have a Grinch-style change of heart, and instead of demanding conformity, they begin to appreciate and even celebrate difference.

Books like these make it possible for children to imagine nonheterosexual desires as livable. Even more, they focus less on the family unit, which almost always reproduces heterosexual conventions in LGBTQ+ children's picture books, and more on the queer couple as partners who find joy in sharing their lives together. The children's picture books discussed in my third chapter focus less on the joy of queer relationships and more on acceptance of queer families, so these books add an important reality, albeit in nonhuman form, to the field of LGBTQ+ children's picture books.

Sexing Childhood: Sea Stories

My research turned up a couple of delightfully quirky and surprisingly sensual queer picture books that take place in or near the sea. Written and illustrated by Eric Jon Nones, *Caleb's Friend* (1993) offers a queerly seductive representation of same-gender desire. Caleb is a tan-skinned boy of about twelve. As an orphan who appears to work full-time on a boat, Caleb blurs the line between adult and child. One day, as Caleb works on the ship, he accidentally drops a harmonica into the sea. An icy-blue-skinned merboy surfaces, returning the harmonica to him. The human boy and the merboy become infatuated with each other and continue to meet, exchanging objects like shells and flowers instead of kisses. These scenes are gorgeously rendered, often lingering on the merboy's eroticized form. Framed through Caleb's gaze, the merboy is constructed as a queer object of desire. His reciprocating gaze demonstrates that he is also a desiring subject. Caleb's isn't the only gaze that lingers on the merboy's figure. One day, he is caught in a fisher's net and sold to a merchant, who puts him on display for a paying audience, riveted by his otherworldly form. In this instance, the merboy is objectified and commodified, enslaved and branded a beautiful monster.

Caleb bravely saves the merboy and sets him free. Like the reciprocated gaze, the merboy reciprocates this favor by saving Caleb and his shipmates during a storm. Caleb and the merboy eventually part ways, although the text ends by noting that Caleb returns to the village annually to throw armfuls of flowers into the sea. *Caleb's Friend* dabbles in the trope of doomed queer love that frequently appears in LGBTQ+ culture.

Interestingly, most book reviewers did not read Caleb and the merboy's relationship as queer. Perhaps the artistry of image and text or the prestige of the press, Farrah, Straus and Giroux, kept this book from being widely acknowledged as a queer love story. *Kirkus Reviews* refers to the boys as friends. Even more, the reviewer displaces Caleb and the merboy's sensual relationship onto a reading of the relationship between the book's illustrations and text: "Almost more a mood piece than a story, the quietly elegiac text and enigmatic tone are perfectly in harmony with skillfully rendered art" (Kirkus Reviews). A *Publishers Weekly* review similarly transfers the romance between boy and merboy onto the relationship between image and text: "In a powerful union of graphics and words, Nones uses a dusk-colored palette for his haunting, strikingly detailed depictions of the sailing vessels and dress of a simpler time" (Publishers Weekly; Kirkus Reviews). Apparently, mainstream reviewers recognized a harmonious union but could not acknowledge the relationship between merboy and boy as its clearest expression. This is a significant erasure of queer possibility in a text that reproduces numerous romantic conventions from gift exchanges and minor flirtations to grand heroics.

Ingrid Godon and Andre Sollie's *Hello, Sailor* (2003) was published in the Netherlands before being translated into English and published by Macmillan Children's Books in the US. It is a subtle love story about a man named Matt who lives in a lighthouse and his mostly missing beloved. Every night, Matt guides ships safely home with the hope that the sailor he loves and longs for will be on one of the ships. The whimsical drawings have a folkish charm that captures the forlorn mood of the text. At first, it seems like this will be a story of doomed gay love as seen in *Caleb's Friend*; after all, Matt waits day after day, night after night, absorbed in the task of helping his love land safely at the shore. However, the book has a surprisingly happy ending. Sailor does come back for Matt, and he whisks him away to sea.

Both books introduce queer desire to young audiences in ways that position them to identify with homosexual possibilities, and to identify these possibilities as desirable. *Caleb's Friend* does this through the romantic story of a twelve-year-old boy and a merboy. Although Godon and Sollie's *Hello, Sailor* features adult men, the absence of a focalizing child character allows young readers to identify with the desiring adult characters, particularly Matt, whose persistent love and loyalty are rewarded.

In the next section, I turn to fairy tales that appropriate and subtly queer heteronormative tropes of desire. Similar to *Hello, Sailor*, these books highlight adult romance, but they do so in a way that allows young readers to imagine themselves being swept away by love.

Sexing Childhood: Fairy Tales

Many fairy tales, at least after being adapted by Disney, center two opposite-gender heterosexuals who must overcome obstacles to be rewarded with a life that includes matrimony as an essential component of living "happily ever after." These stories, at least in their contemporary iterations, are most often consumed by young girls who are bombarded with tales of fearless knights and charming princes riding horses or bearing glass slippers to rescue pretty, sweet, and necessarily vulnerable young women from conniving older women. Although the queer fairy tales discussed in this section demonstrate an awareness of fairy-tale conventions, they defamiliarize all but the happy ending.

Queer fairy tales are a recent phenomenon. The first, *King and King*, written by Linda de Hann and illustrated by Stern Nijland, was originally written in Dutch and published in the Netherlands. In 2003, three years after its original publication, it was translated into English and published by Tricycle Press. The premise of the story is simple. The queen, the crown prince, and their pet cat all live together. Early in the story, the queen demands that her son marry, so he can rule the kingdom. As in many fairy tales, princesses come from all around to be paraded in front of the royal family. Also, like in many fairy tales, the prince finds true love, and the book ends with a sumptuous wedding. Heterosexism permeates the text, most notably present in the assumption that the prince is heterosexual, but also in the subtler idea that maturity is linked to marriage. After all, a prerequisite to ruling is marrying, even though, ironically, the queen herself appears to be single.

The royal mother has an antagonistic relationship to her son. She is overbearing, monstrous even. Early in the text, the queen is depicted shouting at the prince, demanding he marry. In a corresponding image, spittle rains from her mouth. After a day of bullying, the prince concedes to his mother's wishes. She quickly arranges to have a group of young women paraded in front of him. Most of the princesses are excessively unattractive: one is overweight, another has bad teeth, a third is extremely tall with grotesquely long arms. None of them embody the conventional beauty associated with fairy-tale princesses.

However, the last princess *is* fairy-tale pretty, with long blond hair and an impossible hourglass figure. If this were a traditional (a.k.a. heterosexual) fairy tale, the prince would have found his future queen, but it isn't. The unreasonably attractive princess has a companion—her brother, Prince Lee. It's the two princes who fall in love at first sight. They quickly marry and become known as King and King. Of course, they live happily ever after.

Linda de Hann followed *King and King* with *King and King and Family* in 2004. The second story was also illustrated by Stern Nijland and published in the US by Tricycle Press. In this picture book, the couple's story picks up on their honeymoon to a faraway land. Their pet cat stows away in their suitcase. As the threesome make their way through a generic jungle, the newlyweds delight in watching animals with their offspring. This makes King Bertie wish he had a child of his own.

Wishes come true in this story—it's a fairy tale, after all. When the couple and their cat arrive home from their honeymoon, a little girl of perhaps seven or eight years old, wearing a bright-colored tank top and a patterned skirt, pops out of their suitcase. The racially ambiguous young stowaway is welcomed into the family. There is no discussion of her life in the generic jungle, including her motivation for hiding in the couple's suitcase. This queer family-making scenario negates the politics of transnational adoption as well as the challenges of adopting a child as a same-sex couple, although the girl's official adoption is gestured toward in an image of one king completing a lot of paperwork at the end of the book. While this pair of picture books represents the first depictions of gay fairy-tale romance, they aren't the last.

Kendal Nite's self-published picture book, *The Prince and Him: A Rainbow Bedtime Story* (2007), illustrated by Y. Brassel, dabbles in queer eroticism The story starts off, much like *King and King*, with Prince Edmond's parents urging him to marry a princess and enter adulthood. Also, similarly to *King and King*, a group of young women are paraded in front of the prince so he can choose a wife. Instead of simply looking at the women, the prince kisses each of them, but there is no spark. This book does dabble in representations of physical intimacy, which positions young readers to identify with the prince as he rejects each would-be princess. None of this cluster of texts is at all feminist, quite the contrary. Linda de Hann's depictions of women are grotesque, and Nite's women characters lack both depth and agency. Both authors appear to problematically link the desirability of queerness to the undesirability of women.

Like de Hann's overbearing queen, Nite's royal mother steers her son toward heterosexual love. When he is unable to pick a future wife from the women paraded in front of him, the queen assumes he needs more women to choose from. She gives him money and sends him into the world to find love. However, although he keeps kissing maidens, he doesn't find his bride. That is, until he sees a muscular young man, naked and bathing in a pond. Readers are positioned to see the naked man through the prince's gaze, and, by extension, the reader is invited to mirror the prince's arousal. The prince quickly kisses the man, and follows the kiss with a declaration of love. The two return to Prince Edmond's home, where they are met by his delighted parents. The equally accepting villagers cheer their new kings. Unlike in *King and King*, sexual attraction is foregrounded in *The Prince and Him: A Rainbow Bedtime Story*. Both books explore queer desire, but the queer gaze is far more elaborately developed and deployed in *The Prince and Him: A Rainbow Bedtime Story*, which makes the text more likely to prompt readers to identify with queer desire.

Daniel Haack authored two high-quality fairy-tale love stories: *Prince and Knight* (2018) and *Maiden and Princess*, which was co-authored with Isabel Galupo (2019). In a June 2019 email correspondence, Haack shared the benefits of working with an established press:

My two titles, *Prince & Knight* (2018) and *Maiden & Princess* (2019), were published by Little Bee Books and distributed through Simon & Schuster. Working with a large publisher can offer more credibility, a wider audience and greater marketing and business support. The publishing team has been incredibly supportive, both in terms of just the books themselves as well as the broader effort to improve LGBTQ representation in children's literature. In particular, they've partnered with GLAAD to amplify the books as part of a greater campaign to offer LGBTQ representation in children's media. This has opened so many doors and helped get these books in front of press, celebrities and more.

Haack recognizes that the material and creative support his work receives is connected to the resources available to established publishing houses like Simon and Schuster. Both illustrations and text are polished, demonstrating professionalism and skill often missing in LGBTQ+ children's picture books that are self-published or published by smaller presses. Haack added to his response, noting:

I'm skeptical of self-publishing for myself personally, as I really rely on the wonderful input from my agent and editors, nor do I have an interest in all the additional work and financing that comes with it. At the same time, I acknowledge that there has historically been limited support for LGBTQ children's stories from major publishers until recent years.

Haack's point, that established presses are beginning to publish LGBTQ+ picture books, which has not historically been the case, explains the quality of many recent publications. In fact, if one were to turn to the beginning of this book and flip through the images of book covers included, a brief visual history of changing publishing practices and their effect on LGBTQ+ picture book quality would emerge.

Importantly, established presses have not fully embraced queerness in all its complexity. There remain notable absences, particularly with authentic representations of racial and ethnic diversity. As noted by my colleague Danelle Adeniji, authentic Black queer representations are lacking in most LGBTQ+ children's picture books, which instead include incidental racial and ethnic diversity. Authentic queer, of color representations in LGBTQ+ children's picture books have not made their way past traditional press

Figure 14 *Prince and Knight* (2018), written by Daniel Haack, illustrated by Stevie Lewis, published by Little Bee Books

gatekeepers, and it remains necessary to go to smaller presses like Flamingo Rampant Press and Reflection Press for picture books that take complex intersectional representations of diversity seriously. However, although both presses publish high-quality books, marketing and distribution remain challenges for smaller presses.

Incidental racial and ethnic diversity doesn't prompt young readers to think critically about racial power dynamics or the specificity of racial and ethnic experience. In other words, there's no depth to racial and ethnic difference in many LGBTQ+ children's picture books. Instead, surface-level diversity appears innocuous and insignificant to the lives of characters. For instance, the cover of *Prince and Knight*, which is expertly illustrated by Stevie Lewis, shows a rosy-cheeked, young, white man surrounded by fawning women of different races. The prince stares, not at the women, but away from them at a racially ambiguous knight, who leans casually against a horse (figure 14). I note the depiction of diversity beyond sexuality in this text because it is indicative of a larger trend. Representational strategies can quickly become formulas that become traps for creators. The new norm appears to be representing surface-level differences untethered from socio-cultural specificity—to put it bluntly, diversity as decoration.

Prince and Knight opens with an image of a majestic castle surrounded by water. The proximate depiction of far simpler homes enhances the castle's grandeur. The facing page zooms in on the rosy-cheeked, golden-haired prince, who sits on a balcony staring off into the distance, appearing to wistfully wait for something to happen. His position echoes that of princesses, most notably Rapunzel, waiting to be rescued. From the beginning, *Prince and Knight* subverts fairy-tale tropes by inhabiting them with a queer difference. For instance, the text's conflict is quite conventional: the prince must be married to inherit the kingdom. In a two-page spread, the prince and his parents sit together at a long dining room table. The king and queen glance at their son worriedly. The text reads: "His parents knew that soon, it would be time he took the throne. But with a kingdom so grand, the prince could not rule alone." The three set off to find the dapper prince a "worthy bride." This echoes the exigence for the text's action in both *King and King* and *The Prince and Him: A Rainbow Bedtime Story* as well as far more traditional fairy tales. Like in those previously discussed texts, this one introduces the prince to a stream of bejeweled young women. Also, like those previously discussed texts, in this one, the prince rejects princess after princess, telling his parents he is "looking for something special in a partner." He goes off in search of his true love.

The prince's quest for true love is interrupted when he learns a dragon is attacking his home. He bravely mounts a horse and rides through a lush green forest to save his village from sure destruction. The brave prince confronts the open-mouthed dragon, sword drawn, but he doesn't face the dragon alone. A knight in full armor stands on a cliff behind the dragon. The prince and the knight work together intuitively; it is as if fate has brought them together. The knight uses his shield to direct sun into the dragon's eyes, using intelligence instead of brute strength. The prince takes the opportunity to leap onto the distracted dragon, subduing him with fancy knot work that gestures to kink sensibilities. Prince and Knight have defeated the dragon, but just as it seems danger has passed, the prince trips and begins to fall. The knight jumps onto his horse and races to the prince's aid. He swoops in and scoops the prince up before he contacts the ground. The knight continues to hold the prince as they each excitedly exclaim that they saved the other's life. These two are partners, perhaps worthy of ruling the kingdom together.

The next image in the text depicts the villagers gathered around the town square as the prince and the knight share an intimate embrace on top of a large fountain. Inside the castle, the king and the queen are elated that their son has found a partner to help him rule. The prince and the knight, eyes closed, fingers entangled, lean in to kiss each other. The text reads: "And on the two men's wedding day, the air filled with cheer and laughter, for the prince and his shining knight would live happily ever after." As in the other two picture books depicting queered fairy tales centered on gay men, this one challenges compulsory heterosexuality without challenging heteronormativity. Marriage remains an unquestioned marker of adulthood and maturity. In fact, far from critiquing heterosexual norms, the text reinforces them by constructing gay couples as interchangeable with heterosexual couples. Queer difference is dampened by collapsing any distinctions between queer and straight couples. However, it is also true that these gay-centered fairy tales unapologetically make queer desire accessible to young readers even as queer desire is constrained by genre conventions. In fact, in a personal correspondence with Haack, he wrote: "My focus has been on telling stories about LGBTQ people who take on traditionally 'heroic' roles, while also allowing them to be romantic leads in a supportive and welcoming environment." (See appendix B for full quote.) The quick acceptance of queer love is a deliberate choice, as is the portrayal of queer characters in heroic roles.

Daniel Haack followed this book with a coauthored picture book written with Isabel Galupo and illustrated by Becca Human. *Maiden and Princess* (2019) plays with gender roles and challenges assumptions of heterosexuality to create a delightfully queer feminist take on love. Like in other fairy tales discussed, the royal family, this time depicted with warm brown skin, throw a ball to help their son find a wife. A maiden who knows the prince from battle attends the ball. Attendees agree she will make a wonderful wife for the prince, but the maiden has other ideas and escapes the chatter only to find herself alone with and enamored by the prince's sister. Neither the maiden nor the princess knows of each other's relationship to the prince, and they feel an immediate romantic connection. The text ends with them happily married.

Another very new title, *The Bravest Knight Who Ever Lived* (2019), written by Daniel Errico and illustrated by Shiloh Penfield, shadows a quick-witted boy named Cedric who begins life on a pumpkin farm. Cedric has the opportunity to serve as a knight's squire after using his wits to outsmart a thief. He quickly impresses the king and queen with his heroics, and they offer him their daughter in marriage. Cedric surprises them by asking to marry the prince instead. At first distressed by Cedric's request, the king quickly realizes that the prince and knight were meant for each other. A royal wedding ensues.

These picture books incorporate fairy-tale plot formulas and genre conventions while positioning young readers as queerly desiring subjects. As previously mentioned, although compulsory heterosexuality is challenged, heteronormativity continues to constrain the imaginative possibilities found within the pages of most LGBTQ+ children's picture books, and fairy tales are no exception. However, newer queer fairy tales offer images of married life that aren't anchored in domesticity and disrupt heteronormative gender roles. For instance, post-marriage, *Maiden and Princess*'s title characters are depicted, swords drawn, in battle. Instead of marital lives marked by reproduction, the princesses and princes of queer fairy tales appear to embrace child-free futures, at least in the short-term.

A Young Boy's Crush x 2

Most queer characters available for children to identify with are hardly mirrors into young queer subjectivity or real-life experience. Instead, these characters, ranging from worms to fairy-tale princes, are proxies for queer youth. Of course, I include a couple of books, *Julián Is a Mermaid* and *The Boy Who Cried Fabulous*, that do represent what I interpret as proto-gay youth characters. However, in those books, both characters' queerness is presented through embodiments of camp and fabulousness respectively, not romantic desire. Their gayness is deferred, maintaining a line between children and adolescents. This section explores two recent books that render children's romantic desire possible by representing boy-boy crushes. Although the tone of each book as well as the parent-child relationships depicted are radically different, both books can serve as essential mirrors for children experiencing same-gender attraction.

Thomas Scotto's *Jerome by Heart*, illustrated by Olivier Tallec, is a French-language book that was translated into English by Claudia Bedrick and Karin Snelson in 2018. This first-person narrative, from the point of view of a young boy named Raphael, explores the child's nascent infatuation with another

Figure 15 *Jerome by Heart* (2018), written by Thomas Scotto, illustrated by Olivier Tallec, translated from the French by Claudia Zoe Bedrick and Karin Snelson, published by Enchanted Lion Books

boy. It opens with an image of two boys holding hands while riding bikes (see figure 15). Oblivious to the world around them, the boys' activity literally stops traffic, disrupting the normative flow of the adult world, much to the chagrin of the scowling drivers depicted in unmoving vehicles behind them. The text that accompanies the illustration reads: "He always holds my hand. / It's true. / Really tight." Scotto's first-person narrative strategy creates a quick sense of intimacy as Raphael divulges his feelings about Jerome.

One two-page spread depicts the boys on a class trip. The other children are clustered together viewing a painting, but the boys are not among their peers. Instead, on the facing page, Jerome and Raphael stand together in front of a different painting. The text reads: "On field trips to the art museum, / It's me he chooses as his buddy. / That's why I love Jerome. / It doesn't bother me at all. / Raphael loves Jerome. I can say it. / It's easy." The proclamation of love does not necessarily queer the boys' relationship, but the fact that the narrator disavows shame and stigma, claiming prototypical gay pride, inserts queer possibility into the narrative—these boys are not "just" friends.

In scene after scene, the boys are shown in proximity and clear affinity, delighting in one another. In one two-page image, Jerome is seen on a soccer field ignoring the game and instead chasing butterflies. Raphael stands next to him, hands clenched at chest-level, eyes closed, smile wide, enjoying Jerome's happiness. On the facing page, Raphael's father sits on a bench watching two girls aggressively chase a ball. The text reads: "My dad thinks it's a "pity" / that Jerome doesn't play soccer. / But just because Jerome doesn't play rough / doesn't mean he's not strong. / He is strong." The term *strength* is resignified in the text; it is not about physical strength and prowess, but instead one's ability to know and perform desire.

Raphael's unrelenting praise of Jerome gestures toward the potential queerness of all childhood intimacies. Another two-page spread features vignettes of the boys playing together, laughing together, running together, talking together, and holding hands. The accompanying text reads: "I've made up my mind. / From now on, every day is for Jerome. / Mornings are happy from the start! / By lunch, we've laughed so hard our stomach hurts. / And by dinner, I've stocked up on enough of Jerome to last me the whole night. / That's important." Rafael counts time by his love for Jerome and is sustained by him. Their relationship moves beyond friendship even as it is not described in erotic terms but instead those of intense affection.

Whereas the fairy tales discussed provide readers with requisite happy endings and do not represent sexual identity as a source of conflict within the family or greater community, in *Jerome by Heart*, Raphael's feelings for Jerome are met with open hostility from his parents. For instance, in a two-page spread following Raphael's blissful description of his feelings for Jerome, Raphael is depicted with his back to his parents, who tower over him. In fact, their bodies stretch outside of the frame. This is reminiscent of Rex Ray's illustrations of Bailey's parents in Marcus Ewert's *10,000 Dresses* and, as in Ewert's picture book, the disproportionately large parents represent the power adults have over children. Also, similar to Bailey's parents, Raphael's lack faces, which dehumanizes and accentuates the textual focus on Raphael and his love interest, Jerome. The text accompanying Tallec's significant illustration reads:

This morning at breakfast, I burst out: / "I had the best dream last night! / It was good in a Jerome kind of way." / Dad stares at his shoelaces, like he doesn't hear a word I'm saying. / Mom digs through my backpack and

sighs. / [Raphael continues to talk about Jerome until his father says:] "Now
that's enough." / Dad's voice is like sharp fish bones in my hot chocolate. /
Grownups must not be able to think straight in the morning. / Because if I
can't talk about Jerome anymore . . .

In this powerful exchange, filtered through Raphael's perspective, the child
acknowledges his father's disdain without registering what motivates it. It's
easy to read this as an example of accidental resilience through naivete, but at
points, for instance in the first passage quoted, Raphael does seem to have an
understanding of stigma and shame even if it isn't fully articulated in the text.

The fraught family scene is followed by one of Raphael alone in his bedroom, which I've often noted is a domestic space frequently depicted in
LGBTQ+ children's picture books to provide readers access to the queer
child's psychic life. Alone with his thoughts, Raphael stands, one hand quiz-
zically resting on his chin, as he tries to understand his parents' reaction.
However, Raphael does not spend much time fretting about his parents. His
thoughts quickly return to Jerome, specifically to finding a gift he can give
Jerome. The quick shift from thinking about his parents' anger to thinking
about bringing Jerome joy is a meaningful demonstration of the persistence
of queer desire despite the hostility of heteronormative gatekeepers lurking
in the kitchen. Raphael's imagination wanders as he considers possible ways
to demonstrate his love to Jerome, knowing he wants "something strong as a
fortress / that will last forever." The future is not given to the reader, but not
knowing what will happen next does not detract from the real joy and desire
experienced in the text's present. In fact, the lack of resolution is, perhaps,
one of the text's queerest elements.

When We Love Someone We Sing to Them: Cuando Amamos Cantamos
(2018), written by Ernesto Javier Martinez, illustrated by Maya Gonzalez, and
translated from Spanish by Jorge Gabriel Martinez Feliciano, explores the
relationship between a father and son as well as the son's crush on another boy.
The text opens with a whimsical image of the father surrounded by butterflies
against a purple sky as he strums an instrument. The lyrical text mirrors the
dreaminess of the illustrations and unfolds from the point of view of the
son. The boy's father explains that a serenata is a song sung to a beloved and
reminds the boy about a song the two of them once sang to the boy's mother.
His father tells him that when he starts "to feel the Xochipilli way" he will help
him sing "what's in your heart." The story subtly expresses the imbrication

of cultural and familial traditions through the father-son relationship before shifting to an exploration of the boy's nascent crush on another boy.

In a dreamy image, the boy and his crush, André, sit astride a large blue bird that carries them through the sky. The boys stare into each other's eyes, and the corresponding text reads: "My heart? / My heart zoomed like a bird the day we met." In subsequent images, the child recollects "what's in his heart."

When the text returns to the father and son relationship, the boy shares: "And so, one day, I asked Papi to help me sing my butterfly song, my serenade for a boy in town, for a boy bright brown, who smelled like fresh rain, wet earth, and lemonade." After André shares his feelings, his father is at first silent. He sighs before asking his son what song they should sing for his "friend." The child ignores the weight of the euphemism "friend" and explains that he wants a song about a boy who loves boys. The text reads: "Papi thought for a while, then, he thought a bit more, saying, let's make a new song, a great song, for your butterfly-garden-love-joy." Father and son spend days creating and practicing a song before driving to André's home, where the boy will serenade him as his father witnesses.

Both *Jerome by Heart* and *When We Love Someone We Sing to Them: Cuando Amamos Cantamos* allow their child protagonists to experience romantic desire, a representation that remains rare. In fact, when queer children are the focus of LGBTQ+ children's picture books, they are almost always represented as challenging regimes of gender normativity, which is why I devote two chapters to these representations. In pink boy texts as well as those representing nonbinary and transgender youth, questions of sexual desire and identity never surface, even as the threat of queer sexuality fuels stigma around nonnormative gender identities. These texts disrupt notions of childhood innocence, even as the most physical intimacy glimpsed is passionate hand-holding. The boys at the center of these sweet love stories desire, and their crushes expand queer possibilities for young readers.

Romancing the Reader

Throughout this chapter, I demonstrate that children's picture books can provide meaningful access points to queer desire. Whereas most pre-2010 books featuring lesbian and gay adults in love are focalized through child characters who are related to them, which I argue positions young readers as witnesses of queerness, not as themselves queer, the books identified in this chapter give young readers the opportunity to identify with queerness, even more, as queer. By romancing the reader, they position children to identify queer desire as itself possible and desirable. This is most clear in fairy tales but is also present in other picture books explored. In fact, books like *The Boy Who Cried Fabulous* and *Julián Is a Mermaid* claim pleasure itself for queerness. Roger, the protagonist of Newman's *The Boy Who Cried Fabulous*, inadvertently resists the social imperative to manage time for ultimate productivity, instead frolicking through parks and shops in a demonstration of pure joy. The title character in *Julián Is a Mermaid* identifies with a fantasy sea creature, although what that means remains ambiguous throughout the text. Other books, like *Odd Bird Out*, also explore the desirability of queerness by demonstrating that it is a powerful draw, even by those who disavow it most strongly.

Chapter Seven

Queer Histories

The Politics of Representing the Past

Nonfiction refers to truth-oriented texts that seek primarily to inform or instruct (Gerard). As Penny Colman writes: "Nonfiction is writing about reality (real people, places, events, ideas, feelings, things) in which nothing is made up" (260). Although the goal of nonfiction may be truth oriented, truths themselves, particularly historical truths, are multiple, fractured, and implicated in relations of power. This is not to suggest that no truth statements can be made about the past, or for that matter the present, but instead that perception inevitably plays a role in recording reality, and, because existing LGBTQ+ nonfiction children's picture book titles are so sparse, the danger of a single story is amplified (Adichie).

This chapter's central claim is that the histories on children's bookshelves represent versions of the past considered inheritable by a vast network of adult gatekeepers. These books archive historical actors and events that are deemed acceptable, and even necessary, to pass down to children, because of the realities, personal and collective, they memorialize. Until very recently, LGBTQ+ histories have been notably absent from children's bookshelves. This absence both reflected and reproduced stigma surrounding LGBTQ+ identities, cultures, and histories. As of early 2019, most nonfiction LGBTQ+ children's picture books were created by two authors: Rob Sanders and Gail E. Pitman. Sanders authored a biography of Harvey Milk and a history of the Stonewall riots.[1] Pitman's early nonfiction LGBTQ+ children's picture books were biographical, although they can also be read as cultural histories. One is about Gilbert Baker; the other is about Phyllis Lyon and Del Martin.

A related line of argument explored in this chapter suggests that the lack of nonfiction LGBTQ+ children's picture books available and accessible to young people makes it difficult for queer youth to imagine themselves as part of a transhistorical queer collective that has contributed in significant ways to local and national life by building communities, challenging unjust laws, demanding visibility, and creating vibrant cultures. This is exacerbated by the fact that most LGBTQ+ youth are isolated in cisgender heterosexual families that neither reflect nor support their experiences of gender and sexuality. An expanded archive of LGBTQ+ children's nonfiction could do important work helping young people understand themselves as part of an LGBTQ+ collective. Even more, incorporating LGBTQ+ nonfiction into school curriculum would demonstrate the specificity of queer experience to all students while also serving to construct a more nuanced and accurate picture of our shared history.

To represent queer realities is to gesture toward an experience beyond the individual and toward a collective, both material and imagined, that has most frequently been ignored in fictive LGBTQ+ children's picture books, which tend to focus on the family unit. This leads to a new question: what can nonfiction LGBTQ+ children's picture books do? I suggest that non-fiction LGBTQ+ children's picture books have the potential to go beyond promoting empathy to enabling and encouraging affective identifications across differences as well as inspiring collective action. By this I mean that nonfiction has the potential to facilitate understanding of and emotional connection with queer people, community, and experience. Furthermore, nonfiction content can foster critical awareness of oppressive social systems and prompt action. Throughout this chapter, I continue to frame my readings through critical optimism in order to explore the limits and possibilities of the existing archive.

Remembering Differently, Imaging Differently

Activist and scholar Charlene Carruthers's *Unapologetic: A Black, Queer, and Feminist Mandate for Radical Social Change* (2018) explores the importance of passing on radical histories to encourage the transformative thinking and action necessary for collective liberation. This text, more than any other, has influenced my feelings about the potential of nonfiction to inspire critical queer consciousness. Carruthers's book is one of several texts by queer scholars of color to politicize and mobilize hope as a strategy for social change (Muñoz; Chambers-Letson; Moore). Privileging hope over skepticism prompts several queer theorists of color to identify and strategize alternatives to present and historical social injustices, similarly to much recent work in the field of transgender studies. For Carruthers and others taking this approach, there is an understanding that the world can change because it must. Hope for these scholars isn't that of liberal progress narratives that assume the inevitability of positive social change while ignoring the role of collective action in creating it. Instead, a demand is placed on social agents acting in the present to make change happen, and the past is a resource.

Carruthers introduces the idea of a Black queer feminist (BQF) lens as a model to perceive unjust realities and enact justice-oriented change. She describes the BQF lens as "a political praxis (practice and theory) based in Black feminist and LGBTQ traditions and knowledge, through which people and groups see to bring their full selves into the process of dismantling all systems of oppression" (10). According to Carruthers, if we think and act through the intersectional model offered by the BQF lens, we can "effectively prioritize problems and methods that center historically marginalized people in our communities" (10). Centering the lived experience of marginalized people, perhaps marginalized "others," demands an acknowledgment of various modes of difference and a reckoning with complex systems of privilege, power, and oppression. My readings of the handful of nonfiction LGBTQ+ children's picture books that currently exist suggest that material histories of struggle as well as the internal diversity of the LGBTQ+ community are both obscured, which constrains readers' ability to understand the past in ways that could meaningfully contribute to imagining and enacting change in the present leading to a transformed future.

In my introduction, I discuss queer love as an affective identification with and investment in an "other." In chapter four, I read the creative and activist work of parent-advocates who are queered by affective investment in their queer children as an example of queer love. As seen in that chapter, most notably in Cheryl Kilodavis's *My Princess Boy*, love for the queer child can create a strong enough affective bond to trouble the distinction between self and other. I wonder at the possibility of imagining and enacting this affective investment in the "other" beyond the confines of the normative family, and I wonder about the role of culture in this project. Engaging literature seems like a possible mode of producing affective relations beyond the historical present as well as providing the ability to recognize the ghosts that continue to haunt it. I see nonfiction as particularly useful for queer youth, who are often unable to turn to family members for a sense of affirming and anchoring historical continuity or shared experiences of marginalization. Even more, histories of queer culture and queer resistance are essential to helping young queers imagine acceptance beyond acquiescence to cisgender heterosexual norms and inclusion in dominant institutions. However, the histories inherited in picture books must be as complex as the histories lived outside of them.

Carruthers gestures toward the political possibilities of expanded cultural archives when discussing the significance of including Black queer voices in the canon of Black radical literature to weave "a more complete story" about Black liberation. Although she is not considering children's literature specifically, the logic and significance of her claim are applicable to an argument for expanding queer representations in children's picture books (49). Carruthers suggests that studying Audre Lorde, Joseph Beam, and Lorraine Hansberry could change the contours of the thinkable (59). According to Carruthers, omitting Black queer people or obscuring queer specificity prevents an intersectional understanding of historical struggles and allows scholars and activists to refuse to acknowledge the complex organization and manifestation of power within and outside collectives. Even more, it fails to account for how gender and sexuality affect Black people, and limits the ability to identify injustice as well as to imagine and enact solutions. Carruthers connects expanding the Black radical tradition to developing the Black imagination, specifically the ability to imagine "alternative economics, alternative family structures, or something else entirely" (39). Carruthers passionately argues that envisioning and enacting a just future needs to account for the most vulnerable among us. In other words, we need to envision a world in which justice is extended to everyone.

My hope for nonfiction LGBTQ+ children's picture books mirrors my hope for LGBTQ+ children's picture books generally. I hope that representations of queerness will prompt critiques of heteronormative institutions that reproduce inequality, not toward the inclusion of queer subjects into existing social institutions, but toward new visions of what we mean by "the good life," how we understand and evaluate success, and how we relate to our many others. To that end, I'm particularly critical of representations and representational strategies in LGBTQ+ picture books that foreground the individual without paying significant attention to context or community, because these texts foreclose imaginative possibilities. Even more, focusing on individuals instead of communities, particularly community action, reproduces problematic liberal investments in the individual as an agent of free will, free thought, and free action.

I am also critical of picture books that create an opposition between the past and present. As Heather Love writes in *Feeling Backward: Loss and the Politics of Queer History*: "Backward feelings serve as an index of the ruined state of the social world; they indicate continuities between the bad gay past and the present; and they show up the inadequacy of queer narratives of progress. Most important, they teach us that we do not know what is good for politics" (27). As of early 2019, the small archive of nonfiction LGBTQ+ children's picture books all create a binary between "the bad gay past and the present." Although many substantial changes have indeed been made, these texts too often simplify struggle. There is no sense of continuity, but instead an awkward rupture between "then" and "now" that fails to account for the persistence of queer shame and the power of the sex-gender-sexuality system to oppress.

Inheritable Queer Histories

Published in 2017, Gayle E. Pitman's *When You Look Out the Window: How Phyllis Lyon and Del Martin Built a Community*, illustrated by Christopher Lyles, unfolds in the first-person plural, producing a sense of intimacy as protagonist-narrators Phyllis Lyon and Del Martin reflect on San Francisco's transformation into a LGBTQ+-affirming community. To track the city's transformation in time, Pitman takes readers on a queer tour of San Francisco's landmarks that can be seen from the couple's home. This technique could allow the narrative to develop as both an intimate personal story and a community history, but the text does not live up to this potential. Instead, by constructing the text as a reflection on progressive change, Pitman creates a binary between the "then" of a homophobic past and the "now" of a transformed present that problematically excludes the work of community building and community struggle required for the social transformation it celebrates. Moreover, by focusing on a couple in the private sphere of the home, queer community and public culture are downplayed.

The book opens with an image of a young Lyon and Martin, arms around each other, with the Golden Gate Bridge in the background. The image locates them in love and in San Francisco. On the next page, the young couple are seen in their newly purchased home as they peer out their window while holding hands. They critique the imperative that lesbian love must remain private and lament the lack of community they experience in San Francisco. Pitman writes: "We saw, quiet streets. / Doors tightly shut. / So many women / who didn't have rights." The critique reads as ironic, since the queer utopia the text presents is centered on the home and the lesbian couple.

The next page further develops a critique of "old" San Francisco, focusing on the couple's social isolation and introducing their experience of homophobia. The couple recall what they saw when they left the privacy and security of their home: "People who were afraid of us. / People who didn't think we should love each other. / No feeling of community." The associated illustration depicts five people whose expressions include horror, disgust, and anger at the sight of a lesbian couple. The use of past tense to describe homophobia and lack of community frames time oppositionally, a then and a now to be traversed in the turn of a page.

In fact, the next illustration does just that. The two-page spread offers readers a bird's eye view of the city that provides a sense of expansiveness in contradistinction to the busy San Francisco street that greeted the lesbian couple in the previous illustration. Although the spread portrays space, it represents a temporal crossing between San Francisco's homophobic past and its queer-affirming present. The sentence "So we worked to change that" accompanies the image, gesturing toward a history of collective struggle and activism that isn't visually represented or described in the text. Instead, progress appears to be something that occurs naturally as time passes. Image and text contradict each other, as confused as the representational slippage between space and time.

The book ends with images of "new" San Francisco—a city decorated with rainbows, a church that welcomes everyone, and shopping queer couples. Pitman closes the text: "We see a big rainbow community." Again, image and text tell different stories as the spectacle of rainbow objects stand in for actual community. Queerness appears to be commodified, packaged, and sold. Rainbows identify spaces that welcome queers without depicting queer cultural specificity or community. Instead, queer couples have been accepted into society and can shop and attend church alone or in pairs.

Young readers asked to explain who Lyon and Martin are and what important contributions they made to society—in other words, why they were significant enough figures to warrant a quasi-biography—would be hard pressed to think of anything to say. There is, however, detailed back matter. In contradistinction to the picture book, Pitman's "Reading Guide" is rich with historical detail and specific references to time. The purchase date of the couple's home is referenced as 1953, and their participation in the 1955 founding of Daughters of Bilitis (DOB) as well as the 1966 founding of the National Organization for Women (NOW) are discussed. In this case, the text's back matter does not supplement the historical tale; it is the only place history makes an appearance. In Pitman's "Note to Parents, Caregivers, and Educators" she writes: "Children from historically marginalized groups don't always see positive and empowering images of themselves in books or other forms of media, and their histories aren't always well represented in school materials." Although Pitman has created a positive image of lesbians and introduced children to homophobia, the text doesn't provide readers with access points to identify with the narrators or encourage them to develop an understanding of homophobia, community, or transformative action.

Pitman continues to create problematic binaries in her 2018 picture book *Sewing the Rainbow: The Story of Gilbert Baker*. This book, which is beautifully illustrated by Holly Clifton-Brown, explores the life of Gilbert Baker. Pitman introduces Baker to readers when he is a child, and many young readers will likely identify with him as a result of this strategy. At the start of the book, a young proto-gay Gilbert Baker negotiates "gray and dull and flat" Kansas. Kansas is represented as boring and uninspiring, a decidedly unqueer geographical site for such a creative child to call home. However, even in the seemingly straightest of states, Baker finds creative inspiration. His grandmother's love of fashion encourages his own, and he creates "beautiful gowns and costumes." Baker's father doesn't approve of his predilection for design and is depicted angrily tearing up Baker's sketchbook. Pitman describes young Baker's reaction to his father's outburst, suggesting that without his art Baker's "colorful, sparkly glittery personality started to fade." Young Baker "became gray and dull and flat, just like the Kansas landscape." Pitman suggests that Baker cannot be himself in Kansas, where he is instead stifled by the state's provincialism and his father's toxic masculinity.

In fact, Baker's geographic location is emphasized throughout the text, eventually producing a binary between the "there" of Kansas that young Baker suffers through and the "here" of San Francisco where adult Baker flourishes. The spatial opposition between Kansas and San Francisco can be mapped onto a temporal opposition between the "then" of childhood as well as the "then" of the "bad gay past" and the "now" of adulthood with movement across time and space represented as progress à la the It Gets Better Project ("It Gets Better").

Within the text's reality, young Baker lacks agency and mobility. He envisions adulthood as a threshold he will cross into freedom. Ironically, although Baker imagines choice and control as features of adulthood, when he turned eighteen, he "received a letter that knocked every last bit of sparkle out of him." Details of the letter are not revealed, but the next page depicts Baker in a military uniform doing push-ups. The reader with historical competency can contextualize Baker's personal life within a larger national framework, identifying this as the Vietnam War and understanding that Baker was drafted. Of course, this troubles the idea of agency as a feature of adulthood, since Baker's movements and actions are circumscribed by the state when he turns eighteen years old.

Baker's time in the military appears to be short-lived. Because of his inaction, specifically his refusal to shoot a gun, "they sent him to San Francisco, where he would never have to pick up a gun again." Adult Baker is again positioned in a passive role. He ends up in San Francisco not by choice but because "they" sent him there. Even more, Baker appears to be transformed by San Francisco. He experiences a rebirth that is a reversion to the person he was before his father tore up his sketchpad, before the United States drafted him to fight in a war. Pitman writes: "He could be his colorful, sparkly, glittery self." The text is accompanied with an image of Baker standing near the Golden Gate Bridge, smiling widely as confetti rains down on him, a queer baptism.

Although Kansas represents a time and place Baker dreamed of escaping, traces of his time there also inspire him once he is in San Francisco. Pitman writes: "He thought about his grandmother's clothing store. / He thought about the drawings his father tore up. / And he realized he wanted all of that back." Baker put his skill as a designer and tailor to use creating fashions for queer cultural figures as well as by participating in community building and political projects in San Francisco. For instance, he created banners for political protests and "was making the city more and more colorful by the day."

Gilbert is finally represented as putting things into the world, although the community he helped create isn't present in the text. In fact, most illustrations depict Baker by himself, visually emphasizing the individual, much as Pitman's earlier biography emphasizes the queer couple over queer community.

Of course, as the title suggests, this is a book not only about Gilbert Baker but also about queer history, specifically the creation of the rainbow flag. Details surrounding the creation of the flag are not given full expression. Instead, a two-page spread depicts Baker sitting comfortably in a chair across from a man referred to as "his friend." The man is shown smiling as Baker holds up a vertical rectangle with eight striped color blocks—a prototype of the Pride flag. Text on the facing page identifies Baker's friend as a man named Harvey, and the culturally competent reader will know that "Harvey" is Harvey Milk. It is Harvey who suggests the need for a symbol to unite the gay and lesbian community under a sign of Pride. This gestures toward collaboration while maintaining the focus on Baker found throughout the text.

After the two friends' brief exchange, Baker is portrayed creating what becomes the rainbow flag. Although the narrative states that a group of friends helped Baker create the flag, this is not depicted in illustrations, which continue to show Gilbert alone cutting, dyeing, and sewing two flags. This is a missed opportunity to visually represent the community discussed throughout both of Pitman's biographies but present in neither.

In fact, when community is present in *Sewing the Rainbow: The Story of Gilbert Baker*, it is described as a "crowd" that stands in opposition to and judgment of the text's protagonist. After Gilbert completes his project, he prepares to display the flags. Pitman writes: "The big day arrived. A crowd gathered around City Hall. Gilbert held his breath. Would people understand his flags?" The use of the singular possessive pronoun "his" depicts the flag less as a community project and community symbol and more as a personal creation, as does the visual focus on Gilbert. The "community" is a crowd of people that Gilbert is literally and figuratively apart from. The accompanying image is of a white building with a dome shaped roof. A group is shown with their heads turned toward the building on which the flags are displayed. The image on the next page zooms in on a small, racially diverse "crowd" of eight people standing under the flags as they blow in the breeze.

The text concludes with a two-page spread of Gilbert wearing a paper crown underneath the rainbow flag. Pitman writes: "Today, the rainbow flag is everywhere. Even in the small town in Kansas where Gilbert grew up. /

Whenever you see a rainbow flag, you'll know that it's okay to be your colorful, sparkly, glittery self." As in Pitman's previous biography, it is the Pride flag that will welcome queers and empower them to be themselves, not a collective of queers struggling against oppressive gender and sexual norms. Community is not represented by the symbol; it is subsumed under the symbol. Even more, this text, like Pitman's previous one, represents the past and present oppositionally, disallowing a sense of continuity and collectivity.

In both of Pitman's books, instead of complementing each other, image and text often appear to be telling different stories. Even more, queer community is thematized in both books, but it is never presented within the text. Instead, it is an idea that is gestured toward. Pitman's picture books don't encourage young readers to imagine themselves as part of a collective. Neither do they encourage queer subjectivity formation, identification with shared or similar experiences and desires. Instead of showing and sharing the community building that Gilbert Baker, Phyllis Lyon, and Del Martin participated in, a homophobic "before" and queer-affirming "after" are represented with the collective struggle and action that occurred in between largely left out of both picture books.

Rob Sanders's *Pride: The Story of Harvey Milk and the Rainbow Flag* (2018), published the same year as Pitman's biography of Gilbert Baker, tells the story of the Pride flag through Harvey Milk's role in its creation. Illustrated by Steven Salerno, the relationship between image and text works to produce a story that reads as both personal and community history. Salerno illustrates the book with a touch of whimsy. It begins with a barefoot Harvey Milk lying on a green paisley background that's reminiscent of grass but clearly artificial. The world is visually positioned at his feet. The text reads: "Harvey Milk was an ordinary man, but he had an extraordinary dream. That dream would change history." Milk's dream, that "he and his friends would be treated like everyone else," is visually represented through an image of two white men with wavy brown hair sharing a two-seater bike with a "Just Married" banner floating behind them. Representing being "treated like everyone else" through access to marriage seems like an anachronistic choice, since it was decades before white, middle-class gays and lesbians galvanized behind the single issue. Just as the focus on marriage gestures toward the future, characterizing Milk as a dreamer conjures associations with Martin Luther King Jr. and gestures toward the past while bringing gay rights activism into conversation with civil rights activism. This is a

Figure 16 *Pride: The Story of Harvey Milk and the Rainbow Flag* (2018), written by Rob Sanders, illustrated by Steven Salerno, published by Penguin Random House

generative slippage that doesn't so much collapse time and identity-based differences as subtly bring to light their affinities.

Throughout the book, Sanders emphasizes that Milk sought to change laws by going into politics and motivating his community to demand change. He is a leader, not a loner. Even more, the homophobia experienced and challenged is visually present in Salerno's illustrations, which depict signs with phrases including: "Gays Must Go" and "God Says No." By presenting homophobia, a reality impossible to avoid in a biography of Milk, Sanders thematizes stigma without introducing feelings of shame. In fact, although Sanders creates an affectively complex text likely to produce feelings of sadness, discomfort, or even anger, he avoids depictions of shame, replacing shame with a story of queer resilience.

It is in his role as an activist and community builder that Milk begins to consider the need for a symbol that will unite the queer community during future marches. A pensive Milk is depicted standing alone in a sea of symbols that include peace signs and recycling signs. The next two-page spread introduces Milk's friend Gilbert Baker, who is depicted at a sewing machine working on a rainbow flag. Unlike in Pitman's version, three people are shown in the background cutting and dyeing cloth. It is a subtle but significant difference from the focus on individual actors and actions foregrounded in Pitman's biography of Gilbert Baker.

The next two-page spread shows the finished project flowing across a cityscape. Milk is illustrated in the left corner, hands raised, smiling in front of street signs that locate him at the intersection of Castro and Market Streets. The text reads: "On June 25, 1978, when it was time for the march, a breeze stirred in San Francisco." Small details like marking time and space provide a sense of history lacking in Pitman's version of the text. Even more, Sanders represents the unveiling of the Pride flag as part of a larger community event, whereas Pitman describes it as one man's moment to shine. Here the flag unites a community; there the flag was an individual achievement to be judged by a crowd.

The representation of the march as a community event continues in the next two-page spread, which shows a community of queers marching behind Harvey as he leads them through the streets of San Francisco under the unifying banner of the rainbow flag. Although Harvey is leading, the collective is present in word and image. Sanders writes: "Harvey and the people asked for equality. / They asked to be treated like everyone else. / They asked to live and love as they pleased. / They hoped the march would make a difference." Words like "the people" and "they" remind the reader that social action must be collective action to be successful action.

The tone of the text soon changes from one of celebration to one of sorrow. A newspaper with the headline "Moscone, Milk Killed" leaps from a two-page spread. The dates and text of the paper are illegible, but the image still serves as a reminder that this is nonfiction, historical fact, a point reiterated by the corresponding text, which reads: "Five months later—on the morning of November 27, 1978—Harvey and the mayor of San Francisco, George Moscone, were assassinated. Their lives were taken by a man who did not think like Harvey, or feel like him, or love like him." Sanders is not reticent in his representation of homophobic violence.[2] The reality that people have been and can be murdered for challenging gender and sexual norms, as well as for demanding social change, is a painful one. Sanders's depiction allows readers to feel a sense of loss, which effectively collapses time, encouraging "backward feelings."

The subsequent two-page spread depicts a community in mourning walking through the streets of San Francisco while carrying candles to honor Milk. The mood is contemplative. Although a grieving community is depicted, the collective feeling of loss emphasizes the gains made by Milk as a community builder. The queer collective is his legacy. This is reiterated on the next two-page spread, which depicts rainbow flags spelling the word *hope*. Complementary text reads: "More rainbow flags were created. / . . . / More and more people began to think of the flag as their flag. / And they began to feel pride. / They began to feel hope." Several other depictions of the Pride flag are shown, demonstrating that Milk's legacy of community building and community activism lives on, at least symbolically.

Gilbert Baker is reintroduced as the story flashes forward to 1994, the year he redesigned the Pride flag with six instead of eight stripes. Other images depict the spatial and temporal reach of Milk's legacy. For instance, one image shows the rainbow flag's global reach, another depicts the White House lit up in the colors of the rainbow flag on June 26, 2015, again subtly linking liberation and marriage. The book ends with Milk, sporting a rainbow tie and waving a rainbow flag, dressed up, megaphone at his hip, against a paisley green background like the one in the book's opening image. However, unlike the opening image, which depicts Milk as a dreamer with his eyes closed, here his eyes are wide open. The text reads: "Equality. / Pride.

/ Hope. / Love. / Harvey's dream / became a flag for all of us." Harvey, the individual, the dreamer, the leader, frames the story, but his isn't the whole story. This fact-heavy picture book successfully works as a biography and a community history.

The rainbow flag as a sign of pride has a forty-year history, but it is not a history without internal conflict. In fact, many queers have been very critical of the false universality it represents as well as issues of transphobia and racism within the LGBTQ+ community obscured under the unifying symbol of the rainbow. In 2018, Daniel Quasar redesigned the Pride flag and created a Kickstarter campaign to offset production costs. Quasar's version is deliberately inclusive of transgender and other marginalized members of the LGBTQ+ community (Quasar). Quasar describes the symbolism of this updated flag: "The trans flag and marginalized community stripes were shifted to the Hoist of the flag and given a new arrow shape. The arrow points to the right to show forward movement, while being along the left edge shows that progress still needs to be made." Quasar's flag isn't the first update; brown and black stripes were added to symbolize racial inclusion around 2017 in Philadelphia as a response to racism in gay bars, and there are likely other iterations used in various localities (Abad-Santos). Importantly, neither Pitman nor Sanders explores critiques of the Pride flag.

I appreciate the challenge of shifting focus from the individual to the collective as well as creating accessible and engaging nonfiction picture books for children. I think Sanders does a very good job responding to both difficulties. His more recent children's picture book, *Stonewall: A Building. An Uprising. A Revolution.* (2019), represents the Stonewall riots of 1969. Jamey Christoph illustrates the text with atmospheric images that recall the grit of New York and capture a sense of possibility and danger with thoughtful use of color throughout. The story is told from the point of view of the Stonewall Inn itself à la *If These Walls Could Talk* (Cher and Savoca). It doesn't begin in 1969, but instead in the 1840s, when the inn was built as two stables used to board horses. The inn narrates its story in the first-person plural even after the stables are converted to one building in the 1930s. In one two-page spread, the inn, then called Bonnie's Stone Wall Restaurant, opens its doors to a group of patrons, including Black customers. Poets and jazz musicians are depicted in the 1950s, highlighting the inn's changing patrons and purposes.

The narrative slows and lingers on the 1960s, particularly 1967, when the Stonewall Inn received its current name and its patrons became overwhelmingly queer. One two-page spread portrays nightlife inside the inn. Three friends—two white and masculine presenting, one Black and feminine presenting—are at the center of the image. To their left, two white men talk. To their right, a gay couple dances. Sanders writes: "Women and men, young and old, teenagers, transgender people, drag queens, veterans, businesspeople, students, people of different colors, religions, and cultures, gathered, chatted, laughed, and danced under one roof." The inn, like the Pride flag, appears to envelop a queer collective. It unites disparate queers under one roof as the Pride flag unites them under one symbol.

Children's literature scholar Laura Jimenez is critical of the picture book, particularly Jamey Christoph's illustrations, which she claims enforce a "strict gender binary. The men are masculine appearing in a sort of Abercrombie & Fitch metro-sexual way, whereas the women remind me of Marlo Thomas from *That Girl!*" (L. Jimenez, "Erasure by Any Other Name"). Jimenez argues that Sanders and Christoph's representational practices "actively erase the contributions of people of color, trans, bi, butch and femme in favor of a more palatable White, heteronormative mimicry" (L. Jimenez, "Erasure by Any Other Name"). I don't think this critique is entirely correct. Many of the images throughout the text depict racially diverse subjects. Additionally, in the two-page spread referenced above, the feminine-presenting Black character is quite a bit taller than the two masculine-presenting characters and could be read as a drag queen, especially because of the hyperfemininity performed relative to other characters in the spread. I do agree that most characters appear to be cisgender. I agree that more could have been done to represent queer genders, but I wouldn't go so far as to label the book's visual representations as "heteronormative mimicry."

I find other issues more problematic. I especially find the focalization of the text through the Stonewall Inn limiting. For instance, one two-page spread depicts the arrest of two feminine characters and one masculine character. A couple of police officers frame them, one with his baton drawn, which introduces the specter of violence to the text without depicting it outright. The Stonewall Inn narrates: "After each raid, those who hadn't been arrested left quietly, angrily, disappearing into the darkness. We stood tall and kept opening our doors. People kept coming." Although very creative, this narrative strategy weakens the text's ability to encourage identification with a queer collective. The inn witnesses its queer patrons' anger at injustice but feels nothing itself. As a result, an affective connection to queer trauma, queer history, and queer community isn't likely. Readers, like the inn, are witnesses.

Even more, by focalizing the story through the inn, a contested history lived by variously positioned subjects is reduced to a single story delivered with a false sense of omnipresence and objectivity. The inn simply observes. This is particularly problematic because the history represented, the history of the Stonewall Inn uprising, is a challenging and a challenged one. For instance, a recent article in *Perspectives on History: The News Magazine of the American Historical Association* noted: "With little hard evidence and numerous firsthand accounts—many of which contradict one another—the messy events at Stonewall and the myths it generated have become a matter of intense debate among historians and other scholars of the past" (Mitchell). It may have been interesting to incorporate shifting focalizers who experience queer vulnerability and by extension the riots differently.

Prior to the 1969 uprising, police raided the inn on multiple occasions, harassing, arresting, and otherwise terrorizing its customers. On June 28, 1969, the inn's patrons fought back. In the first image of the riot, a dozen people are depicted outside the inn as a police officer guides a short-haired woman into a police car. By the next page, the crowd has grown exponentially as the inn's queer patrons form a unified front. Only a few of the patrons' faces are depicted in detail, but each represents a different emotion, from anger to surprise. No clear displays of violence are depicted, although Sanders does make it apparent that the riots lasted "on and off for several days and nights." They are depicted across a set of three two-page spreads. Christoph's illustrations show a larger crowd on subsequent nights. The steely blue images are accompanied by text that acknowledges the "rage" of protestors and their defiant screams that become demands for freedom from police brutality. In the last image of the riot, Sanders writes: "A new day was dawning for the gay rights movement.")

The next two-page spread fast-forwards a full year to June 28, 1970. Instead of a dark, moody sky, police in riot gear, and fed-up protestors, the two-page spread shows a sunny sky and smiling crowd under a banner reading "Christopher Street Gay Liberation Day 1970." The shift from night to day symbolizes a cultural transformation in queer visibility as the LGBTQ+ community takes to the streets in broad daylight instead of slinking into the Stonewall Inn under the cover of night. Sanders's description of marchers repeats the language previously used to describe the inn's patrons, with one notable exception: "At first, hundreds marched. Then thousands of women and men, young and old, teenagers, transgender people, drag queens, veterans, businesspeople, students, people of different colors, religions, and cultures, *and* their friends and families joined to parade through the streets of New York City." Here, Sanders intimates another important shift. Queers have come out and come into the supportive arms of family and friends willing to march with them. Although some could argue that this is a too generous simplification, it doesn't need to represent a universally experienced shift to acceptance to correctly capture a significant cultural transformation in the publicness and acceptance of queer identities.

Like the handful of other nonfiction LGBTQ+ children's picture books available, this one ends in the present. The Stonewall Inn is depicted with a neon light in its window and a rainbow flag over its front door, rendering queerness visible under the sun. Text on the facing page reads: "Many things *are* different now. / Some things *have* changed. Even some laws have changed. / Now two men who love each other, or two women who love each other, can marry." Marriage is the only concrete example of change offered in the text, which harkens to Sanders's biography of Milk, whose vision of equality is anachronistically linked to marriage. Additionally, Sanders notes that Pride parades are still celebrated in June, linking the past to the present. It is noted that these parades "celebrate freedom" and "celebrate equality." This, disappointingly, demands nothing of readers. Equality, which is conflated with marriage, has been achieved. Although Sanders implies that there is more work to be done when he writes that "some" things have changed, he does not prompt his reader to identify what change is needed.

Like other examples of queer historical nonfiction children's picture books discussed, this text contains back matter, including "The History of the Stonewall Inn," pictures, and even an interview with a participant. In fact, it is the interview that I found most telling. In his story, Sanders paints a picture of surface-level inclusivity, a melting pot of queers, but his interview with Martin Boyce, an LGBTQ+ activist and participant in the uprising, reveals far more internal divisions within the queer community than depicted in the picture book. Sanders asks Boyce if he understood he was making history when he joined the Stonewall Inn uprising. Boyce's response illustrates the not-so-subtle privileging of gay men in the space: "It's also important to note the role of lesbians that night. It was not their bar, but they were with us." Far from melting into a queer mélange, lesbians are othered, a "them," to the gay "our" that Boyce uses to casually claim ownership over the inn and, even more, the movement. Far from begrudging him his casual possessiveness, I wish Sanders had teased division through the text to highlight the incommensurability of queer identities (Muñoz).

The Future of Queer History

The transformative potential of nonfiction LGBTQ+ children's picture books published in and before early 2019 is limited by investments in liberal ideals of equality before the law, most often represented through marriage equality. Even more, significant embodied differences within the LGBTQ+ community are ignored, and the presence of various markers of privilege—particularly cisgender, male, white, and middle-class identities and embodiments—are unexplored. Additionally, the lackluster representation of actual queer communities in their specificity constrains the transformative potential of these texts.

The dangers of a single story are very real when the archive of representations available number so few. That is, of course, not the fault of Pitman and Sanders, whose work makes an important contribution to the field of LGBTQ+ children's picture books. Building a rich bookshelf of nonfiction LGBTQ+ children's picture books can play a significant role in helping young people develop queer consciousness. I think it is possible to imagine becoming queer as a project in empathy and understanding that forces us to rethink attachments to oppressive ideas, identities, and institutions that reproduce oppression, indignity, and injustice for a newly conceptualized all of us. History can be a resource, but the scant queer histories children are currently inheriting is not.

There is reason for optimism. Sanders and Pitman have only very recently begun publishing nonfiction LGBTQ+ children's picture books, and texts are in the works. Little Bee Books, an imprint of Simon and Schuster, is coming out with a board book series marketed as helping parents "celebrate the accomplishments of LGBTQ heroes and introduce their little ones to the trailblazers who have shaped our world" (Simon and Schuster). The first three biographies released are of lesbian entertainer Ellen DeGeneres, gay political figure Harvey Milk, and African American, gay drag queen RuPaul Charles. RuPaul and DeGeneres are each activists and pioneers of LGBTQ+

representations who certainly deserve to be recognized for their contributions to LGBTQ+ visibility. In addition to this emerging collection of board books for very young children, Joy Michael Ellison, an activist, educator, and scholar, has authored a biography about transgender activists Marsha Johnson and Sylvia Rivera called *Sylvia and Marsha Start a Revolution!* (2021), which is illustrated by Teshika Silver. Other post-2020 biographies of transgender historical figures include *Were I Not a Girl: The Inspiring and True Story of Dr. James Barry* (2020) by Lisa Robinson and Lauren Simkin Berke and *The Fighting Infantryman: The Story of Albert D. J. Cashier, Transgender Civil War Soldier* (2020), written by Rob Sanders and illustrated by Nabi H. Ali. Like other subfields of LGBTQ+ children's picture books, I have every reason to suspect the quantity and quality of LGBTQ+ nonfiction children's picture books will expand, providing readers with rich opportunities to develop knowledge, empathy, and points of identifications with historical and contemporary queer realities.

Concluding Thoughts

In many ways I recognize that this book, even at its conclusion, is just an introduction to an archive. There is so much work to do. I've traced the historical shift from queer silences to queer stories, arguing that we should take the myriad picture books currently available seriously as worldmaking projects and historical archives. Importantly, this genealogy of LGBTQ+ children's picture books does not reveal linear progression toward an abundance of queerness; instead, representational shifts follow larger sociocultural transformations in the meaning made of gender and sexual identities, experiences, and communities. By cataloguing and describing texts, a primary goal of this project, trends emerge, and those trends are themselves stories. Some of these trends are subtle—for instance, the coding of queer adult relationships through the word *friend*, the appearance and disappearance of picture books about HIV/AIDS, the formalization and legalization of gay and lesbian marriages, and the depiction of children as agents of desire with self-knowledge. There are many opportunities to dive deeper into specific time periods, representations, and tropes.

One of my principal motivations in writing this book has been pushing back against dismissive readings of LGBTQ+ children's picture books as homonormative, assimilationist, and undelightful (Ford; Lester; Huskey; Taylor). The picture books in this archive are a significant part of children's literary and cultural history, as well as LGBTQ+ history, that provide essential pathways to queer visibility. Beyond historical archives, with value because of the pasts they reflect, many of the picture books in my archive are important worldmaking projects that challenge an oppressive sex-gender-sexuality system, especially the role of culture in normalizing gender- and sexual-role expectations, expressions, and identifications.

This brings me to my interpretive reading of LGBTQ+ children's picture books through the lens of critical optimism. I have been able to account for legitimate critiques of homonormativity and the limited transformative potential of most existing children's picture books, while also arguing that explicit LGBTQ+ representations do the radical work of disrupting the ubiquity of cisgender heterosexual children's culture. By accounting for the meaningful cultural work LGBTQ+ children's picture books accomplish, one can produce more nuanced readings, readings that account for multiple scenes of cultural politics, and celebrate the ripples that help change the tide.

I recognize that several areas remain underexplored in this book. In fact, as I complete final revisions in spring 2021, I am working with a wonderful group of scholars on an edited collection about LGBTQ+ children's picture books. These scholars take up notable absences in my project, including 1) critical analysis of nonhuman characters, 2) transgender and nonbinary parents, 3) religion and ritual, 4) the lack of authentic Black queer representation, 5) gay sex, and 6) drag queens. Other contributions dive deeper into areas explored, including 1) child agency, 2) marriage equality, 3) transgender youth, 4) queer exceptionalism, and 5) LGBTQ+ nonfiction. I see this project as an exciting collaboration among scholars similarly invested in LGBTQ+ studies and children's literature. I am particularly enthusiastic about the collection, since it will provide researchers the opportunity to examine very recent LGBTQ+ children's picture books that are unaccounted for in this book.

Appendix A: Jane Severance

The following excerpt is from an email correspondence with Jane Severance that took place on August 6, 2018.

When I decided I wanted to write a children's book featuring a lesbian mother I was very young—only a few years out of high school. I was heavily involved in the women's/lesbian movement, mostly concentrated on working at Woman to Woman Bookstore in Denver. This was a time period where suddenly a number of women's/lesbian presses sprung up and began putting out books such as *Rubyfruit Jungle*, *The Cook and the Carpenter*, and *You Can Have It When I'm Done with It*. Some were adult presses, but there were also a few small presses printing books for children. We were at the height of great change and parents were looking for books showing children with different families, children making nontraditional choices and being supported for making those choices and even books showing adults in unexpected roles. For example, one of Lollipop's books, which were really more like pamphlets, was the story of a farmer who cared for a sheep, sheared it and then knitted a warm sweater from the wool. The twist? The farmer was a woman. This probably doesn't seem like such a big deal to you, but at the time I had never seen a picture book in which a woman was called a farmer. As opposed to a farm woman. I had seen plenty of women in aprons feeding the chickens and hanging up wash. They were always secondary characters and always the real farmer's wife.

I have gotten a lot of flack because I showed a lesbian family in a "negative" way—the mother was breaking up with her partner. (Who she would have called "her lover." We were a long way from partner.) Again, you must understand the time in which I was living. Now it is common for a lesbian or lesbians to choose to have children—at the time I wrote Megan I did not know one single lesbian who had a planned child. Everyone who I knew who had children, and there weren't a lot, had them from a previous marriage to a man. I worked with kids and liked kids in the work setting, but I couldn't imagine anything worse than having one. It would have totally cramped my style. I wanted to have lots of sex with lots of women and I avoided women with children like the plague. It was, in fact, as if they had the plague. I didn't see a lot of support for lesbians with children in the community in which I lived at the time. There was always childcare at concerts and events, but I didn't see it going much further than that. It led to a vicious spiral—the lesbian mothers I saw were generally not supported, which meant they couldn't always make good parenting choices (such as getting a babysitter rather than bringing children to parties where there was alcohol and drugs). The mothers were usually poor, because we all were poor, but it's a lot easier to live in one room with forty dollars of food stamps when you don't have kids. Poor can also lead to bad choices out of desperation. For example, several times when I offered to babysit, the mother and her girlfriend just disappeared, and an overnight commitment turned into several days. I look back now and realize that those women, who were mostly not much older than me, just kind of melted down because they hadn't had an opportunity to get away from their child (often an infant) for weeks. They hadn't slept through the night for months. But because they had been unable to express their need to me (who was probably very superior about the choices I had made, which did not include sleeping with men) what ended up was me being furious and spreading the news so that no one in my house would babysit again. Which meant bad choices about bringing kids to parties or leaving them home alone, which led to kids who were pretty unlikeable. So when I needed a little story to hang my book on, I chose breaking up. We write about what we see. I couldn't write about Pridefest or anything like that. There was no Pridefest.

Additionally, I was getting a degree in Early Childhood Education, which meant I had taken classes in Children's Literature, where one of the hot topics was books showing children of divorce. So I kind of thought I'd kill two birds with one stone. As I mentioned, this was a time of change in children's books, in mainstream literature as well as in small presses. Now days you see children's books covering all kinds of children and all kinds of families. But

I remember the project I did for my Children's Lit class. I went to the library and went through the stacks and found between ten or fifteen picture books that showed illustrations of Black children. I brought them to class and made a display. I didn't even write about them. The fact that I had found them at all was unique enough to make the project stand on its own.

The wretched parenting that I saw came from this combination of factors. Children with alcoholic or mentally ill lesbian moms who didn't know how to get help and were estranged from a family that might otherwise have helped them. Children whose mothers chose partners who resented them. Children whose mothers were scrambling so hard just to survive that there wasn't a lot of time for anything else. Or children whose mothers were attempting to raise them outside patriarchal rules in experiments that didn't work so well. Like, they had decided that their children were to be treated like adults, no rules, no bedtime, no respect for adults. Which created a lot of kids who nobody liked. And when nobody likes you, well, that just makes things more difficult for everyone.

I knew one or two mothers who dragged their kids everywhere with them, including late night parties where there was drinking and drugging. We were raising each other, remember? Unless you had family in town—and most of the young lesbians I know had moved to be away from family for reasons of lesbianism—these women didn't have babysitters or money to pay babysitters.

The one child who I saw who was truly being raised in a caring, communal situation was being raised that way because his mother gave him away. She decided she was tired of taking care of a five-year-old, and four complete strangers stepped in to keep him from going into a foster home. Do I think there were great lesbian mothers during that time? You betcha. Were you a lesbian mom who did a great job? Thank you—it must have been hard, and you must have made a lot of sacrifice. I wish I could have known you. If I did know you and blew you off because you had kids, I'm sorry.

Appendix B: Daniel Haack

The following excerpt is from an email correspondence with Daniel Haack that took place on June 6, 2019.

Why do you write books that explicitly represent LGBTQ characters and experiences?
I've worked in children's media (TV, digital video and apps) for several years and received my master's degree in education, so I'm cognizant of the power that media, including literature, can have on shaping a young person's worldview and beliefs. In many ways, children's media is the final frontier for LGBTQ representation. My own titles have been challenged at libraries and schools, and there's a concern that LGBTQ portrayals may be too mature for kids or alienating to certain audiences. However, by erasing LGBTQ people from our stories, we are essentially communicating the message that there's something shameful about it all. The publishing industry has been a bit more progressive in this space than film or television (among many reasons, it has a lower barrier of entry and financial success), and so there's a greater opportunity there for offering rich, interesting LGBTQ characters for children.

I think it's just as important to offer these representations to children who, for example, have two dads or two moms as it is for the many kids who have little or no LGBTQ exposure in their lives. Approaching it in a matter-of-fact way helps kids understand and appreciate both our similarities and differences, which I hope extends beyond sexual orientation to also include myriad identities and communities.

In particular, my focus has been on telling stories about LGBTQ people who take on traditionally "heroic" roles, while also allowing them to be romantic leads in a supportive and welcoming environment. I prefer writing human characters, as research suggests these are more relatable and resonant for young readers than anthropomorphic characters.

Appendix C: Archive of LGBTQ+ Children's Picture Books (1991-2018)

The following tables organize my archive chronologically by decade. I provide information about authors, illustrators, and publishers. Additionally, I identify central tropes and themes. Finally, I include notes on race and ethnicity as well as whether characters are human or animal.

I include this to aid future researchers and educators as well as to help readers visualize the data I've collected about LGBTQ+ children's picture books.

Please, note: this table is not exhaustive. It includes titles I was able to identify and access.

TABLE A: 1970–1979

Title	Author	Illustrator	Year	Publisher	Tropes/ Themes	Race/Ethnicity/ Nonhuman
William's Doll	Charlotte Zolotow	William Pène du Bois	1972	Harper and Row, Publishers	Sissy boy; single father	All white
Exactly Like Me	Lynn Phillips	Lynn Phillips	1972	Lollipop Power Inc.	Tomboy	Primarily white
Nice Little Girls	Elizabeth Levy	Mordicai Gerstein	1974	Delacorte Press	Tomboy	Primarily white
X: A Fabulous Child's Story	Lois Gould	Jacqueline Chwast	1978	Daughters Publishing Company	Nonbinary	Primarily white
When Megan Went Away	Jane Severance	Tea Schook	1979	Lollipop Power Inc.	Lesbian parents; divorce	All white
Oliver Button Is a Sissy	Tomie dePaola	Tomie dePaola	1979	Voyager Books, Harcourt Brace and Company	Sissy boy; queer exceptionalism	All white
Jesse's Dream Skirt	Bruce Mack	Marian Buchanan	1979	Lollipop Power Inc.	Boy-meets-skirt; single mother	Primarily white

TABLE B: 1980–1989

Title	Author	Illustrator	Year	Publisher	Tropes/ Themes	Race/Ethnicity/ Nonhuman
Lots of Mommies	Jane Severance	Jan Jones	1983	Lollipop Power Inc.	Communal living; lesbian parenting; gender roles	Multiracial family
Tough Eddie	Elizabeth Winthrop	Lillian Hoban	1985	E. P. Dutton	Sissy boy	All white
Jenny Lived with Eric and Martine	Susanne Bösche Louis Mackay (translator)	Andreas Hansen	1987	Gay Men's Press	Gay parents; some homophobia	All white
The Boy Toy	Phyllis Hacken Johnson	Lena Shiffman	1988	Lollipop Power Inc.	Gender norms	Primarily white
Losing Uncle Tim	MaryKate Jordan	Judith Friedman	1989	Albert Whitman	HIV/AIDS; gay uncle	All white
Heather Has Two Mommies	Lesléa Newman	Diane Souza	1989	Copublished with author; republished by Alyson Wonderland Books in 1990	Lesbian parents	Primarily white

TABLE C: 1990–1999

Title	Author	Illustrator	Year	Publisher	Tropes/ Themes	Race/ Ethnicity/ Nonhuman
Daddy's Roommate	Michael Willhoite	Michael Willhoite	1990	Alyson Wonder-land Books	Gay parents	All white
Asha's Mums	Rosamund Elwin	Michele Paulse	1990	Women's Press	Lesbian moms; homophobia	Primarily Black
Bonjour, Mr. Satie	Tomie dePaola	Tomie dePaola	1991	Putnam	Gay uncle	Nonhuman
The Generous Jefferson Bartleby Jones	Forman Brown	Leslie Trawin	1991	Alyson Wonderland Books	Gay parents	Primarily white
Gloria Goes to Pride	Lesléa Newman	Russell Crocker	1991	Alyson Wonderland Books	LGBTQ+ culture	Primarily white
Belinda's Bouquet	Lesléa Newman	Michael Willhoite	1991	Alyson Wonderland Books	Lesbian parents; inci-dental queer-ness; body acceptance	All white
The Duke Who Outlawed Jelly Beans	Johnny Valentine	Lynette Schmidt	1991	Alyson Wonderland Books	Gay parents, lesbian parents	Racial and ethnic diversity
Whisper Whisper Jesse, Whisper Whisper Josh: A Story About AIDS	Eileen Pollack	Bruce Gilroy	1992	Advantage/Aurora Publications	Gay uncle; HIV/AIDS	All white
The Day They Put a Tax on Rainbows and Other Stories	Johnny Valentine	Lynette Schmidt	1992	Alyson Wonderland Books	Gay parents, lesbian parents	Primarily white
A Boy's Best Friend	Joan Alden	Catherine Hopkins	1992	Alyson Wonderland Books	Lesbian parents	All white
The Daddy Machine	Johnny Valentine	Lynette Schmidt	1992	Alyson Wonderland Books	Lesbian parents	All white

Title	Author	Illustrator	Year	Publisher	Tropes/ Themes	Race/ Ethnicity/ Nonhuman
Caleb's Friend	Eric Jon Nones	Eric Jon Nones	1993	Farrah, Straus and Giroux	Queer youth desire	Racial ambiguity; merboy
Saturday Is Patty Day	Lesléa Newman	Annette Hegel	1993	New Victoria Publishers	Lesbian parents; divorce	All white
Uncle What-Is-It Is Coming to Visit!!	Michael Willhite	Michael Willhite	1993	Alyson Wonderland Books	Queer uncle; gay stereotypes	All white
Is Your Family Like Mine?	Lois Abramchik	Alaio Bradshaw	1993	Open Heart, Open Mind	Family diversity	Racial and ethnic diversity
Mr. Pam Pam and the Hullabazoo	Trish Cooke	Patricia Aggs	1994	Candlewick Press	Subtle gay parenting	All black
One Dad, Two Dads, Brown Dad, Blue Dads	Johnny Valentine	Melody Sarecky	1994	Alyson Wonderland Books	Gay parents	Nonhuman
Anna Day and the O-Ring	Elaine Wickens	Elaine Wickens	1994	Alyson Wonderland Books	Lesbian parents	All white
Tiger Flowers	Patricia Quinlan	Janet Wilson	1994	Dial	HIV/AIDS; gay uncle	All white
Too Far Away to Touch	Lesléa Newman	Catherine Stock	1995	Clarion Books	HIV/AIDS; gay uncle	All white
Who's in a Family?	Robert Skutch	Laura Nienhaus	1995	Tricycle Press	Family diversity (human and animal)	Racial and ethnic diversity
My Two Uncles	Judith Vigna	Judith Vigna	1995	Albert Whitman	Gay uncles	All white
Amy Asks a Question . . . Grandma— What's a Lesbian?	Jeanne Arnold	Barbara Lindquist	1996	Mother Courage Press	Lesbian grandmothers; lesbian subculture; HIV/AIDS; gay uncle	All white

Title	Author	Illustrator	Year	Publisher	Tropes/ Themes	Race/ Ethnicity/ Nonhuman
My Dad Has HIV	Earl Alexander, Sheila Rudin, and Pam Sejkora	Ronnie Walter Shipman	1996	Fairview Press	HIV-positive father	All white
Daddy's Wedding	Michael Willhoite	Michael Willhoite	1996	Alyson Wonderland Books	Gay parents; gay marriage	All white
Lucy Goes to the Country	Joseph Kennedy	John Canemaker	1998	Alyson Wonderland Books	Gay pet parents	All white
A Name on the Quilt	Jeannine Atkins	Tad Hills	1999	Atheneum	HIV/AIDS; gay uncle	All white
Best Best Colors/Los Mejores Colores	Eric Hoffman	Celeste Henriquez	1999	Redleaf Press	Lesbian parents	Primarily Latinx

TABLE D: 2000–2009

Title	Author	Illustrator	Year	Publisher	Tropes/ Themes	Race/ Ethnicity/ Nonhuman
King and King	Linda de Hann	Stern Nijland	2000	Tricycle Press	Coming out; marriage; family acceptance	All white
Are You a Boy or a Girl?	Karleen Pendleton Jimenez	Karleen Pendleton Jimenez	2000	Green Dragon Press	Gender non-conformity	Racially ambiguous
Hello, Sailor	Ingrid Godon with words by Andre Sollie	Ingrid Godon	2000/ 2003	Macmillan Children's Books	Gay men in love	All white
Pugdog	Andrea U'Ren	Andrea U'Ren	2001	Farrar, Straus and Giroux	Gender non-conformity	Animal
A Cowboy Named Ernestine	Jacqueline K. Ogburn	Nicole Rubel	2001	Dial	Cross-dressing	All white
The Harvey Milk Story	Kari Krakow	David Gardner	2001	Two Lives Publishing	Biography; political fig-ure; activism	All white
Max: The Stubborn Little Wolf	Marie-Odile Judes Joan Robins (translation)	Martine Bourre	2001	HarperCollins Publishers	Gender stereotypes	Nonhuman
Bedtime for Baby Teddy	Tamara Arc-Dekker	Jenni Boettcher	2002	Rainbow Babies Books	Lesbian parents	Nonhuman
Felicia's Favorite Story	Lesléa Newman	Adriana Romo	2002	Two Lives Publishing	Lesbian parents; adoption	White and Latinx
The Mommy Book	Todd Parr	Todd Parr	2002	LB Kids	Family diversity	Nonhuman
The White Swan Express: A Story About Adoption	Jean Davies Okimoto and Elaine M. Aoki	Meilo So	2002	Clarion Books	International adoption; les-bian parents	Racial and ethnic diversity
The Sissy Duckling	Harvey Fierstein	Henry Cole	2002	Simon and Schuster	Feminine boy duck	Nonhuman

Title	Author	Illustrator	Year	Publisher	Tropes/ Themes	Race/ Ethnicity/ Nonhuman
Pearl's Christmas Present	Thomas Scott Wurst	Thomas Scott Wurst	2004	Pearl and Dotty Press	Sissy boy	All white
All Families are Special	Norma Simon	Teresa Flavin	2004	Albert Whitman	Family diversity	Racial and ethnic diversity
How My Family Came to Be— Daddy, Papa and Me	Andrew R. Aldrich	Mike Motz	2003	New Family Press	Interracial adoption; gay parents	Multiracial family
King and King	Linda de Hann	Stern Nijland	2003	Tricycle Press	Gay romance and mar-riage; fairy tale	All white
Carly: She's Still My Daddy	Mary Boenke	Dolores Dudley	2004	The Transgender Network (TNET) of Parents, Families and Friends of Lesbians and Gays (PFLAG)	Transgender parent	All white
A Fire Engine for Ruthie	Lesléa Newman	Cyd Moore	2004	Clarion Books	Tomboy	All white
The Boy Who Cried Fabulous	Lesléa Newman	Peter Ferguson	2004	Tricycle Press	Camp; proto-gay boy	All white
Molly's Family	Nancy Garden	Sharon Wooding	2004	Farrar, Straus and Giroux	Lesbian parents	All white
Everywhere Babies	Susan Meyer	Marla Frazee	2004	Harcourt	Family Diversity	Racial and ethnic diversity
Mom and Mum are Getting Married	Ken Setterington	Alice Priestley	2004	Second Story Press	Gay uncle; lesbian parents	All white

Title	Author	Illustrator	Year	Publisher	Tropes/ Themes	Race/ Ethnicity/ Nonhuman
The Princess Knight	Cornelia Funke	Kerstin Meyer	2004	Chicken House	Gender roles	All white
Flying Free	Jennifer C. Gregg	Janna Richards	2004	BookSurge	Lesbian parents	All white
What Are Parents?	Kyme and Susan Fox-Lee	Randy Jennings	2004	StoryTyme Publishing	Lesbian parents	Racial and ethnic diversity
While You Were Sleeping	Stephanie Burks	Kelli Bienvenu	2004	Burks Publishing	Lesbian parents; interracial adoption	Racial and ethnic diversity
King and King and Family	Linda de Hann	Stern Nijland	2004	Tricycle Press	Gay parents; fantasy international adoption; fairy tale	Primarily white with brown-skinned "adoptee"
And Tango Makes Three	Justin Richardson and Peter Parnell	Henry Cole	2005	Simon and Schuster	"Gay" parents in nature	Nonhuman
Emma and Meesha My Boy: A Two Mom Story	Kaitlyn Considine	Binny Hobbs	2005	Two Mom Books	Lesbian parents	All white
Uncle Aiden	Laurel Dykstra	Laurel Dykstra	2005	BabyBloc Publishing	Gay uncle; hint of polyamory	Racial and ethnic diversity
Antonio's Card	Rigoberto González	Cecilia Concepcion Alvarez	2005	Children's Book Press	Lesbian parents	Bilingual; Latinx
Time to Get Up, Time to Go	David Milgrim	David Milgrim	2006	Clarion Books	Boy and doll	All white
The Not-So-Only Child	Heather Jopling	Lauren Page Russell	2006	Nickname Press	Gay parents; family diversity	All white
Monicka's Papa Is Tall	Heather Jopling	Allyson Demoe	2006	Nickname Press	Gay parents; interracial family	Multiracial family

Title	Author	Illustrator	Year	Publisher	Tropes/ Themes	Race/ Ethnicity/ Nonhuman
Ryan's Mom Is Tall	Heather Jopling	Allyson Demoe	2006	Nickname Press	Lesbian parents	All white
Buster's Sugartime	Marc Brown	Marc Brown	2006	Little, Brown	Lesbian parents	Animal
The Different Dragon	Jennifer Bryan	Danamarie Hosler	2006	Two Lives Publishing	Lesbian parents	All white
Ballerino Nate	Kimberly Brubaker Bradley	R. W. Alley	2006	Dial	Sissy boy	Nonhuman
The Prince and Him: A Rainbow Bedtime Story	Kendal Nite	Y. Brassel	2007	Self-published	Gay romance	All white
Rough, Tough Charley	Verla Kay	Adam Gustavson	2007	Tricycle Press	Transgender	All white
Mini Mia and Her Darling Uncle	Pija Lindenbaum Elisabeth Kallick Dyssegaard (translator)	Pija indenbaum	2007	R & S Books	Gay uncle	All white
My Two Aunts	Deb Bixler	Deb Bixler	2007	Author House	Lesbian aunts	All white
We Belong Together	Todd Parr	Todd Parr	2007	Little, Brown	Family diversity	Nonhuman
10,000 Dresses	Marcus Ewert	Rex Ray	2008	Seven Stories Press	Transgender child	All white
Uncle Bobby's Wedding	Sarah S. Brannen	Sarah S. Brannen	2008	Putnam	Same-sex marriage	Nonhuman
My Mommy Is a Boy	Jason Martinez	Karen Winchester	2008	Lulu.com	Transgender parent	Racially ambiguous
Dear Child	John Farrell	Maurie J. Manning	2008	Boyds Mills Press	Family diversity	Racial and ethnic diversity

Title	Author	Illustrator	Year	Publisher	Tropes/ Themes	Race/ Ethnicity/ Nonhuman
The Turklebees of Turkledorf	Jennifer Ingerman Miller	Jennifer Ingerman Miller	2008	CreateSpace	Politicizes gay marriage	Nonhuman
Daddy, Papa, and Me	Lesléa Newman	Carol Thompson	2009	Tricycle Press	Gay parents	Multiracial family
Mommy, Mama, and Me	Lesléa Newman	Carol Thompson	2009	Tricycle Press	Lesbian parents	Multiracial family
And Baby Makes Four	Judith Benjamin	Judith Freeman	2009	Motek Press	Lesbian parents	All white
In Our Mothers' House	Patricia Polacco	Patricia Polacco	2009	Philomel Books	Lesbian parents; interracial adoption	Multiracial family
Arwen and Her Daddies	Jarko de Witte van Leeuwen	Jarko de Witte van Leeuwen	2009	Self-published	Transnational/ interracial adoption; gay parents	Multiracial family
Two Daddies . . . and Me!	Robbi Anne Packard	Lori Ann McElroy	2009	Author House	Gay parents; interracial adoption	Multiracial family

TABLE E: 2010–2018

Title	Author	Illustrator	Year	Publisher	Tropes/ Themes	Race/ Ethnicity/ Nonhuman
Be Who You Are!	Jennifer Carr	Ben Rumback	2010	Author House	Transgender girl	All white
My Princess Boy	Cheryl Kilodavis	Suzanne DeSimone	2010	Aladdin	Pink boy; boy-meets-dress	Primarily Black
A Tale of Two Daddies	Vanita Ohlschlager	Kristin Blackwood and Mike Blanc	2010	VanitaBooks	Gay parents	All white
A Tale of Two Mommies	Vanita Ohlschlager	Kristin Blackwood and Mike Blanc	2010	VanitaBooks	Lesbian parents	Multiracial family
Chimpy Discovers His Family	James LaCroce	James LaCroce	2010	CreateSpace	Gay men; "adoption"	Multiracial couple
City Time	Jeannelle Ferreira	J. Cecelia Haytko	2010	Books for All Families	Lesbian parents	Unavailable
The Family Book	Todd Parr	Todd Parr	2010	Little, Brown	Family diversity	Nonhuman
The Boy with Pink Hair	Perez Hilton	Jen Hill	2011	Celebra Children's Books/ Penguin Group	Gay exceptional-ism; camp flamboyance	Primarily white
When Kathy Is Keith	Wallace Wong	Wallace Wong	2011	Xlibris US	Transgender child	All white
Keesha and Her Two Moms Go Swimming	Cheril N. Clarke and Monica Bey-Clarke	Aiswarya Mukherjee	2011	My Family!/ Dodi Press	Lesbian parents	Primarily Black
Operation Marriage	Cynthia Chin-Lee	Lea Lyon	2011	PM Press	Lesbian parents; marriage	All white
All I Want To Be Is Me	Phyllis Rothblatt	Phyllis Rothblatt	2011	CreateSpace	Gender diversity	Racial and ethnic diversity

Title	Author	Illustrator	Year	Publisher	Tropes/ Themes	Race/ Ethnicity/ Nonhuman
Donovan's Big Day	Lesléa Newman	Mike Dutton	2011	Tricycle Press	Lesbian parenting; marriage	All white
My Uncle's Wedding	Eric Ross	Tracy K. Greene	2011	Self-published	Gay uncles; marriage	Primarily white
The Lopez Family: Science Fair Day	Monica Bey-Clarke and Cheril N. Clarke	Aiswarya Mukherjee	2011	My Family!/ Dodi Press	Gay parents; incidental queerness	Latinx
Odd Bird Out	Helga Bansch	Helga Bansch	2011	Gecko Press	Camp flamboyance	Nonhuman
Who's In My Family?: All About Our Families	Robie H. Harris	Nadine Bernard Westcott	2012	Candlewick	Family diversity	Racial and ethnic diversity
The Adventures of Tulip, Birthday Wish Fairy	S. Bear Bergman	Suzy Malik	2012	Flamingo Rampant	Transgender	Primarily Black
Backwards Day	S. Bear Bergman	KD Diamond	2012	Flamingo Rampant	Transgender	Nonhuman
Hugs of Three: My Daddies and Me	Stacey Bromberg and Joe Taravella	Jessica Warrick	2012	Forward Footsteps	Gay parents; interracial family	Multiracial family
Hello, It's Only Me! The Diary of a Transgendered Kid	Layde Aphrodite	Jordan A Brewer, Janae A Brewer-Robinson, Idasia Beanca Brewer, Layde Aphrodite	2012	CreateSpace	Transgender	Racial and ethnic diversity
When Leonard Lost His Spots: A Transparent Tail	Monique Costa	Marina Shupik	2012	My Family!/ Dodi Press	Transgender	Nonhuman

Title	Author	Illustrator	Year	Publisher	Tropes/ Themes	Race/ Ethnicity/ Nonhuman
Goblinheart: A Fairy Tale	Brett Axel	Terra Bidlespacher	2012	East Waterfront Press	Transgender allegory	Nonhuman
My Mommy Is a Boy	Jason Martinez	Karen Winchester	2013	Self-published	Transgender parent	Racial ambiguity
Roland Humphrey Is Wearing a What?	Eileen Kiernan-Johnson	Katrina Revenaugh	2013	Huntley Rahara Press	Gender non-conforming	Primarily white
When Kayla Was Kyle	Amy Fabrikant	Jennifer Levine	2013	Avid Readers Publishing Group	Transgender child	All white
What Makes a Baby?	Cory Silverberg	Fiona Smyth	2013	Triangle Square	Reproduction	Nonhuman
The Purim Superhero	Elisabeth Kushner	Mike Byrne	2013	Kar-Ben Publishing	Gay parents; Jewish holiday (Purim)	Jewish
Adopting Ahova	Jennifer Byrne	Oana Vaida	2013	Dodi Press	Lesbian parents	Jewish
A Girl Like Any Other	Sophie Labelle	Sophie Labelle	2013	Self-published/ crowd funded	Transgender girl	Racial and ethnic diversity
Michael and Me	Margaret Baker-Street	Margaret Baker-Street	2014	Xlibris US	Transgender	Racial and ethnic diversity
The Christmas Truck	J. B. Blankenship	Cassandra Bolan	2014	NarraGarden	Gay parents; Christmas	Racial and ethnic diversity
Made by Raffi	Craig Pomranz	Margaret Chamberlain	2014	Frances Lincoln Children's Books	Sissy boy; possible neurodiversity	Racial and ethnic diversity
This Day in June	Gayle Pitman	Kristyna Litten	2014	Magination Press	LGBTQ history; biography	All white
I Am Jazz	Jessica Herthel and Jazz Jennings	Shelagh McNicholas	2014	Dial Books	Transgender girl; autobiography	Primarily white

Title	Author	Illustrator	Year	Publisher	Tropes/ Themes	Race/ Ethnicity/ Nonhuman
Zak's Safari: A Story about Donor-Conceived Kids of Two-Mom Families	Christy Tyner	Ciaee	2014	Self-published	Lesbian parents; donor inception	Multiracial family
Morris Micklewhite and the Tangerine Dress	Christine Baldacchino	Isabelle Malenfant	2014	Groundwood Books	Pink boy; boy-meets-skirt	Primarily white
Call Me Tree/ Llamame arbol	Maya Christina Gonzalez	Maya Christina Gonzalez	2014	Children's Book Press	Gender independent	Bilingual/ Latinx
Jacob's New Dress	Sarah and Ian Hoffman	Chris Case	2014	Magination Press	Pink boy; boy-meets-skirt	Primarily white
The Newspaper Pirates	j wallace skelton	Ketch Wehr	2015	Flamingo Rampant	Gay parents; subtle gender non-conformity; gender-creative child; apartment setting	Racial and ethnic diversity
M Is for Mustache: A Pride ABC Book	Catherine Hernandez	Marisa Firebaugh	2015	Flamingo Rampant	Queer inclusive	Racial and ethnic diversity
Are You a Boy or a Girl?	Sarah Savage	Fox Fisher	2015	Jessica Kingsley Publishers	gender non-conformity	Primarily white
Is That for a Boy or a Girl?	S. Bear Bergman	Rachel Dougherty	2015	Flamingo Rampant	Queer	Racial and ethnic diversity
The Zero Dads Club	Angel Adeyoha	Aubrey Williams	2015	Flamingo Rampant	Family diversity	Racial and ethnic diversity

Title	Author	Illustrator	Year	Publisher	Tropes/ Themes	Race/ Ethnicity/ Nonhuman
A Princess of Great Daring	Tobi Hill-Meyer	Elenore Toczynski	2015	Flamingo Rampant	Lesbian parents; transgender child	Racial and ethnic diversity
Love Is in the Hair	Syrus Marcus Ware	Syrus Marcus Ware	2015	Flamingo Rampant	Gay uncles	All Black
Rumplepimple	Suzanne Dewitt Hall	Kevin Scott Gierman	2015	Self-published	Lesbian pet parents	White/ racially ambiguous couple
Large Fears	Myles E. Johnson	Kendrick Daye	2015	Self-published	Queer child	All Black
Annie's Plaid Shirt	Stacey D. Davids	Rachel Balsaitis	2015	Upswing Press	Gender non-conformity; single mom	Racial ambiguity
Square Zair Pair	Jase Peeples	Christine Knopp	2015	Self-published	Same-sex marriage allegory	Fantasy
A Peacock Among Pigeons	Tyler Curry	Clarione Gutierrez	2015	Mascot Books	Camp	Nonhuman
Introducing Teddy: A Gentle Story about Gender and Friendship	Jessica Walton	Dougal MacPherson	2016	Bloomsbury	Transgender teddy bear	Nonhuman
A Family Is a Family Is a Family	Sara O'Leary	Qin Leng	2016	Groundwood Books	Family diversity	Racial and ethnic diversity
Rosaline	Daniel Errico	Michael Scanlon	2016	Pajama Publishing	Lesbian love; fairy tale	All white
The Boy and the Bindi	Vivek Shraya	Rajni Perera	2016	Arsenal Pulp Press	Hindu culture; gender expression	Asian
One of a Kind, Like Me/Único Como Yo	Laurin Mayeno	Robert Liu-Trujillo	2016	Blood Orange Press	Gender expression	Latinx; bilingual

Title	Author	Illustrator	Year	Publisher	Tropes/ Themes	Race/ Ethnicity/ Nonhuman
Yetta & the Fantastic Mom Suits	Jano Oscherwitz	Kate Yarrow	2016	Prancing Goat Books	Lesbian parents; Jewish folktale (dybbuk)	Jewish; white
The Flower Girl Wore Celery	Meryl G. Gordon	Holly Clifton-Brown	2016	Kar-Ben Publishing	Lesbian parents; wedding	Jewish; white
Old Dog Baby Baby	Julie Fogliano	Chris Raschka	2016	Roaring Brook Press	Lesbian parents	All white
Uh-Oh!	Shutta Crum	Patrice Barton	2016	Alfred A. Knopf	Lesbian parents	All white
Home At Last	Vera B. Williams	Chris Raschka	2016	Greenwillow Books	Adoption; gay parents	All white
Worm Loves Worm	J. J. Austrian	Mike Curato	2016	Balzer + Bray	Same-sex marriage allegory	Nonhuman
Keesha's South African Adventure	Cheril N. Clarke and Monica Bey-Clarke	Julia Selyutina	2016	My Family!/ Dodi Press	Lesbian parents	Black family
Families	Jesse Unaapik Mike and Kerry McCluskey	Lenny Lishchenko	2017	Inhabit Media	Diverse family forms	Inuit
Rumplepimple Goes to Jail	Suzanne Dewitt Hall	Kevin Scott Gierman	2017	Self-published	Lesbian pet moms	Racial ambiguity
When You Look Out the Window: How Phyllis Lyon and Del Martin Built a Community	Gayle E. Pitman	Christopher Lyles	2017	American Psychological Association	LGBTQ+ history	All white
Bell's Knock Knock Birthday!	George Parker	Sam Orchard	2017	Flamingo Rampant	Nonbinary child; queer parents	Racial and ethnic diversity
47,000 Beads	Koja Adeyoha, Angel Adeyoha	Holly McGillis	2017	Flamingo Rampant	Two-spirit	Indigenous culture

Title	Author	Illustrator	Year	Publisher	Tropes/ Themes	Race/ Ethnicity/ Nonhuman
The Last Place You Look	j wallace skelton	Justin Alves	2017	Flamingo Rampant	Nonbinary kid and adult; queer parents/ caregivers	Jewish
Moondragon in the Mosque Garden	El-Farouk Khaki, Troy Jackson	Katie Commodore	2017	Flamingo Rampant	Nonbinary kid; queer parents/ caregivers	Muslim
Super Power Baby Shower	Tobi Hill-Meyer and Fay Onyx	Janine Carrington	2017	Flamingo Rampant	Nonbinary kid; nonbinary adult; queer parents/ caregivers	Black; Muslim
Rachel's Christmas Boat	Sophie Labelle	Sophie Labelle	2017	Flamingo Rampant	Transgender parents	Racial diversity
From the Stars in the Sky to the Fish in the Sea	Kai Cheng Thom	Li Kai Yun Ching and Wai-Yant Li	2017	Arsenal Pulp Press	Nonbinary	Racial diversity
Santa's Husband	Daniel Kibblesmith	Ap Quach	2017	Harper Design	Gay Santa	Interracial couple
The Gender Wheel	Maya Gonzalez	Maya Gonzalez	2017	Reflection Press	Gender wheel	Racial and ethnic diversity
They She He Me: Free to Be	Maya Gonzalez and Matthew Smith-Gonzalez	Maya Gonzalez	2017	Reflection Press	Gender diversity	Racial diversity
A Church For All	Gayle E. Pitman	Laure Fournier	2018	Albert Whitman and Company	Religion and LGBTQ inclusion	Racial diversity
Prince and Knight	Daniel Haack	Stevie Lewis	2018	Little Bee Books	Gay romance	Primarily white
A House for Everyone	Jo Hirst	Naomi Bardoff	2018	Jessica Kingsley Publishers	Queer inclusive	Multiracial family

Title	Author	Illustrator	Year	Publisher	Tropes/ Themes	Race/ Ethnicity/ Nonhuman
Vincent the Vixen	Alice Reeves	Phoebe Kirk	2018	Jessica Kingsley Publishers	Transgender allegory; adult trans-gender role model	Nonhuman
When We Love Someone We Sing to Them: Cuando Amamos Cantamos	Ernesto Javier Martinez	Maya Christina Gonzalez	2018	Reflection Press	Youth same-sex desire	Mexican culture; Latinx; bilingual
Pride: The Story of Harvey Milk and the Rainbow Flag	Rob Sanders	Steven Salerno	2018	Random House Books for Young Readers	Gay biogra-phy; LGBTQ history	Primarily white
Jack (Not Jackie)	Erica Silverman	Holly Hatam	2018	Little Bee Books	Transgender girl	All white
Jamie Is Jamie: A Book About Being Yourself and Playing Your Way	Afsaneh Moradian	Maria Bogade	2018	Free Spirit Publishing	Nonbinary	All white
Neither	Airlie Anderson	Airlie Anderson	2018	Little, Brown	Nonbinary	Nonhuman
Jessie's Hat Collection	Nick Barnes	Nick Barnes	2018	Self-published	Transgender boy	All white
Love Is Love	Michael Genhart	Ken Min	2018	Little Pickle Press	Queer love	Racial and ethnic diversity
Pink Is for Boys	Robb Pearlman	Eda Kaban	2018	Running Press Kids	Disrupt gender stereotypes	Racial and ethnic diversity
"What's 'Gay'?" Asked Mae	Brian McNaught	Dave Woodford	2018	Self-published	Birds explain what gay means to two children	All white
Julián Is a Mermaid	Jessica Love	Jessica Love	2018	Candlewick	Queer fabulousness	Latinx

Title	Author	Illustrator	Year	Publisher	Tropes/ Themes	Race/ Ethnicity/ Nonhuman
Jerome by Heart	Thomas Scotto Claudia Bedrick and Karin Snelson (translators)	Olivier Tallec	2018	Enchanted Lion Books	Gay romance	All white
Phoenix Goes to School	Michelle and Phoenix Finch	Sharon Davey	2018	Jessica Kingsley Publishers	Transgender girl	All white

Notes

Chapter One: What Can Picture Books Do?
The Politics of LGBTQ+ Children's Literature

1. LGBTQ+ refers to lesbian, gay, bisexual, transgender, and queer. The plus represents identities beyond those listed, such as two-spirit and asexual.

2. BIPOC refers to Black, Indigenous, and people of color and has gained popularity in recent years as an anacronym that highlights shared experiences of marginalization within white supremacist national contexts.

3. I refer to Jody Norton with feminine pronouns as that seems most common. However, it is difficult to know what pronouns Norton would now use given the shifting availability of language to describe gender identifications and shifts in the meaning of language frequently used.

As of the publication of this manuscript, it is customary to treat the term *trans* as an adjective and leave a space between it and the noun it modifies—for instance, writing trans children, trans girl, trans boy, trans woman, or trans man instead of, for example, transchildren.

4. My understanding of the normative or dominant sex-gender-sexuality system is derived from feminist theorists including Gayle Rubin, Anne Fausto-Sterling, and Judith Butler. In her 1975 publication, "The Traffic in Women: Notes on the 'Political Economy' of Sex," Rubin theorized the relationship between sex, gender, and sexuality, arguing that normative links between them are socially constructed. For Rubin, sex is raw material that socialization transforms into gender. Even more, she argues that heterosexuality requires a binary sex-gender system to naturalize and normalize itself. Later scholars, including Anne Fausto-Sterling and Judith Butler, challenge the naturalness of the sexed body, arguing that it too is a social construct.

5. I am grateful to the anonymous reviewer of my book proposal for pointing this out to me. By creating a false binary, I was engaging in the kind of simplistic analysis Kenneth Kidd warns against.

Chapter Two: A Genealogy of LGBTQ+
Children's Picture Books: The Early Years

1. *Jesse's Dream Skirt* was reissued on its fortieth anniversary in 2019, introducing readers to the urtext in the boy-meets-skirt field.

2. Although I discuss several Alyson Wonderland publications in this chapter, the press published several significant texts that I do not discuss, including: *The Duke Who Outlawed Jelly Beans* (1991), written by Johnny Valentine and illustrated by Lynette Schmidt; *The Entertainer: A Story in Pictures* (1992), written and illustrated by Michael Willhoite; *The Day They Put a Tax on Rainbows and Other Stories*, written by Johnny Valentine and illustrated by Lynette Schmidt; *A Boy's Best Friend* (1992), written by Joan Alden and illustrated by Catherine Hopkins; *The Daddy Machine* (1992), written by Johnny Valentine and illustrated by Lynette Schmidt; *Uncle What-Is-It Is Coming to Visit!!* (1993), written and illustrated by Michael Willhite; *One Dad, Two Dads, Brown Dad, Blue Dads* (1994), written by Johnny Valentine and illustrated by Melody Sarecky; *Anna Day and the O-Ring* (1994), written and illustrated by Elaine Wickens; *Daddy's Wedding* (1996), written and illustrated by Michael Willhoite; and *Lucy Goes to the Country* (1998), written by Joseph Kennedy and illustrated by John Canemaker.

3. See also *Who's in a Family?* (1995), written by Robert Skutch and illustrated by Laura Nienhaus.

Chapter Three: Virtually Normal: Lesbian and
Gay Grown-Ups in Children's Picture Books

1. Deb Bixler wrote, illustrated, and self-published *My Two Aunts* in 2007. It is the only picture book focused on lesbian aunts that I've identified. Like most "gay uncle" books, this one is told from the point of view of a young child. It is quite amateurish and, like many self-published LGBTQ+ children's picture books, was motivated by the author's desire to provide a "window" into her lesbian relationships for her young nieces and nephews.

2. This much-loved classic was recently revised and rereleased (2020) by Little Bee Books. New illustrations are provided by Lucia Soto, who transformed the nonhuman characters into a gorgeously rendered multiracial family.

Chapter Four: Beyond the Sissy Boy: Pink Boys and Tomboys

1. Sociologists J. L. Johnson and Amy Best refer to parent-advocates as "radical normals" and note that they are "made deviant not by their own actions, but by association with another" (324). According to Johnson and Best, radical normals become allies and activists to support their children and, in doing so, perform their normative familial role as protectors (324).

Chapter Five: Queer Youth and Gender: Representing Transgender, Nonbinary, Gender-Creative, and Gender-Free Youth

1. "Queer and Trans-Themed Books for Young Readers: A Critical Review" by Robert Bittner, Jennifer Ingrey, and Christine Stamper is essential reading for those interested in transgender and nonbinary representations in children's and young adult literature. The authors suggest queer- and trans-themed texts may "begin to form a pedagogy of possibility that is rooted in gender equity and social justice" (951).

2. This section doesn't include all LGBTQ+ children's picture books featuring transgender children. My formal study of LGBTQ+ children's picture books ended in 2018, and several very good, relevant books have since been published, including *Sam!* (2019), written by Dani Gabriel and illustrated by Robert Liu-Trujillo; *Call Me Max* (2019), written by Kyle Lukoff and illustrated by Luciano Lozano; and *Casey's Ball* (2019), written by Kit Yan and illustrated by Holly McGillis. Several very amateurish self-published picture books were also published in the last decade, including *When Kathy Is Keith* (2011), written and illustrated by Wallace Wong; *A Girl Like Any Other* (2013), written and illustrated by Sophie Labelle; *Michael and Me* (2014), written and illustrated by Margaret Baker-Street; *Jessie's Hat Collection* (2018), written and illustrated by Nick Barnes; and *A Girl Named Adam* (2019), written by Jordan Scavone and illustrated by C. N. J. Zing. These texts demonstrate a growing investment in representing transgender youth. Additionally, several Flamingo Rampant Press publications feature young transgender characters, including *The Adventures of Tulip, Birthday Wish Fairy* (2012), written by S. Bear Bergman and illustrated by Suzy Malik; *Backwards Day* (2012), written by S. Bear Bergman and illustrated by KD Diamond; and *A Princess of Great Daring* (2015), written by Tobi Hill-Meyer and illustrated by Elenore Toczynski. Because of the exponential growth in LGBTQ+ children's picture books after 2010, it is not possible to discuss all of the more recent publications. Instead, I highlight texts that exemplify trends or expand representations. I hope that by mapping the field of LGBTQ+ children's picture books more scholars are enticed to study the field from literary and cultural studies perspectives.

3. See also *What Riley Wore* (2019), written by Elana K. Arnold and illustrated by Linda Davick.

Chapter Seven: Queer Histories: The Politics of Representing the Past

1. A second, much earlier biography of Harvey Milk, Kari Krakow's *The Harvey Milk Story*, was published in 2001. I don't discuss it in chapter seven, because it is the only nonfiction text to be published before the late 2010s.

2. Although Sanders suggests that homophobia motivated Dan White to assassinate Milk and Moscone, their former colleague's motivation for murder continues to be debated.

Selected Bibliography

This bibliography includes all of the scholarly works consulted. The full archive of LGBTQ+ children's picture books reviewed during the research for this book and discussed within the book is included in the tables in Appendix C.

Abad-Santos, Alex. "Philadelphia's New, Inclusive Gay Pride Flag Is Making Gay White Men Angry." *Vox*, June 20, 2017. https://www.vox.com/culture/2017/6/20/15821858/gay-pride-flag-philadelphia-fight-explained.

Abate, Michelle Ann. "Trans/Forming Girlhood: Transgenderism, the Tomboy Formula, and Gender Identity Disorder in Sharon Dennis Wyeth's Tomboy Trouble." *The Lion and the Unicorn* 32, no. 1 (2008): 40–60. Project MUSE. https://doi.org/10.1353/uni.2008.0007.

Adichie, Chimamanda Ngozi. "The Danger of a Single Story." TED. 2009. https://www.ted.com/talks/chimamanda_adichie_the_danger_of_a_single_story.

Afanador, Ruven. "The Rise of Nonbinary Fashion." *Washington Post*, November 20, 2019. https://www.washingtonpost.com/magazine/2019/11/20/rise-nonbinary-fashion-photo-essay/.

American Library Association. "Caldecott Medal—Terms and Criteria." Association for Library Service to Children (ALSC). November 30, 1999. http://www.ala.org/alsc/awardsgrants/bookmedia/caldecottmedal/caldecottterms/caldecottterms.

American Library Association. "Rainbow Book Lists." Accessed November 2, 2019. https://glbtrt.ala.org/rainbowbooks/rainbow-books-lists.

Anderson, Benedict. *Imagined Communities: Reflections on the Origin and Spread of Nationalism*. Revised ed. New York: Verso, 1998.

Bakhtin, Mikhail. *Rabelais and His World*. Bloomington: Indiana University Press, 2009.

Bansch, Helga. *Odd Bird Out*. Wellington, New Zealand: Gecko Press, 2011.

Berlant, Lauren. *Cruel Optimism*. Durham, NC: Duke University Press, 2011.

Bishop, Rudine Sims. "Windows, Mirrors, and Sliding Glass Doors." *Perspectives: Choosing and Using Books for the Classroom* 6, no. 3 (1990).

Bittner, Robert, et al. "Queer and Trans-Themed Books for Young Readers: A Critical Review." *Discourse: Studies in the Cultural Politics of Education* 37, no. 6 (2016) 948–64.

Botelho, Maria José, and Masha Kabakow Rudman. *Critical Multicultural Analysis of Children's Literature*. New York: Routledge, 2009.

Brand, Susan Trostle, and Susan L. Maasch. "Updating Classroom Libraries and Cross-Curricular Activities: Celebrating Gender Identity and Diversity Through LGBTQ Books." *Childhood Education* 93, no. 5 (September 2017): 430–39. https://doi.org/10.1080/00094056.2017.1367240.

Brody, Jane E. "Boyhood Effeminancy and Later Homosexuality." *New York Times,* December 16, 1986. https://www.nytimes.com/1986/12/16/science/boyhood-effeminancy-and-later-homosexuality.html.

Burke, Brianna R., and Kristina Greenfield. "Challenging Heteronormativity: Raising LGBTQ Awareness in a High School English Language Arts Classroom." *English Journal* 105, no. 6 (2016): 46.

Butler, Judith. *Bodies That Matter: On the Discursive Limits of Sex.* New York: Routledge, 1993.

Butler, Judith. *Gender Trouble: Feminism and the Subversion of Identity.* New York: Routledge, 2006.

Carruthers, Charlene. *Unapologetic: A Black, Queer, and Feminist Mandate for Radical Movements.* Boston: Beacon Press, 2018.

Chambers-Letson, Joshua. *After the Party: A Manifesto for Queer of Color Life.* New York: New York University Press, 2018.

Cher, and Nancy Savoca, dirs. *If These Walls Could Talk.* 1996; Imports, 2013.

Coletta, Jennifer. "The Missing B Word: Compulsory Binarization and Bisexual Representation in Children's Literature." *Jeunesse: Young People, Texts, Culture* 10, no. 1 (Summer 2018): 85–108.

Collins, Patricia Hill. *Black Feminist Thought: Knowledge, Consciousness, and the Politics of Empowerment.* New York: Routledge, 2008.

Colman, Penny. "A New Way to Look at Literature: A Visual Model for Analyzing Fiction and Nonfiction Texts." *Language Arts* 84, no. 3 (2007): 257–68. JSTOR.

Crisp, Thomas. "Setting the Record 'Straight': An Interview with Jane Severance." *Children's Literature Association Quarterly* 35, no. 1 (February 2010): 87–96. Project MUSE. https://doi.org/10.1353/chq.0.1950.

Curwood, Jen Scott, Megan Schliesman, and Kathleen T. Horning. "Fight for Your Right: Censorship, Selection, and LGBTQ Literature." *English Journal* 98, no. 4 (2009): 37–43. JSTOR.

Davis, Heath Fogg. *Beyond Trans: Does Gender Matter?* New York: New York University Press, 2017.

de Haan, Linda, and Stern Nijland. *King and King.* Berkeley, CA: Tricycle Press, 2003.

de Lauretis, Teresa. "Queer Theory. Lesbian and Gay Sexualities: An Introduction." Special issue, *Differences: A Journal of Feminist Cultural Studies* 3, no. 2 (Summer 1991): iii–xviii.

de Lauretis, Teresa. *Technologies of Gender: Essays on Theory, Film, and Fiction.* Bloomington: Indiana University Press, 1987.

DePalma, Renée. "Choosing to Lose Our Gender Expertise: Queering Sex/Gender in School Settings." *Sex Education* 13, no. 1 (January 2013): 1–15. https://doi.org/10.1080/14681811.2011.634145.

Diverse BookFinder. "Our Categories." Accessed May 19, 2021. https://diversebookfinder.org/our-categories/.

Dodge, Autumn M., and Paul A. Crutcher. "Inclusive Classrooms for LGBTQ Students." *Journal of Adolescent and Adult Literacy* 59, no. 1 (2015): 95–105. Wiley Online Library. https://doi.org/10.1002/jaal.433.

Dreger, Alice. "Gender Identity Disorder in Childhood: Inconclusive Advice to Parents." *Hastings Center Report* 39, no. 1 (2009): 26–29. JSTOR.

Dreger, Alice. "Pink Boys: What's the Best Way to Raise Children Who Might Have Gender Identity Issues?" *Pacific Standard*. Accessed September 18, 2019. https://psmag.com/social -justice/pink-boys-gender-identity-disorder-62782.

du Gay, Paul. Introduction to *Doing Cultural Studies: The Story of the Sony Walkman*, edited by Paul du Gay, Stuart Hall, Linda Janes, Anders Koed Madsen, and Keith Negus. 2nd ed. London: SAGE Publications, 2013.

Duggan, Lisa. "After Neoliberalism? From Crisis to Organizing for Queer Economic Justice." *S&F Online*. Accessed March 15, 2016. http://sfonline.barnard.edu/a-new-queer-agenda /after-neoliberalism-from-crisis-to-organizing-for-queer-economic-justice/.

Duggan, Lisa. "The New Homonormativity: The Sexual Politics of Neoliberalism." In *Materializing Democracy: Toward a Revitalized Cultural Politics*, edited by Russ Castronovo and Dana Nelson. Durham, NC: Duke University Press, 2002. https://queer .newark.rutgers.edu/resources/new-homonormativity-sexual-politics-neoliberalism.

Duggan, Lisa. *The Twilight of Equality? Neoliberalism, Cultural Politics, and the Attack on Democracy*. Boston: Beacon Press, 2012.

Dwyer, Colin. "Merriam-Webster Singles Out Nonbinary 'They' for Word of the Year Honors." NPR, December 10, 2019. https://www.npr.org/2019/12/10/786732456/merriam -webster-singles-out-nonbinary-they-for-word-of-the-year-honors.

Egan, Timothy. "Oregon Measure Asks State to Repress Homosexuality." *New York Times*, August 16, 1992. https://www.nytimes.com/1992/08/16/us/oregon-measure-asks-state-to -repress-homosexuality.html.

Epstein, B. J. *Are the Kids All Right? Representations of LGBTQ Characters in Children's and Young Adult Literature*. London: HammerOn Press, 2013.

Epstein, B. J. "The Case of the Missing Bisexuals": Bisexuality in Books for Young Readers." *Journal of Bisexuality* 14, no. 1 (February 2014): 110–25.

Epstein-Fine, Sadie, and Makeda Zook, eds. *Spawning Generations: Rants and Reflections on Growing Up with LGBTQ+ Parents*. Toronto, Ontario: Demeter Press, 2018.

Essi, Cedric. "Queer Genealogies across the Color Line and into Children's Literature: Autobiographical Picture Books, Interraciality, and Gay Family Formation." *Genealogy* 2, no. 43 (2018).

Everett, Merrikay. *History of Lollipop Power, Incorporated: Small Press with a Vision*. Chapel Hill: University of North Carolina Press, 1984.

Fausto-Sterling, Anne. *Sexing the Body: Gender Politics and the Construction of Sexuality*. New York: Basic Books, 2000.

Flamingo Rampant. "About Flamingo Rampant." Accessed March 11, 2021. https://www .flamingorampant.com/about.

Flamingo Rampant. "Flamingo Rampant." Accessed January 16, 2020. https://www.flamingo rampant.com.

Ford, Elizabeth A. "H/Z: Why Leslea Newman Makes Heather into Zoe." In *Over the Rainbow: Queer Children's and Young Adult Literature*, edited by Kenneth Kidd and Michelle Ann Abate, 201–14. Ann Arbor: University of Michigan Press, 2011.

Frow, John. "Cultural Studies and the Neoliberal Imagination." *Yale Journal of Criticism* 12, no. 2 (1999): 424–30.

Garry, Candi Pierce. "Selection or Censorship? School Librarians and LGBTQ Resources." PhD diss., Miami University, 2014. ProQuest. https://search.proquest.com/docview /1646484627/abstract/D51904E235DF4C77PQ/1.

Gerard, Philip. *Creative Nonfiction: Researching and Crafting Stories of Real Life, Second Edition*. 2nd ed. Long Grove, IL: Waveland Press, 2017.

Gill-Peterson, Jules. *Histories of the Transgender Child*. Minneapolis: University of Minnesota Press, 2018.

GoFundMe. "GoFundMe: #1 Fundraising Platform for Crowdfunding." Accessed February 9, 2021. https://www.gofundme.com/.

Gomez, Betsy. "Banned Spotlight: *And Tango Makes Three*." Banned Books Week. September 5, 2018. https://bannedbooksweek.org/banned-spotlight-and-tango-makes-three/.

Gonzalez, Maya Christina. "Mission & Values." Reflection Press, Accessed May 20, 2021. https://reflectionpress.com/about-us/mission-values/.

Goodrich, Kristopher M., and Melissa Luke. "Queering Education in Response to the Needs of LGBTQQIA Students in P–12 Schools." *Journal of Homosexuality* 61, no. 3 (January 2014): 361.

Grady, Jonathan, Rigoberto Marquez, and Peter McLaren. "A Critique of Neoliberalism with Fierceness: Queer Youth of Color Creating Dialogues of Resistance." *Journal of Homosexuality* 59, no. 7 (August 2012): 982–1004. https://doi.org/10.1080/00918369.2012.699839.

Green, Richard. "One-Hundred Ten Feminine and Masculine Boys: Behavioral Contrasts and Demographic Similarities." *Archives of Sexual Behavior* 5, no. 5 (September 1976): 425–46. https://doi.org/10.1007/BF01541335.

Green, Richard. "The Significance of Feminine Behavior in Boys." *Journal of Child Psychology and Psychiatry* 16, no. 4 (October 1975): 341.

Green, Richard. *The "Sissy Boy Syndrome" and the Development of Homosexuality*. New Haven, CT: Yale University Press, 1987. https://uta.alma.exlibrisgroup.com.

Green, Richard, Katherine Williams, and Marilyn Goodman. "Masculine or Feminine Gender Identity in Boys: Developmental Differences between Two Diverse Family Groups." *Sex Roles* 12, no. 11–12 (June 1985): 1155–62. https://doi.org/10.1007/BF00287825.

Green, Richard, Marielle Fuller, Brian R. Rutley, and Jared Hendler. "Playroom Toy Preferences of Fifteen Masculine and Fifteen Feminine Boys." *Behavior Therapy* 3, no. 3 (July 1972): 425–29. https://doi.org/10.1016/S0005-7894(72)80142-4.

Halberstam, Jack. *Female Masculinity*. Durham, NC: Duke University Press, 1998.

Halberstam, Jack. *In a Queer Time and Place: Transgender Bodies, Subcultural Lives*. New York: New York University Press, 2005.

Hall, Stuart. "Encoding/Decoding." In *Culture, Media, Language*, edited by Stuart Hall, Dorothy Hobson, Andrew Lowe, and Paul Willis, 128–38. New York: Routledge, 1980.

Hall, Stuart. "Introduction to Media Studies at the Center." *Culture, Media, Language*, edited by Stuart Hall Dorothy Hobson, Andrew Lowe, and Paul Willis, 117–21. New York: Routledge, 1980.

Hall, Stuart. *Representation: Cultural Representations and Signifying Practices*. London: Sage, 1997.

Harris, Gerald. "Bill to Restrict Transgender Healthcare before Puberty Advances out of Tennessee House Committee." WKRN News 2, 2021, https://www.wkrn.com/news/tennessee-news/bill-to-restrict-transgender-healthcare-before-puberty-advances-out-of-tennessee-house-committee/.

Hermann-Wilmarth, Jill, and Caitlin Ryan. "Queering Chapter Books with LGBT Characters for Young Readers: Recognizing and Complicating Representations of Homonormativity." *Discourse: Studies in the Cultural Politics of Education* 37, no. 6 (2016): 846–66.

Hoffman, Sarah. "My Son, the Pink Boy." *Salon*, February 22, 2011, about:reader?url=http%3
A%2F%2Fwww.salon.com%2F2011%2F02%2F22%2Fson_looks_great_in_dress%2F.

Hoffman, Sarah. "Pink Boys: Another Way." *Sarah & Ian Hoffman*, December 6, 2010. http://
www.sarahandianhoffman.com/2010/12/pink-boys-another-way/.

Hoffman, Sarah, and Ian Hoffman. *Jacob's New Dress*. Chicago: Albert Whitman and
Company, 2014.

Holmes, Juwan. "Tennessee's Governor Signs Bill That Bans Trans Youth in Sports into Law."
LGBTQ Nation, March 27, 2021, https://www.lgbtqnation.com/2021/03/tennessees
-governor-signs-bill-bans-trans-youth-sports-law/.

Human Rights Campaign. "About Us." Human Rights Campaign. Accessed October 16, 2019.
https://www.hrc.org/hrc-story/about-us/.

Human Rights Campaign. "HRC Foundation." Human Rights Campaign. Accessed October
16, 2019. https://www.hrc.org/hrc-story/hrc-foundation/.

Human Rights Campaign. "Our Victories at HRC." Human Rights Campaign. Accessed
October 16, 2019. https://www.hrc.org/hrc-story/our-victories/.

Hurley, Nat. "The Little Transgender Mermaid: A Shape-Shifting Tale." In *Seriality and Texts
for Young People: The Compulsion to Retreat*, edited by Mavis Reimer, Nyala Ali, Deanna
England, and Melanie Dennis Unrau, 258–80. London: Palgrave Macmillan, 2014.

Huskey, Melynda. "Queering the Picture Book." *The Lion and the Unicorn* 26, no. 1 (2002):
66–77. https://doi.org/10.1353/uni.2002.0005.

Hyland, Nora E. "Social Justice in Early Childhood Classrooms What the Research Tells Us."
Young Children 65, no. 1 (January 2010): 82–90.

Inhabit Media. "About." Accessed January 17, 2020. https://inhabitmedia.com/about/.

It Gets Better. "It Gets Better Project." Accessed April 15, 2021. https://itgetsbetter.org/.

Jacqueline. "What Awaits in Public Schools Thru Children's Books." *Deep Roots at Home*.
August 26, 2017. https://deeprootsathome.com/gay-agenda-permeates-public-schools
-with-childrens-books/.

Janmohamed, Zeenat. "Queering Early Childhood Studies: Challenging the Discourse of
Developmentally Appropriate Practice." *Alberta Journal of Educational Research* 56, no. 3
(December 2010): 304.

Jiménez, Karleen Pendleton. "Queering Classrooms, Curricula, and Care: Stories from
Those Who Dare." *Sex Education* 9, no. 2 (May 2009): 169–79. https://doi.org/10.1080
/14681810902829638.

Jimenez, Laura. "Erasure by Any Other Name. . . . " *Booktoss*, June 4, 2019, https://booktoss
.blog/2019/06/04/erasure-by-any-other-name/.

Jimenez, Laura M. "Trans People Aren't Mythical Creatures." *Booktoss*, September 24, 2018,
https://booktoss.org/2018/09/24/trans-people-arent-mythical-creatures/.

Johnson, J. L., and Amy L. Best. "Radical Normals: The Moral Career of Straight Parents as
Public Advocates for Their Gay Children." *Symbolic Interaction* 35, no. 3 (2012): 321–39.
https://doi.org/10.1002/symb.23.

Jung, Susanne. *Bouncing Back: Queer Resilience in Twentieth and Twenty-First Century
English Literature and Culture*. N.p.: transcript publishing, 2020.

Kaiser, Niki, and Carey-Anne Morrison. "Closets of Fear, Islands of Love: Coming of Age in
the 1980s." In Epstein-Fine and Zook, *Spawning Generations*, 56–70.

Kidd, Kenneth. "Introduction: Lesbian/Gay Literature for Children and Young Adults."
Children's Literature Association Quarterly 23, no. 3 (1998): 114–19.

Kidd, Kenneth, and Michelle Ann Abate, eds. *Over the Rainbow: Queer Children's and Young Adult Literature*. Ann Arbor: University of Michigan Press, 2011.

Kilodavis, Cheryl. "To Acceptance!" *My Princess Boy*. Accessed January 28, 2020. https://myprincessboy.com/.

Kirkus Reviews. Review of *Caleb's Friend*, by Eric Jon Nones. June 15, 1993. https://www.kirkusreviews.com/book-reviews/eric-jon-nones/calebs-friend/.

Kohl, Herbert. "A Plea for Radical Children's Literature." In *Should We Burn Babar?*, 57–93. New York: New Press, 1995.

Krischer, Hayley. "Beyond Androgyny: Nonbinary Teenage Fashion." *New York Times*, August 14, 2019. https://www.nytimes.com/2019/08/14/style/nonbinary.html.

Lebovitz, P. S. "Feminine Behavior in Boys: Aspects of Its Outcome." *American Journal of Psychiatry* 128, no. 10 (April 1972): 1283.

Lester, Jasmine Z. "Homonormativity in Children's Literature: An Intersectional Analysis of Queer-Themed Picture Books." *Journal of LGBT Youth* 11, no. 3 (July 2014): 244–75. https://doi.org/10.1080/19361653.2013.879465.

Letts, William J., and James T. Sears, eds. *Queering Elementary Education: Advancing the Dialogue about Sexualities and Schooling*. Lanham, MD: Rowman and Littlefield Publishers, 1999.

Leuzzi, Tony, and Leslea Newman. "Too Far Away to Touch." *Harvard Educational Review* 66, no. 2 (1996): 389.

Leve, Annabelle M. *The Circuit of Culture as a Generative Tool of Contemporary Analysis: Examining the Construction of an Education Commodity*. Joint AARE APERA International Conference, Sydney. 2012.

Little Bee Books. *RuPaul Charles*. Illustrated by Vincent Chen. New York: Little Bee Books, 2020.

Little Miss Hot Mess. *The Hips on the Drag Queen Go Swish, Swish, Swish*. Illustrated edition. Philadelphia: Running Press Kids, 2020.

Love, Heather. *Feeling Backward: Loss and the Politics of Queer History*. Cambridge, MA: Harvard University Press, 2009.

Machlin, Sherri. "Banned Books Week: And Tango Makes Three." New York Public Library, September 23, 2013. https://www.nypl.org/blog/2013/09/23/banned-books-week-and-tango-makes-three.

Mack, Bruce, and Marian Buchanan. *Jesse's Dream Skirt*. Chapel Hill, NC: Lollipop Power, 1984.

Marks, Jadyn. "What's Wrong with the Human Rights Campaign." *Daily Emerald* (Eugene, OR), February 17, 2017. https://www.dailyemerald.com/opinion/columns/marks-what-s-wrong-with-the-human-rights-campaign/article_faa8f768-b908-52d7-9065-05473c462613.html.

Mason, Derritt. "What Having Two Mommies Looks Like Now: Queer Picture Books in the Twenty-First Century." *Literary Cultures and Twenty-First-Century Childhoods*, edited by Rachel Conrad and L. Brown Kennedy, 109–37. Cham, Switzerland: Palgrave Macmillan, 2020.

Matos, Angel Daniel. "Rabbit Weddings, Animal Collectives, and the Potentialities of Perverse Reading: Children's Literature and Queer Worldmaking in *A Day in the Life of Marlon Bundo*." *QED: A Journal in GLBTQ Worldmaking* 5, no. 3 (Fall 2018): 28–41.

Mattel. "You Can Be Anything." Barbie. Accessed March 30, 2021. https://barbie.mattel.com/en-us/about/you-can-be-anything.html.

McRuer, Robert. "Reading and Writing 'Immunity': Children and the Anti-Body." *Children's Literature Association Quarterly* 23, no. 3 (1998): 134.

Meadow, Tey. *Trans Kids: Becoming Gendered in the Twenty First Century*. Berkeley: University of California Press, 2018.

Meronek, Toshio. "Human Rights Campaign Under Fire in LGBT Community." Truthout, January 11, 2015. https://truthout.org/articles/human-rights-campaign-under-fire-in -lgbt-community/.

Merriam-Webster. "Merriam-Webster's Words of the Year 2019: They." Accessed December 16, 2019. https://www.merriam-webster.com/words-at-play/word-of-the-year.

Miller, Jennifer. "For the Little Queers: Imagining Queerness in 'New' Queer Children's Literature." *Journal of Homosexuality*, vol. 66, no. 12 (September 2018): 1–26. https://doi .org/10.1080/00918369.2018.1514204.

Miller, Jennifer. "A Little Queer: Ambivalence and the Work of Gender Play in Children's Literature." In *Heroes, Heroines, and Everything in Between: Challenging Gender and Sexuality Stereotypes in Children's Entertainment Media*, edited by CarrieLynn D. Reinhard and Christopher J. Olson, 35–49. Lanham, MD: Lexington Books, 2017.

Miller, Jennifer. "Queering the Straight World?: Mommy Blogs, Queer Kids, and the Limits of Digital Advocacy." In *The Dialectic of Digital Culture*, edited by David Arditi and Jennifer Miller, 99–112. Lanham, MD: Lexington Books, 2019.

Miller, Jennifer. "Thirty Years of Queer Theory." In *LGBTQ+ Studies: An Open Textbook* (Beta Edition), edited by Deborah Amory and Sean Massey. N.p.: Lumen Learning, 2020. https://courses.lumenlearning.com/suny-lgbtq-studies/chapter/introduction/.

Mitchell, Christopher Adam. "Stonewall's Contested History." *Perspectives on History: The Newsmagazine of the American Historical Association*, November 18, 2015. https://www .historians.org/publications-and-directories/perspectives-on-history/november-2015 /stonewalls-contested-history.

Moore, Madison. *Fabulous: The Rise of the Beautiful Eccentric*. New Haven, CT: Yale University Press, 2018.

Muñoz, José Esteban. *Cruising Utopia: The Then and There of Queer Futurity*. New York: New York University Press, 2009.

Naidoo, Jamie Campbell. *Rainbow Family Collections: Selecting and Using Children's Books with Lesbian, Gay, Bisexual, Transgender, and Queer Content*. Santa Barbara, CA: Libraries Unlimited, 2012. Open WorldCat, http://public.eblib.com/choice/publicfull record.aspx?p=894796.

Napoles, Desmond. *Be Amazing: A History of Pride*. New York: Farrar, Straus and Giroux, 2020.

Newman, L. E. "Treatment for the Parents of Feminine Boys." *American Journal of Psychiatry* 133, no. 6 (June 1976): 683.

Newman, Lesléa. *Gloria Goes to Gay Pride*. Boston: Alyson Books, 1991.

Newton, Esther. "Selections from Mother Camp." In *The Transgender Studies Reader*, edited by Susan Stryker and Stephen Whittle, 121–30. New York: Routledge, 2006.

Nickname Press. "About Nickname Press." Accessed March 11, 2021. https://www.nicknam epress.com/about.htm.

Norton, Jody. "Transchildren and the Discipline of Children's Literature." In *Over the Rainbow: Queer Children's and Young Adult Literature*, edited by Kenneth Kidd and Michelle Ann Abate. Ann Arbor: University of Michigan, 2011.

Pitman, Gayle. "Censorship." *Gayle E. Pitman*, Accessed April 19, 2019. https://gaylepitman .com/censorship.

Puar, Jasbir. *Terrorist Assemblages: Homonationalism in Queer Times*. Durham, NC: Duke University Press, 2007.

Publishers Weekly. Children's Book Review: *Caleb's Friend* by Eric Jon Nones. Accessed September 19, 2019. https://www.publishersweekly.com/978-0-374-31017-2.

Quasar, Daniel. "'Progress' A PRIDE Flag Reboot." Kickstarter. Accessed July 21, 2019. https://www.kickstarter.com/projects/danielquasar/progress-a-pride-flag-reboot.

Rich, Adrienne. "Compulsory Heterosexuality and Lesbian Existence." *Signs* 5, no. 4 (1980): 631–60.

Riesco, Stephanie. "'Because I like Them.'" *Boulder Weekly*, February 28, 2013. https://www.boulderweekly.com/entertainment/books/lsquobecause-i-like-themrsquo/.

Robertson, Mary Anna. *Growing Up Queer: Kids and the Remaking of LGBTQ Identity*. New York: New York University Press, 2019.

Robinson, Charlotte. "'Arwen and Her Daddies.'" *OutTake Voices*, May 27, 2010. https://charlio.podbean.com/e/%e2%80%9carwen-and-her-daddies%e2%80%9d/.

Robinson, Kerry. "Doing Anti-Homophobia and Anti-Heterosexism in Early Childhood Education: Moving beyond the Immobilising Impacts of 'Risks,' 'Fears' and 'Silences.' Can We Afford Not To?" *Contemporary Issues in Early Childhood* 6, no. 2 (2005): 175–88.

Rofes, Eric. "Innocence, Perversion, and Heather's Two Mommies." *Journal of Gay, Lesbian, and Bisexual Identity* 3, no. 1 (1998): 3–26.

Royce, Ellie. *Auntie Uncle: Drag Queen Hero*. Illustrated edition. New York: Pow! Kids Books, 2020.

Rubin, Gayle. "The Traffic in Women: Notes on the 'Political Economy' of Sex." In *Toward an Anthropology of Women*, edited by Rayna R. Reiter, 157–210. New York: Monthly Review Press, 1975.

Rudolph, Dana. "The Mombian Database of LGBTQ Family Books, Media, and More." *Mombian*. Accessed January 11, 2021. https://mombian.com/database/.

Rudolph, Dana. *Mombian: Sustenance for Lesbian Moms*. Accessed November 2, 2019. https://www.mombian.com/.

Ruti, Mari. *The Ethics of Opting Out: Queer Theory's Defiant Subjects*. New York: Columbia University Press, 2017.

Ryan, Caitlin L., and Jill M. Hermann-Wilmarth. "Already on the Shelf: Queer Readings of Award-Winning Children's Literature." *Journal of Literacy Research* 45, no. 2 (June 2013): 142–72. https://doi.org/10.1177/1086296X13479778.

Ryan, Caitlin L., and Jill M. Hermann-Wilmarth. *Reading the Rainbow: LGBTQ-Inclusive Literacy Instruction in the Elementary Classroom*. New York: Teachers College Press, 2018.

Sadjadi, Sahar. "View of Deep in the Brain: Identity and Authenticity in Pediatric Gender Transition." *Cultural Anthropology* 34, no. 1 (2019): 103–29. https://journal.culanth.org/index.php/ca/article/view/3728/430.

Sanders, April, and Janelle Mathis. "Gay and Lesbian Literature in the Classroom: Can Gay Themes Overcome Heteronormativity?" *Journal of Praxis in Multicultural Education* 7, no. 1 (April 2013). https://doi.org/10.9741/2161-2978.1067.

Sass, Sammy. "Gathering Voices: An Interview Project with Young Adults Raised in Queer Families." In Epstein-Fine and Zook, *Spawning Generations*, 32–37.

Sciurba, Katie. "Flowers, Dancing, Dresses, and Dolls: Picture Book Representations of Gender-Variant Males." *Children's Literature in Education: An International Quarterly* 48, no. 3 (2017): 276.

Sears, James T. "Interrogating the Subject: Queering Elementary Education, 10 Years On." *Sex Education* 9, no. 2 (May 2009): 193–200. https://doi.org/10.1080/14681810902829653.

Sedgwick, Eve Kosofsky. *Epistemology of the Closet.* 2nd ed. Berkeley: University of California Press, 2008.

Sedgwick, Eve Kosofsky. "How to Bring Your Kids Up Gay." *Social Text* no. 29 (1991): 18–27. JSTOR, https://doi.org/10.2307/466296.

Sedgwick, Eve Kosofsky. "Paranoid Reading and Reparative Reading, or, You're So Paranoid, You Probably Think This Essay Is About You." In *Touching Feeling: Affect, Pedagogy, Performativity.* Durham, NC: Duke University Press, 2002.

Seven Stories Press. "Seven Stories Press." Accessed February 28, 2020. https://www.seven stories.com/.

Simon and Schuster. "People of Pride." Little Bee Books. Accessed April 22, 2020. https://www.simonandschuster.com/series/People-of-Pride.

Smolkin, Laura B., and Craig A. Young. "Missing Mirrors, Missing Windows: Children's Literature Textbooks and LGBT Topics." *Language Arts* 88, no. 3 (January 2011): 217–25.

Sontag, Susan. "Notes on Camp." In *Against Interpretation, and Other Essays.* New York: Farrar, Straus and Giroux, 1966.

Sosin, Kate. "Jennifer Carr Tells Kids to 'Be Who You Are'—Gay Lesbian Bi Trans News Archive." *Windy City Times* (Chicago), April 27, 2011. http://www.windycitymediagroup.com/lgbt/Jennifer-Carr-tells-kids-to-Be-Who-You-Are/31567.html.

Stern, Mark Joseph. "What Was It Like Writing an LGBTQ Picture Book in 1989? What's It Like Now?" *Slate Magazine*, August 3, 2016. https://slate.com/culture/2016/08/lgbtq-childrens-book-authors-leslea-newman-and-christine-baldacchino-interviewed.html.

Stoller, R. J. "Psychotherapy of Extremely Feminine Boys." *International Journal of Psychiatry* 9 (January 1970): 278.

Sullivan, Andrew. *Virtually Normal.* New York: Alfred A. Knopf, 1995.

Swartz, Patti Capel. "Bridging Multicultural Education: Bringing Sexual Orientation into the Children's and Young Adult Literature Classrooms." *Radical Teacher* no. 66 (2003): 11–16.

Taylor, Nathan. "U.S. Children's Picture Books and the Homonormative Subject." *Journal of LGBT Youth* 9, no. 2 (2012): 136–52.

Tea, Michelle. *Tabitha and Magoo Dress Up Too.* New York: Amethyst Editions, 2020.

The Trevor Project. "Research Brief: Diversity of Youth Gender Identity." October 29, 2019. https://www.thetrevorproject.org/2019/10/29/research-brief-diversity-of-youth-gender-identity/.

Travers, Ann. *The Trans Generation: How Trans Kids (and Their Parents) Are Creating a Gender Revolution.* New York: New York University Press, 2018.

Truth and Tails. "About Us." Accessed March 12, 2020. http://www.truthandtails.com/about/.

Tuber, Steven, and Susan Coates. "Interpersonal Phenomena in the Rorschachs of Extremely Feminine Boys." *Psychoanalytic Psychology* 2, no. 3 (1985): 251–65. https://doi.org/10.1037/0736-9735.2.3.251.

20/20. "My Secret Self: A Story of Transgender Children." Hosted by Barbara Walters. ABC News, 2007.

Valentine, David. *Imagining Transgender: An Ethnography of a Category.* Durham, NC: Duke University Press, 2007.

Vidal, Gabriela. "'Call Me Max': A Children's Book about a Transgender Boy Stirs Controversy at Eanes ISD." CBS Austin, March 10, 2021. https://cbsaustin.com/news/local/call-me-max-a-childrens-book-about-a-transgender-boy-stirs-controversy-at-eanes-isd.

Warner, Michael. *The Trouble with Normal: Sex, Politics, and the Ethics of Queer Life*. New Ed edition. Cambridge, MA: Harvard University Press, 1999.

"When Kayla Was Kyle." 2014. http://www.whenkaylawaskyle.com/.

Williams, Raymond. *Marxism and Literature*. New York: Oxford University Press, 1978.

Yampell, Cat. "Alyson Wonderland Publishing." *Bookbird* 37, no. 3 (1999): 31.

Index

About the Author

Photo Credit: University of Texas at Arlington

Jennifer Miller is a non–tenure track English lecturer and women's and gender studies affiliate faculty at the University of Texas at Arlington. Her research interests include LGBTQ+ children's picture books, sexual subcultures, and digital cultures. She has published research about LGBTQ+ children's picture books in the *Journal of Homosexuality* and the edited collection *Heroes, Heroines, and Everything in Between*. She also blogs about children's literature at RaiseThemRighteous.com. Miller's scholarship about sexual subcultures appears in *Fast Capitalism* and the *European Journal of American Studies*. She is also the coeditor of *The Dialectic of Digital Culture*, a collection of essays about the possibilities and pitfalls of digital culture, in which she contributed an essay about mommy blogs. Miller is currently editing a collection of essays about LGBTQ+ children's picture books forthcoming with University Press of Mississippi.